DYSTOPIA AND DISPOSSESSION IN THE HOLLYWOOD SCIENCE-FICTION FILM, 1979–2017

Liverpool Science Fiction Texts and Studies, 77

Liverpool Science Fiction Texts and Studies

Editors
David Seed, *University of Liverpool*
Sherryl Vint, *University of California Riverside*

Editorial Board
Stacey Abbott, *University of Roehampton*
Mark Bould, *University of the West of England*
Veronica Hollinger, *Trent University*
Roger Luckhurst, *Birkbeck College, University of London*
Andrew Milner, *Monash University*
Andy Sawyer, *University of Liverpool*

Recent titles in the series

61. Upamanyu Pablo Mukherjee, *Final Frontiers: Science Fiction and Techno-Science in Non-Aligned India*
62. Gavin Miller, *Science Fiction and Psychology*
63. Andrew Milner and J.R. Burgmann, *Science Fiction and Climate Change: A Sociological Approach*
64. Regina Yung Lee and Una McCormack (eds), *Biology and Manners: Essays on the Worlds and Works of Lois McMaster Bujold*
65. Joseph Norman, *The Culture of "The Culture": Utopian Processes in Iain M. Banks's Space Opera Series*
66. Jeremy Withers, *Futuristic Cars and Space Bicycles: Contesting the Road in American Science Fiction*
67. Sabrina Mittermeier and Mareike Spychala, *Fighting for the Future: Essays on Star Trek: Discovery*
68. Richard Howard, *Space for Peace: Fragments of the Irish Troubles in the Science Fiction of Bob Shaw and James White*
69. Thomas Connolly, *After Human: A Critical History of the Human in Science Fiction from Shelley to Le Guin*
70. John Rieder, *Speculative Epistemologies: An Eccentric Account of SF from the 1960s to the Present*
71. Sarah Annes Brown, *Shakespeare and Science Fiction*
72. Christopher Palmer, *Apocalypse in Crisis: Fiction from 'The War of the Worlds' to 'Dead Astronauts'*
73. Mike Ashley, *The Rise of the Cyberzines: The Story of the Science-Fiction Magazines from 1991 to 2020: The History of the Science-Fiction Magazine Volume V*
74. J. Jesse Ramírez, *Un-American Dreams: Apocalyptic Science Fiction, Disimagined Community, and Bad Hope in the American Century*
75. Istvan Csicsery-Ronay, Jr., *Mutopia: Science Fiction and Fantastic Knowledge*
76. Tobi Evans, *Reimagining Masculinity and Violence in* Game of Thrones *and* A Song of Ice and Fire

DYSTOPIA AND DISPOSSESSION IN THE HOLLYWOOD SCIENCE-FICTION FILM, 1979–2017

The Aesthetics of Enclosure

HARRY WARWICK

LIVERPOOL UNIVERSITY PRESS

First published 2023 by
Liverpool University Press
4 Cambridge Street
Liverpool
L69 7ZU

This paperback edition published 2025

Copyright © 2025 Harry Warwick

Harry Warwick has asserted the right to be identified as
the author of this book in accordance with the Copyright, Designs and
Patents Act 1988.

All rights reserved. No part of this book may be reproduced, stored in a
retrieval system, or transmitted, in any form or by any means, electronic,
mechanical, photocopying, recording, or otherwise, without the prior
written permission of the publisher.

British Library Cataloguing-in-Publication data
A British Library CIP record is available

ISBN 978-1-80207-761-2 (hardback)
ISBN 978-1-83624-510-0 (paperback)

Typeset by Carnegie Book Production, Lancaster

Separation is the alpha and omega of the spectacle
> Guy Debord, *The Society of the Spectacle* (1967)

Contents

Acknowledgements		ix
	Introduction – Anticipation: Science Fiction between Spectacle and Speculation	1
	Part 1: Enclosure after Enclosure	
1	Extrapolation: The New Enclosures in New Hollywood	11
2	Privatisation: Conceptualising Enclosure in *RoboCop* and *Total Recall*	43
3	Urbanisation: Images of Los Angeles in *Blade Runner* and *The Truman Show*	65
	Part 2: Dystopia after Dystopia	
4	Expropriation: Marx, Utopia, and the Limits of Political Economy	89
5	Innovation: Intellectual Property in *The Matrix*, *The Island*, and *District 9*	117
6	Speculation: Credit, Crisis, and Foreclosure in *Repo Men* and *The Purge*	147
	Conclusion – Negation: Capitalism at the End of the World	171
Bibliography		181
Filmography		193
Index		197

Acknowledgements

This book grew out of my doctoral thesis, which I researched and wrote, funded by the Wolfson Foundation, at the University of Southampton from 2014 to 2018. I am grateful to Linda Ruth Williams and Michael Hammond for their supervision, to Nicky Marsh and Malcolm Cook for their thoughts on the project at an early stage, and to Lee Grieveson and Stephen Morton for their advice on turning the thesis into this monograph. I would also like to thank David Glover, Stephanie Jones, Neil Ewen, and Sarah Hayden for their general encouragement and support during my time at Southampton.

I wrote much of the book in my first year as a Leverhulme Early Career Fellow at the University of Warwick. My thanks to the Leverhulme Trust for funding my research, and to the Department of English and Comparative Literary Studies for providing a comradely environment in which to complete this project and embark on the next one.

Sarah Smyth and Tomos Hughes have offered incisive comments on various chapters of this book. Stephen Watkins, Sophie Cavey, Bevil Luck, and Lian Patston discussed many of its themes, and much else besides, with me. Andrew Clarke was a meticulous reader and a formidable critic. I want to thank them all.

I am very grateful to Christabel Scaife, at Liverpool University Press, for her guidance during the writing and editing process, and I would also like to thank the book's anonymous peer reviewer.

My deepest thanks, finally, to Charlotte Hallahan, my greatest supporter, and to Susan and Graham Warwick, for everything.

A portion of Chapter 1 has been adapted from *'Alien* and the New Enclosures', *Open Library of Humanities*, 4.2 (2018), 1–23.

Introduction

Anticipation
Science Fiction between Spectacle and Speculation

Science fiction is no more about the future, strictly speaking, than it is about the present or the past. It inclines towards that quite different process called *history*—the thing that binds past, present, and future together—and, to be still more precise, towards our consciousness of that process. Science fiction is the genre proper to societies in which the sense of history roused by capitalism's emergence, particularly by the contrasting rhythms of capitalist and precapitalist modes of production, is in decline, the strange, far-flung phenomena native to the genre—time travel, full automation, utopian societies, alien life-forms, speculative prosthetics—serving, at most, to thematise that decline, the impossibility of conceiving of historical change. Science fiction is therefore not antithetical to the literary realisms of a Scott or a Balzac, say, but, as Fredric Jameson suggests, their successor: a form projecting the future onto the same space on which the historical novel reconstructed the past.[1]

If science fiction is, like realism, the working out of a particular kind of relation to history, what happens when that relation no longer holds? Must science fiction also meet its demise? For much of the period since the genre emerged (on some accounts) in the writings of Jules Verne and H. G. Wells in the second half of the nineteenth century, it would seem that there remained sufficient exteriority to capitalism, sufficient sense of alternative temporalities and lifeworlds, if not for the composition of historical novels, then at least for a genre emphasising the waning of the historical consciousness that underpins such novels.

---

[1] Fredric Jameson, 'Progress versus Utopia; Or, Can We Imagine the Future?', *Science Fiction Studies*, 9.2 (1982), 147–58 (pp. 149–50). For a similar argument about the relation between the two forms, see Carl Freedman, *Critical Theory and Science Fiction* (Middletown: Wesleyan University Press, 2000), pp. 44–62.

This is what began to change in the 1970s, when, responding to the economic crisis of that decade, capital set a new wave of expropriations—what this book, following much of the scholarly literature, will call 'new enclosures'—upon the globe and subsumed still greater zones of human activity under itself. New land grabs, privatisations of energy and water, expansions of intellectual property, 'structural adjustment' programmes, the sale of national forests: these are just a few of the most prominent means through which capital reconstituted its conditions of existence after the crisis.[2]

The present book does not go as far as to pronounce the death of science fiction, but it does suggest that the new enclosures might have wounded or weakened it, depleted its critical energies. My focus in the following pages will be specifically those science fictions released by Hollywood between 1979 and 2017, between Ridley Scott's *Alien* and Denis Villeneuve's *Blade Runner 2049*, a period that begins in the aftermath of the 1970s economic crisis and ends a decade after the irruption of the next one, the 2007–08 crunch. Studying many of the major speculative works of that period, we shall find that the new enclosures, the dispossessions and privatisations consequent on the crisis, occupy them greatly. While *Alien* shows only a dawning awareness of the new enclosures, *RoboCop* (1987) and *Total Recall* (1990) offer critiques of the concept of privatisation; *Blade Runner* (1982) and *The Truman Show* (1998) are concerned with the enclosure of urban space generally and Los Angeles particularly; and *The Matrix* (1999), *The Island* (2005), and *District 9* (2009) articulate a new racial politics through the phenomenon of expanding intellectual property rights. Released in the wake of the second crisis, *Repo Men* (2010) and *The Purge* (2013) attempt to mediate financial collapse and home foreclosure.

Whence then derives the suspicion that science fiction is in decline? Do these texts not offer robust evidence that the genre continues to draw our attention, if not to history itself, then at least to those processes that impede our consciousness of it? What matters is not *that* these films represent the new enclosures in some way, but *how* they do so. Tracing the form's development between 1979 and 2017, this book notes a change in course in the mid-1990s, after which Hollywood's science-fiction cinema begins to naturalise the new enclosures rather than to estrange us from them, and when it thus starts to contradict the vocation of the

---

[2] 'If, today, the reference to enclosure matters, it is because the contemporary mode of extension of capitalism has given it all its actuality' (Isabelle Stengers, *In Catastrophic Times: Resisting the Coming Barbarism* (London: Open Humanities Press, 2015), p. 80).

genre itself. Compare Paul Verhoeven's *RoboCop* with José Padilha's 2014 remake: the original goes as far as to decry 'free enterprise' as a form of theft, while the privatisation of policing, now apparently unworthy of comment, retreats into the background in the latter. The same sort of shift has clearly occurred between Verhoeven's *Total Recall* and Len Wiseman's 2012 version, the latter supplanting the problematic of commodification driving the original with that of overpopulation. These films being remakes, the contrast with their source material is stark, but the transformation we see in them arcs through the period as a whole.

Crucially, the trend towards naturalisation, rather than estrangement or critique, corresponds at the level of genre itself to the shift from a predominantly utopian to a predominantly anti-utopian mode of expression. This is perhaps a counterintuitive claim, since most of the films to which I have just referred are more recognisably dystopias, representing a much worse state of affairs rather than a better one. But dystopia need not be anti-utopian; as we will see in the forthcoming chapters, most of the pre-*Truman Show* films construct an oppressive, seemingly irredeemable dystopian milieu the better to thematise their utopian moment or principle. They do so because of the same historical tendencies noted above: the new enclosures making us, not just more sceptical of the possibilities of revolutionary change, but unable even to imagine it, the utopian dystopia brings into vivid contrast the dystopian and utopian historical logics. Thus RoboCop's surprise subjectivation is that film's utopian moment and persists alongside the corporation's claim to ownership of him, while Truman's (utopian) decision to leave the realm of images comes up against the (dystopian) impossibility of doing so, the world outside the television set being equally in thrall to the spectacle. In these and the other films examined in the first half of the present book, utopia does not win out over dystopia; the denouement reasserts rather than resolves the tension. It is, moreover, precisely this tension, this contrast, that dissipates in the increasingly anti-utopian films of the late 1990s and the new millennium.

In focusing on Hollywood's science fictions, this study situates itself at the intersection between an essentially critical, historicising, estranging genre and one of the most highly commodified cultural industries in the core of the capitalist world-economy. The Hollywood science-fiction film thus offers an exemplary site for the analysis of the relation between capital and culture, spectacle and speculation.[3] My suggestion that the Hollywood science-fiction films released between *Alien* and *The Truman*

---

[3] Hollywood is 'the pole of the global spectacle', Guy Debord writes ('The Decline and Fall of the Spectacle–Commodity Economy', in *Situationist*

Show mount a radical critique of enclosure complicates conventional views of the blockbuster, according to which such films must appeal to broad sections of the American public (in order to recoup their hefty production costs) and can perhaps best do so by confirming rather than troubling their prejudices.[4] Such an argument also runs counter to the prevailing notion of the 1980s as one of the most conservative decades of the postwar United States, its rightward turn manifest on the screen in its hard-bodied action heroes, its Rambos and Terminators.[5] In this political, economic, and industrial climate, why did Hollywood also make so many apparently critical science-fiction films? The answer, we shall see, lies in those films' extrapolative dimension, which happened to coincide with the formal requirements of 'high-concept' cinema, specifically the latter's need to encapsulate the essence of a film in its marketing.

My contention that the politics of Hollywood science-fiction cinema begins to shift in the late 1990s bears certain implications, worth spelling out here, on the question of the form's relation to postmodernism. Since I began by invoking Jameson's thesis that science fiction has its origins in our waning conception of historicity, in the senescence of the historical novel, I ought now to add that Jameson takes this same decline (albeit at a more advanced stage) to be definitive of postmodernity—the age that has 'forgotten how to think historically'—which period begins, in his view, in 1973.[6] The argument of the present work might thus be reformulated as a claim about the relation between science fiction and postmodernism,

---

International Anthology, ed. and trans. by Ken Knabb, revised edn (Berkeley: Bureau of Public Secrets, 2006), pp. 194–203 (p. 198)).

[4] Geoff King, *New Hollywood Cinema: An Introduction* (London: I.B. Tauris, 2002), pp. 79–80.

[5] Susan Jeffords, *Hard Bodies: Hollywood Masculinity in the Reagan Era* (New Brunswick: Rutgers University Press, 1994), p. 13.

[6] Jameson notes that the economic and cultural preconditions of postmodernism were laid down in the 1950s and 1960s, but that 'infrastructure and superstructures [...] somehow crystallized in the great shock of the crises of 1973 [...] which, now that the dust clouds have rolled away, disclose the existence, already in place, of a strange new landscape' (*Postmodernism: Or, The Cultural Logic of Late Capitalism* (London: Verso, 1991), pp. xx–xxi). While Jameson does not discuss the relation between postmodernism and enclosure in any depth in his book, the latter's action, subsuming ever greater areas of our social world under capital, is implicit throughout. At one point, for instance, Jameson observes that 'the waning of our sense of history' has its basis in the 'colonization and absorption' of 'hitherto surviving enclaves of socio-economic difference' by the commodity-form, thus in the 'universalization of capitalism' (*Postmodernism*, p. 405).

namely that the genre charged with thematising our inability to think historically itself eventually succumbed, a little later than other forms had, to a stultifying postmodern ahistoricism. Such a shift comes clearly into focus when we trace the Hollywood science-fiction film's engagement with urbanism, which, as we shall see in my readings of *Blade Runner* and *The Truman Show*, was initially critical, underscoring the enclosures and privatisations of postmodern space. By the time *Repo Men* appeared in theatres in 2010, however, the *Blade Runner*-style metropolis had become mere ornament, the speculative dressing on a white, middle-class suburbia that was little changed, its racial structures naturalised.

This book divides into two parts. Each opens with a historical-theoretical chapter and then proceeds to two chapters that read Hollywood science fictions through crisis and enclosure.

Chapter 1 begins by examining the concept of enclosure. What are enclosures, and on what basis can we distinguish their 'old' from their 'new' forms? Differentiating between those dispossessions wreaked by capital and those that predate the existence of capital as such, I posit that the new enclosures serve to ensure the reproduction of the capital-relation, while the old ones found that relation, bring it into being for the first time. The privatisation of public services is exemplary of the new enclosures; the fencing off of English fields is the elemental form of the old ones. Sweeping across the United States in the 1970s, the new enclosures not only released new assets into circulation at fire-sale prices, preparing the ground for further accumulation, but in doing so boosted the competitiveness of American companies investing in the expropriated assets. Such enclosures thus helped capitalism overcome the 1970s economic crisis, and did so in such a way as to prolong American hegemony in the capitalist world-economy. The second half of the chapter seeks to explain why the new enclosures would become the privileged object of science fiction, and why, additionally, science fictions of this kind proved so attractive to an increasingly blockbuster-driven Hollywood system. I turn to *Alien*—both a blockbuster film and a work of critical, extrapolative science fiction—to illustrate the consonance of science-fictional form and spectacular, high-budget, high-concept cinema.

Released at the end of the 1980s, more than a decade since the inception of the most recent wave of enclosures, Paul Verhoeven's *RoboCop* and *Total Recall* evince greater awareness of the new enclosures than does *Alien*. As Chapter 2 argues, both films mount a critique of the concept of 'privatisation', a term that Reagan and other advocates sought to give currency in the 1980s. *RoboCop* estranges us from the concept by collapsing the public and private spheres—the Omni Consumer

Products boardroom was modelled on the Reagan White House—a trope also employed in *Total Recall*, where the Agency blends corporate and governmental functions. In Chapter 3, I argue that *Blade Runner* and *The Truman Show* ought to be read as responses to the privatisation of urban space. It is no accident that both films place their action in Los Angeles (Truman's Seahaven is a great television set situated there), the postmodern metropolis par excellence. More precisely, since privatisation divides the city ever more sharply between spaces *on* which one looks and spaces *from* which one looks, the two films in question register the intensification of that divide.

Opening this book's second part, Chapter 4 turns to the relationship between utopia and enclosure. I start by arguing that Part Eight of the first volume of Marx's *Capital* (1867) must be read less as proposing a new concept, 'primitive accumulation', more as a critique of the political economists' accounts thereof, which sought to downplay its violence. This clarifies the role of Marx's citations of Thomas More's *Utopia* (1516) in the footnotes of that section, More's work serving not simply as a documentary source for the new social processes unfolding in the English countryside in the fifteenth and sixteenth centuries, but also as an instrument for Marx's critique. Equally, *Utopia* is not a straightforwardly anti-enclosure text; alongside its criticisms of enclosure we find early, inchoate forms of the 'improvement' discourse that, elaborated by John Locke, would come to justify enclosure in Britain and abroad. Arguing that utopias are necessarily anti-enclosure, that they are at root so many efforts to reveal the blindness constitutive of liberal political economy—blindness, that is, to the 'blood and fire' of dispossession—Chapter 4 posits that several other classics of the genre (such as Edward Bellamy's *Looking Backward: 2000–1887* (1888) and H. G. Wells's *A Modern Utopia* (1905)) must also be considered in large part anti-utopian. The chapter ends by discussing why, in the films examined here, utopian moments or fragments coincide with, even require, a much darker, dystopian background.

Chapter 5 calls our attention to a specific kind of enclosure, intellectual property rights, and its expansion since the 1970s, this being one of the United States' major responses to the increasing competitiveness of Japanese manufacturing. By the time *The Matrix* arrived in theatres in 1999, however, Japan no longer seemed the political, economic, and cultural threat to American dominance that it had in the 1980s, when many of that decade's speculative fictions (most notably *Blade Runner*) saw fit to project the future through the lens of 'techno-Orientalism'. I thus argue that *The Matrix*, *The Island*, and *District 9* formulate new representations of race in and through extrapolated biotechnology, the development of this latter being bound up with the growth of intellectual property rights. Chapter 6 moves further into the twenty-first century, up to the 2007–08 crash, of which *Repo Men* and *The Purge* can be read as allegories. Unlike many other post-crisis Hollywood films, *Repo Men* and *The Purge* connect investment banking and foreclosure, show them in their unity. At the same time, both films naturalise the institution of private property, *Repo Men* by constructing an image of white suburbia undisturbed by the revolutionising forces of capital, *The Purge* by treating the lifting of the law as a phenomenon that affects interpersonal but not property relations.

Is it easier to imagine the end of the world than to imagine the end of capitalism? The suspicion that it is—that apocalyptic visions now come more readily to mind than post-capitalist ones, a view that seems to rule out the production of genuinely utopian cultural forms—has found its fullest elaboration in Mark Fisher's *Capitalist Realism* (2009), and it becomes our own focus in this book's conclusion. Fisher's argument that we can no longer even imagine substantial social change seemingly being confirmed by my readings, I try to discern where our propositions diverge. I argue that what Fisher calls 'realism' is, in fact, anti-utopianism—more precisely, a neutral, non-political conception of anti-utopianism, distinct from that term's theorisation in this book. The conclusion proceeds to offer a reading of Alfonso Cuarón's *Children of Men* (2006) that contrasts with Fisher's own, and then with interpretations of several more science-fiction remakes and sequels, which also highlight the difference between the generally critical, utopian films released in the 1980s and 1990s and the anti-utopian ones released afterwards. If imagining the end of capitalism matters, I suggest, this is because it demands reflection on how capitalism persists, how it renews and reproduces itself through the enclosure of proletarian life.

Part 1

Enclosure after Enclosure

Chapter 1

Extrapolation
The New Enclosures in
New Hollywood

To try to grasp the phenomenon of enclosure is to confront its strange temporality. Enclosure 'defies commonsense understandings of historical events as discrete, locatable, and terminal', Carolyn Lesjak points out in her study of British realism and its 'figuration' of the commons. 'How then to capture the historical process of enclosure without doing damage to its non-eventual aspects, or "slow violence" […] perpetrated over the course of multiple centuries but not visible in any simple, transparent way?'[1] Discussing the parliamentary enclosures of the eighteenth and nineteenth centuries, Raymond Williams makes the same point. Such appropriations form just one phase in a longer project: 'The process had been going on since at least the thirteenth century, and had reached a first peak in the fifteenth and sixteenth centuries.' Enclosure, Williams emphasises, 'is continuous from the long process of conquest and seizure: the land gained by killing, by repression, by political bargains'.[2]

The problem of temporality is then also a problem of definition. Can we speak of 'old' and 'new' enclosures? If so, by what criteria should we distinguish them? What separates enclosure proper from the adjacent forms of 'conquest and seizure' that Williams also recalls? I shall begin this chapter with a proposal that we define the old enclosures as those that establish the capital-relation, the new ones as those driven by capital itself. The old enclosures emerge from the breakdown of feudal relations, while the new enclosures avert, at least temporarily, the breakdown of capitalist relations. As David Harvey argues, it is because the new enclosures offer a 'spatial fix' to the overaccumulation of capital that a wave of expropriations followed in the wake of the 1970s economic crisis.

---

[1] Carolyn Lesjak, *The Afterlife of Enclosure: British Realism, Character, and the Commons* (Stanford: Stanford University Press, 2021), p. 22.
[2] Raymond Williams, *The Country and the City* (London: Hogarth, 1993), pp. 96–97.

The best-known example of such expropriations is probably privatisation, but other enclosures prominent in this wave include the expansion of intellectual property rights, the destruction of public housing, and the sale of the electromagnetic spectrum. Introducing a new stream of private property into circulation, these new enclosures allowed capitalists to reinvest their money at profitable rates once again.

The present book contends that the Hollywood science-fiction films of the late twentieth century tend to estrange us from the new enclosures, while those released afterwards tend to naturalise them. Unlike the ensuing chapters, which make the case through readings of science-fiction films, the second half of this chapter ponders why the genre's politics changed thus. The answer lies, I shall argue, in the reason for its genesis, in the universalisation of capitalism during the long nineteenth century, the period of British free-trade imperialism. Science fiction is a response to that universalisation, and to the declining historical consciousness consequent on it; and it is as a result of a similar movement, the new enclosures of our own time, expanding the dominion of capital and further diminishing our sense of historicity, that those enclosures become the genre's prime object of concern. Why did science fiction then cease to estrange us from enclosure—why, on the contrary, did it begin to naturalise it—in the century's closing years? Eventually, in a dialectical twist, by eliminating many of the surviving non-capitalist spaces that served as a contrast to the logic of capitalism, the new expropriations undermined the material basis for science-fictional critique. The same dispossessions that provoked science fiction's critical vigour served, at a later stage of their development, to weaken it.

It is of course one thing to argue that the new enclosures became (and then ceased to be) the privileged object of science-fictional estrangement, quite another to explain why, from the late 1970s, these estrangements so often took the form of the Hollywood blockbuster. Sketching out the industrial context in which the blockbuster became ascendant, the closing sections of this chapter seek to answer that question. Dystopian science fictions function, I shall suggest, by extrapolation, by projecting the depredations and inequalities of their moment into the future. Crucially, the process of extrapolation is consonant with New Hollywood's 'high-concept' marketing tactics, one of whose distinguishing features is that the blockbuster's narrative kernel must be transferable into the advertising materials. Specifically dystopian science fictions combine great critical with great box-office potential—hence their proliferation in the New Hollywood era, and hence also the viability of this book's project to recover the radical, anti-enclosure sentiment of a certain species of blockbuster cinema.

The Prehistory of Capital

For the analyst, capital accumulation always seems to begin *in medias res*. 'The accumulation of capital presupposes surplus-value,' Marx observes in the latter stages of the first volume of *Capital*; 'surplus-value presupposes capitalist production; capitalist production presupposes the availability of considerable masses of capital and labour-power in the hands of commodity producers.'[3] That is, the endless accumulation of capital requires that capitalists make a certain surplus when they sell their goods, which they can then reinvest in their firms (a process Marx calls 'expanded reproduction') with the aim of generating yet more surplus. This presumes specifically capitalist production, which extends the working day beyond the period of time necessary to create the value of an employee's wages and thereby squeezes out the surplus (more properly termed 'surplus-value'). Production of this kind presupposes, in turn, an initial reserve of capital—raw materials intended for use in the production process—and formally 'free' workers, whose labour-power, sold for a certain value, can be used to generate value in excess of that. Yet how does one acquire capital and labour-power (a commodity in its own right) prior to the existence of capitalism itself? It would appear that capital accumulation rests on certain conditions that it creates as a result of its own action. 'The whole movement, therefore, seems to turn around in a never-ending circle,' Marx concludes, in an image to which we will ourselves circle back later in this book.[4]

Where is the true source of the capitalist mode of production, then? What process, or group of processes, places the aforementioned masses of capital and labour-power in the hands of the would-be capitalist? Marx imagines a primal scene in which two very different kinds of commodity-owner come face-to-face:

> on the one hand, owners of money, means of production, means of subsistence, who are eager to valorize the sum of values they have appropriated by buying the labour-power of others; on the other hand, free workers, the sellers of their own labour-power, and thus the sellers of labour. Free workers, in the double sense that they neither form part of the means of production themselves, as would be the case with slaves, serfs, etc., nor do they own the

---

[3] Karl Marx, *Capital: A Critique of Political Economy*, trans. by Ben Fowkes and David Fernbach, 3 vols (London: Penguin, 1976–81), I, 873.

[4] Marx, *Capital*, I, 873. See Chapter 4 for further discussion of this passage, which I read as part of Marx's *critique* of the concept 'primitive accumulation'.

means of production, as would be the case with self-employed peasant proprietors. The free workers are therefore free from, unencumbered by, any means of production of their own.

This division between capitalist and worker, Marx continues, itself requires the separation of the worker from the means of production and subsistence. The vast majority of the population must cease to have direct access to food, clothing, shelter, and so on, as well as the raw materials they would require for their work. The idyllic picture of '[s]o-called primitive accumulation' painted by the political economists must yield, Marx suggests, to a more accurate account, according to which capitalism has its origins in 'the historical process of divorcing the producer from the means of production'—that is, in 'conquest, enslavement, robbery, murder, in short, force'. It is only when people have been thrown off their land, separated from their means of production, that they become labourers, and that those who now own such things become capitalists. 'With the polarization of the commodity-market into these two classes,' Marx argues, 'the fundamental conditions of capitalist production are present.'[5]

Having established the logical necessity of such 'polarization', Marx turns, in the next chapter, to his chief historical illustration of it, the enclosure of the English soil from the late fifteenth century, which process tore the commoners from their land and reconstituted them as a 'free' labour force, ready to be exploited by capital.[6] The dispossession entailed by enclosure consisted as much in the loss of 'common right', the commoners' right of access to property—which they might have used for grazing livestock, gathering dead wood, or gleaning, for instance—as it did in the loss of property itself.[7] 'Enclosure', a complex term, refers most obviously to the fences or walls that the landowner might erect on abrogating common right, but it also signifies a process of holdings consolidation frequently attendant on that.[8] Crucially, stripping from the poor their access to means of subsistence, the enclosures increased their

[5] Marx, *Capital*, I, 874–75.
[6] Marx, *Capital*, I, 878–90.
[7] This right had long been a contested one, the locus of class struggle between poor and rich, as E. P. Thompson recounts, such that its loss cannot unproblematically be equated with enclosure (*Customs in Common* (London: Penguin, 1993), pp. 97–107).
[8] For an overview of the difficulty of defining 'enclosure', which term refers both to the physical enclosure and to a broader process of which fences and walls are particular manifestations, see J. A. Yelling, *Common Field and Enclosure in England 1450–1850* (London: Macmillan, 1977), pp. 5–10.

dependence on wages and thus on the nascent capitalist class. '[O]nly common right stood between the survival of the common-field peasantry and their proletarianization,' J. M. Neeson observes.[9]

At first the lord of the feudal manor was likely to be the primary agent of enclosure, but later enclosure by general agreement (that is, agreement of the majority of landholders) came to predominate.[10] In contradistinction to 'piecemeal' enclosures—where parts of a parish, say, would be enclosed prior to others—these 'general' enclosures were usually large-scale, sweeping up whole settlements, and could be ratified by a Chancery decree. The decisive shift in the history of English enclosures occurred in the middle of the eighteenth century, when parliament became the chief enclosing agent, sanctioning the peasantry's expropriation. 'Gone was the slow, negotiated process of piecemeal enclosure in which closes or woods were taken out of the system and common rights were abated by general agreement,' Neeson notes. 'In its place came a process that dispensed with the need for much agreement and enclosed an entire parish in eight to ten years, and when it was done all common right had gone.'[11] Between 1750 and 1830 more than 4,000 acts of enclosure came into effect, albeit at varying rates.[12] After a sharp rise in the 1760s and 1770s, parliamentary enclosure slowed in the 1780s. It returned to previous levels in the mid-1790s, and another peak followed between 1810 and 1815, after which time almost all common land had been enclosed.[13] 'By the nineteenth century,' Marx thus notes, 'the very memory of the connection between the agricultural labourer and communal property had […] vanished.'[14]

Though England offers the classic example, the enclosure of North America provides instructive contrasts.[15] Allan Greer shows that settlers initially came into ownership of land as much by the imposition of

---

[9] J. M. Neeson, *Commoners: Common Right, Enclosure and Social Change in England, 1700–1820* (Cambridge: Cambridge University Press, 1993), p. 34.

[10] Yelling, p. 20.

[11] Neeson, p. 187.

[12] Ellen Rosenman, 'On Enclosure Acts and the Commons', *BRANCH* [n.d.] <http://www.branchcollective.org/?ps_articles=ellen-rosenman-on-enclosure-acts-and-the-commons> [accessed 17 May 2022] (para. 6 of 13).

[13] Yelling, pp. 15–16.

[14] Marx, *Capital*, I, 889.

[15] Despite the differences, Thompson notes that the ideology of improvement was one of the major justifications for enclosure on both sides of the Atlantic: 'In the English cottager and "the wild Indian" alike there was seen a degrading cultural submission to a picaresque, desultory or vagrant mode of livelihood' (*Customs in Common*, p. 165). For a more recent discussion of improvement discourse in the colonial context, see Brenna Bhandar, *The*

their own commons, which then rivalled Indigenous commons, as by formal means of enclosure. In New Spain, for instance, settlers granted the Indigenous population equal right to the lands on which colonial livestock ranged, but grazing utterly changed the landscape, infringing on native ways of life, and feral cattle and horses pushed Indigenous groups further north and forced them into congregated settlements. This opened the way for the development of haciendas, the granting of individual property rights (sometimes on Indigenous land), and the demarcation of landed property.[16] Here and elsewhere in North America, since livestock was considered private property, settlers let them graze on the Indigenous commons, effecting enclosure by other means.[17] Except in New France, where cold winters, low demand for meat and dairy product, and dense forests limited their expansion, the advance of colonial commons laid the foundations of colonial enclosure.[18]

At the end of the eighteenth century, as the British parliament increasingly took the abrogation of common right into its own hands, Washington started to use treaties to challenge native title. These treaties 'accounted for the majority of land cessions from Indian to non-Indian people', Charles Geisler notes—'an estimated half billion acres'.[19] Mass evictions accelerated the process, as 50,000 Indigenous people had to migrate from the Southeast to the West. Thousands more, forced to leave the Northwest territories, had their land surveyed and plotted by white settlers.[20] Later, in 1887, the Dawes Act intensified the enclosure

---

Colonial Lives of Property: Law, Land, and Racial Regimes of Ownership (Durham, NC: Duke University Press, 2018), pp. 33–75, 115–48.

[16] Allan Greer, 'Commons and Enclosure in the Colonization of North America', *The American Historical Review*, 117.2 (2012), 365–86 (pp. 376–80). Ben Maddison makes a similar point about the colonial function of commons in the context of Australia, where '[r]ules of commons that defined commoners by residence and property-owning status meant the de facto exclusion of indigenous people' ('Radical Commons Discourse and the Challenges of Colonialism', *Radical History Review*, 108 (2010), 29–48 (p. 43)). Together, these studies suggest that nostalgia for the commons is not in itself an effective antidote to pro-enclosure discourse.

[17] Greer, p. 383. This was not without its parallels back in England, where, in the absence of formal methods of enclosure, farmers could overstock and overgraze the commons, making it useless to others who held common right (Neeson, pp. 87–89). In both cases, livestock served as an instrument of *de facto* enclosure.

[18] Greer, pp. 383–84.

[19] Charles Geisler, 'Disowned by the Ownership Society: How Native Americans Lost Their Land', *Rural Sociology*, 79 (2014), 56–78 (p. 64).

[20] Geisler, p. 63.

of the native population: by dividing Indigenous land into parcels, and changing its status from common to private property, the Act opened up new means of dispossession, such as defaulted mortgages and tax forfeiture sales.[21] Thus, between 1887 and 1934, the Native Americans lost more than half their total landholdings. This 'allotment' of native land also challenged native sovereignty, as federal government could begin to impose its rule on the new allotments, removing tribal authorities as mediators between government and individual.[22] As the colonising population spread inland, 'their government enclosed these commons, sequestered surviving Indians onto reservations, and extinguished all but the remnants of aboriginal life and title'.[23]

'New Enclosures'?

As Robert Nichols warns us, however, to describe the dispossession of Native Americans as a kind of enclosure is to risk erasing the differences between European and Anglo-colonial forms of expropriation, which are not parallel but intertwined, co-constituting. The difference is partly one of causation: with the literal use of the term, for instance, the enclosure of the English countryside, it is the emergence of capital from *'noncapital'*—in essence, the breakdown of feudalism—that is being explained, while the enclosure of the Indigenous population involves 'the subsumption of noncapital by *actually existing* capital'.[24] Similarly, the romantic popular and scholarly invocation of 'commons' as an antidote to enclosure not only overlooks its contested, sometimes (as just noted) colonial character, but also ignores the extant traditions of 'care and counterdispossession' cultivated by Indigenous peoples. Indigenous responses to dispossession, Nichols concludes, 'frequently reconfigure

---

[21] David A. Chang, 'Enclosures of Land and Sovereignty: The Allotment of American Indian Lands', *Radical History Review*, 109 (2011), 108–19 (p. 108). On the relationship between the Dawes Act and native sovereignty, see also Nancy Shoemaker, *A Strange Likeness: Becoming Red and White in Eighteenth-Century North America* (Oxford: Oxford University Press, 2004), pp. 19–23.

[22] Chang, pp. 111–12.

[23] Geisler, p. 74.

[24] Robert Nichols, *Theft is Property! Dispossession and Critical Theory* (Durham, NC: Duke University Press, 2020), pp. 69–70. Nichols is here discussing Marx's concept of 'primitive accumulation', which he suggests must be 'disaggregated' into its constituent processes before it can be applied to other contexts.

the relation between rights, property, and power in ways that do not sit neatly with received platitudes about privatization or the commons'.[25]

Further definitional problems arise when we combine this spatial shift with a temporal one and begin to call certain dispossessions occurring in our own time, in the United States and elsewhere, 'enclosures'. What binds processes as novel and widespread as the sale of the electromagnetic spectrum, the privatisation of water, the destruction of public housing, and the commodification of the human genome both to each other and to the fate of the open field? In the first three examples, what we lose is not common right but public property, and in the fourth, our genetic material was perhaps never seen as a form of property in the first place. To describe such things as 'enclosures' is, it would seem, to court trouble: to take an inexact term, whose contours are by no means clear even to the agricultural historian, and superimpose it on a new context, new processes, far spatially, temporally, and conceptually from its rural origins.

Consider, as an illustration of the inexactness to which the concept of new enclosures is prone, the Midnight Notes Collective's 1990 'Introduction to the New Enclosures', one of the earliest and most influential theorisations of the term.[26] In the opening paragraph of their short essay, Midnight Notes posit that the 1980s saw 'the largest Enclosure of the worldly Common in history', and give, as three of its manifestations, the African debt crisis, homelessness, and the collapse of socialism. We might agree with Midnight Notes that these phenomena, though generally treated as separate things, 'deceptively name aspects of a single unified process', but is the correct name for that process

---

[25] Nichols, pp. 155–57. Take, as an example, Massimo De Angelis's contention that '[i]t is either capital that makes the world *through commodification and enclosures*, or it is the rest of us—whoever is that "us"—that makes the world through counter-enclosures and commons' (*The Beginning of History: Value Struggles and Global Capital* (London: Pluto, 2007), p. 135). According to the terms of Nichols's critique, the 'us' left undefined by De Angelis is, in fact, 'Europeans', and thus betrays the Eurocentrism of the latter's theorisation.

[26] Tove Soiland notes that feminist thinkers involved in the housework debates of the 1970s were already beginning to conceptualise housework as a continuous form of capitalist expropriation ('A Feminist Approach to Primitive Accumulation', in *Rosa Luxemburg: A Permanent Challenge for Political Economy*, ed. by Judith Dellheim and Frieder Otto Wolf (London: Palgrave Macmillan, 2016), pp. 185–217 (p. 187)). Additionally, as Soiland goes on to observe, it was Rosa Luxemburg, in *The Accumulation of Capital* (1913), who first postulated the necessity, for capital, of an ongoing 'primitive accumulation'.

really, as they go on to suggest, 'the New Enclosures'?[27] The essay leaves us to guess what defines such processes as 'enclosures': all three bear some relation to dispossession—debt can function as a dispossessing mechanism; homelessness might well be exacerbated by the destruction of public housing; and antisocialism arguably serves as a pretext for further dispossessions—yet these are nonetheless different relations (respectively cause, effect, pretext). To the extent that debt crises, homelessness, and antisocialism are common expressions of something, that thing is surely capitalism generally rather than enclosure specifically.

This loose conceptualisation seems to proceed from an uncertainty, in the Midnight Notes essay, about what kind of a concept 'enclosure' is. Does it refer to a particular political-economic process, one characterised by dispossession and separation, or to 'the large-scale reorganization of the accumulation process [...] underway since the mid-1970s', as they put it at one point, such that it vies with concepts such as 'neoliberalism', 'post-Fordism', and 'globalisation'?[28] The tension between these two usages—between 'enclosure' as particular process and 'Enclosure' as 'large-scale reorganization' encompassing myriad processes—generates two discrepant periodisations. Using the term in the first sense, Midnight Notes can rightly argue that enclosure is 'not a one[-]time process exhausted at the dawn of capitalism', but rather 'a regular return on the path of accumulation and a structural component of class struggle'.[29] On such a view, the 'new' is in fact quite old. When Midnight Notes come to use 'enclosure' in the second sense, however, suddenly the distinction between new and old hinges on a precise date, the mid-1970s, the moment, they argue, that the postwar 'social contract' between labour and capital broke down.

Perhaps it is better not to speak of 'new enclosures' at all. David Harvey's coinage, 'accumulation by dispossession', would seem to allow us to do just that, to account for capital's continuous plunder without perilous analogy to the plight of the English commoners. Correcting Marx's 'assumption' in *Capital* that primitive accumulation served simply to establish capitalism, that such processes disappeared once capital accumulation was up and running (an interpretation of *Capital* my disagreement with which I shall explain in Chapter 4), Harvey identifies, among other things, speculative raiding by hedge funds,

---

[27] Midnight Notes Collective, 'Introduction to the New Enclosures', *Midnight Notes*, 10 (1990) <http://www.midnightnotes.org/pdfnewencl.pdf> [accessed 17 May 2022] (pp. 1–9 (p. 2)).

[28] Midnight Notes, p. 3.

[29] Midnight Notes, pp. 1–3.

the artificial generation of local crises, corporate fraud, privatisation, and the expansion of intellectual property rights as ongoing forms of primitive accumulation. Such dispossessions must persist, Harvey suggests, to solve, at least in the short term, the problem of capital's recurrent overaccumulation (on which more shortly).[30] Suffice it to note here that those phenomena Harvey bundles under the heading 'accumulation by dispossession' also suffer from insufficiently judicious discrimination. As Robert Brenner observes, intensified exploitation, the state's privileging of its own capitalists over others, and the rise of agribusiness at the expense of family farms—all of which Harvey counts as forms of accumulation by dispossession—are 'quite normal aspects or by-products of the already well-established sway of capital'.[31] The notion of accumulation by dispossession being premised on capitalism's inability to sustain itself by its normal functioning, Harvey's conflation of these normal economic processes with exceptional extra-economic ones undermines his concept's very raison d'être.

If we are then to posit the existence of new enclosures, it is incumbent on us to specify, more precisely than Harvey or Midnight Notes do, what these enclosures share with the old ones and where they diverge from them. Let us consider the similarity first. What is essential to enclosure, in the expanded sense in which I will use it here, and also to the original enclosures of the English soil, is the constitution of means of subsistence or production as specifically capitalist private property—hence, as property from which the proletarian has been completely separated.[32] On this view, it matters not whether, prior to its enclosure, the land or object in question was common, public, or even (pre-capitalist) private property.[33] Enclosures, new or old, serve to

---

[30] David Harvey, *The New Imperialism* (Oxford: Oxford University Press, 2003), pp. 145–52. In his book on neoliberalism, in which he returns to the concept, Harvey offers a fourfold characterisation of accumulation by dispossession, which comprises privatisation, financialisation, the manipulation of crises, and regressive state redistributions (*A Brief History of Neoliberalism* (Oxford: Oxford University Press, 2005), pp. 159–65).

[31] Robert Brenner, 'What Is, and What Is Not, Imperialism?', *Historical Materialism*, 14.4 (2006), 79–105 (pp. 100–2).

[32] For De Angelis, too, it is the phenomenon of 'separation' that connects old and new enclosures, while what distinguishes them is the degree of that separation and the context in which it takes place. In this interpretation, enclosure is not a 'primitive' mode of accumulation that precedes capitalism, but must continue as long as does the latter (*Beginning of History*, pp. 137–41).

[33] Regarding this last, Marx notes that the transformation of the 'dwarf-like property of the many'—that is, the private property of the independent artisan or peasant—'into the giant property of the few' is what 'forms the

polarise society ever more sharply between a mass of labourers, who own nothing but their labour-power, must compete for employment, and depend on the market for their survival, and wealth accumulated in a few hands. Separation and consolidation, proletarianisation and accumulation: these are the twin dimensions of enclosure.

What about the difference between old and new forms of enclosure? I want to suggest that we use these adjectives, not (as Midnight Notes sometimes do) to mark some precise date on which enclosure changes its character, but rather to identify the two different agencies that can propel it. As William Clare Roberts notes in his careful reading of *Capital*, what Marx describes in the section on primitive accumulation is not the capitalists' dispossession of workers, but the lords' dispossession of peasants: not capitalist expropriation, in other words, but feudal betrayal, the breakdown of the old social relations, which opened the way for the new.[34] The nascent capitalist class then interposed itself between the 'free' labourers and the landlords, both of whom became dependent on the capitalists, hence Marx's observation that the 'knights of industry [...] only succeeded in supplanting the knights of the sword by making use of events in which they played no part whatsoever'.[35] By contrast with this 'so-called primitive accumulation', the new forms of expropriation that concern us in this book *are*, in fact, motivated by capital. They belong to the period when capitalist production 'stands on its own feet' and capital seeks to maintain and reproduce the proletarian's separation from their means of subsistence and production.[36]

---

pre-history of capital' (*Capital*, I, 927–28). In the rest of this book, when I use the phrase 'private property', I mean property of this specifically capitalist kind, the 'giant property of the few', rather than the scattered private property that preceded capitalism, whose dispersion could not possibly have sustained accumulation on a large scale.

[34] William Clare Roberts, *Marx's Inferno: The Political Theory of* Capital (Princeton: Princeton University Press, 2017), pp. 201–09.
[35] Marx, *Capital*, I, 875.
[36] This conceptualisation aligns with Onur Ulas Ince's distinction between 'capital-positing' and 'capital-preserving' violence: the old enclosures posit capital for the first time, while new enclosures are means by which capital ensures its persistence ('Between Equal Rights: Primitive Accumulation and Capital's Violence', *Political Theory*, 46.6 (2017), 885–914).

Autumn in the World-Economy

Because Marx's focus in the section on 'so-called primitive accumulation' is the origins of capitalism, the burden of explaining why enclosure persists has fallen on his followers, whose writings on the matter typically offer one of two kinds of explanation.[37] The first approach, associated with the autonomists, theorises enclosure as capital's response to proletarian struggle, its effort to overcome the limits established by the latter. Thus, as we have just seen, Midnight Notes construe the new enclosures as a counteroffensive to the 'proletarian initiatives' (the Watts riots, the Prague Spring, the Italian Hot Autumn) that 'transcended the limits of capital's historic possibilities' between 1965 and 1975.[38] Massimo De Angelis conceives enclosure in the same way, as capital's means of subsuming those communal practices that cannot be valorised, that resist integration into the circuits of accumulation. Enclosure therefore opposes itself not only to 'pre-capitalist spaces of autonomy' but also to the more or less continuous 'social contestation' that erects limits to capital's self-expansion.[39] In the autonomist account, the proletariat forms an external barrier to capital, its agency opposing it, impeding it, from the outside.

Positing instead the existence of an internal limit to capital accumulation, a limit arising from capital itself, Harvey's theory of overaccumulation forms the basis of the second approach to the analysis of ongoing enclosures. For Harvey, the downward pressure exerted on the rate of profit as capitalists increasingly implement labour-saving technology, and thereby cut out the living source of surplus-value, makes it increasingly difficult for those same capitalists to reinvest their surplus capital at acceptable rates of return.[40] The result is an overaccumulation crisis, where reserves of capital, perhaps accompanied by reserves of labour, sit idle, losing value. Rising unemployment, a glut of commodities on the market, unused productive capacity, and hoarding typically follow.[41] It is to precisely this kind of malaise that accumulation by dispossession offers capitalists, if not a solution, at least a temporary fix. The new enclosures serve 'to release a set of assets (including labour power) at very low (and in some instances zero) cost', which gives the

---

[37] Stuart Hodkinson notes a similar bifurcation in the scholarly literature in 'The New *Urban* Enclosures', *City*, 16.5 (2012), 500–18 (pp. 506–09).
[38] Midnight Notes, p. 3.
[39] De Angelis, p. 140.
[40] For Harvey's reading of Marx on the rate of profit, see *The Limits to Capital*, 2nd edn (London: Verso, 2006), pp. 156–203.
[41] Harvey, *The New Imperialism*, p. 109.

overaccumulated capital the incentive it needs to return to circulation.[42] Finance must be understood in the same way, Harvey adds—a temporal fix correlative to enclosure *qua* spatial fix. By allowing capitalists to turn the surplus capital locked up in their unsaleable commodities into money, finance permits the transfer of overaccumulated capital into long-term projects, such as construction or research and development, which stimulate the economy and renew the demand for precisely those goods that the capitalist had been unable to sell in the first place.[43]

While Harvey's and the autonomists' explanations start from different premises and develop in quite different directions, they actually offer a false dichotomy. They present the same process from opposite points of view. If, to resolve crises of overaccumulation, capitalists must open up new outlets for investment—by enclosing the commons, or privatising public property—then these resolutions require people to yield their direct access to means of production or subsistence. But, in such a situation, these people are not yet fully proletarianised—they maintain some bond to their means of production, which capital is presently trying to take from them—and thus the capital-relation also does not yet fully obtain. It follows that the effort to resolve crises of overaccumulation by enclosure is always, at the same time, an effort to complete the process of proletarianisation: what De Angelis calls 'disciplinary integration' is ultimately comprehensible as a strategy for resolving economic crisis. But we could also put this the other way around. Since the proletariat's class struggle aims to bring the means of production under common ownership, their victories deprive capitalists of the new, cheap outlets in which the latter would invest their overaccumulated capital. Proletarian struggle intensifies economic crisis, while the 'fixing' of the crisis is nothing but the reassertion of the capital-relation, quelling dissent. Economic crisis is immanent to the terrain of class struggle, and the choice between Harvey's and the autonomists' explanations is a false one.

If the late 1960s and early 1970s formed, as Midnight Notes contend, a high point for proletarian counteroffensives, what were the economic causes of the 1970s crisis? In this instance, overaccumulation had its roots in the declining profitability of American manufacturing, which, during the second half of the 1960s, increasingly found itself competing with

---

[42] Harvey, *The New Imperialism*, p. 149.
[43] Harvey, *The New Imperialism*, pp. 113–14. Going further than Harvey and De Angelis, Werner Bonefeld argues that separation is not merely a solution to crisis, but forms the permanent basis of the capital-relation as such ('Primitive Accumulation and Capitalist Accumulation: Notes on Social Constitution and Expropriation', *Science and Society*, 75.3 (2011), 379–99).

German and Japanese firms producing the same kinds of goods. Lumbered with old fixed capital, and paying relatively higher wages, American firms found that their foreign competitors were producing at much lower cost and could impose cheaper prices on the world market. The result of such systemic over-capacity and over-production, Brenner notes, was a declining aggregate rate of profit in international manufacturing and consequently the beginning of the 'long downturn'.[44] The American response was threefold: to loosen its monetary policy, thereby to make its exports more competitive; to stimulate economic growth by running budget deficits; and to impose 'voluntary export restraints' on its trading partners. Accepting diminished profit margins in this new environment, German and Japanese firms continued to churn out products in the same manufacturing lines, and the problem of overaccumulation worsened. When the oil shocks struck, major recessions followed in 1974–75 and 1979–80, diminished profit rates having left many firms vulnerable to bankruptcy. Only the United States' deficit spending could raise the American economy from the doldrums, yet the manner in which such spending occurred deferred the failure of the high-cost, low-profit firms and perpetuated over-capacity and over-production.[45]

As such an overview suggests, the 1970s economic crisis was at the same time a crisis of American hegemony, what Giovanni Arrighi calls the 'signal' crisis of the United States-led systemic cycle of accumulation. In Arrighi's schema, we ought to note, the United States is the fourth leader of the capitalist world-economy, its hegemony commencing after the Second World War. Genoa, in the fifteenth and sixteenth centuries, was the first leader; the United Provinces, in the seventeenth and eighteenth centuries, was the second; and the United Kingdom, in the nineteenth and early twentieth centuries, was the third. In all of these cases, Arrighi proceeds to note, the hegemon suffered a signal crisis, heralding its decline, and then, some years later, a terminal crisis, marking its usurpation.[46] In every instance, moreover, the hegemon sought a renewed source of profit-making in high finance as their international competitiveness declined. This happened with the United States from 1968 to 1973, during which period, seeking outlets for their overaccumulated capital, American capitalists ploughed ever greater sums into offshore money markets. By the end of the 1970s, the

---

[44] Robert Brenner, *The Boom and the Bubble: The US in the World Economy* (London: Verso, 2002), pp. 16–18.
[45] Brenner, *Boom and the Bubble*, pp. 24–35.
[46] Giovanni Arrighi, *The Long Twentieth Century: Money, Power, and the Origins of Our Times* (London: Verso, 2010), pp. 219–46.

competition between private and public money and the aforementioned looseness of American monetary policy threatened to undermine the dollar's status as world currency. The Federal Reserve, under Paul Volker, decided to return to the time-honoured principles of sound money. Combined with Reagan's militarism abroad and spending at home, this tightening of monetary policy bought the United States one final decade in the sun, the Reagan years thus forming what Arrighi calls the *'belle époque'* of American hegemony.[47]

What Harvey's study of the 'new imperialism' would seem to add to this picture is that finance is only one way to restore profitability, thus to prolong one's hegemonic status. The other, a spatial rather than a temporal fix, is enclosure. This is why the American *belle époque* was also the scene of vast new expropriations: the accelerated contracting out of state and municipal functions; the privatisation of urban space; the expansion of patent, copyright, and trademark protections; the destruction of public housing; and the sale of the electromagnetic spectrum, to name just a few. How these expropriations came into being, what their individual rationales and dynamics were, and in what guise they presented themselves in the light and magic of Hollywood's science-fiction cinema—such are the concerns of later chapters.[48] Suffice it to observe for now that the Reaganite raiding of the American proletariat was as sure a 'sign of autumn' in the long twentieth century as were the capitalists' adventures abroad in Eurodollar markets.

Enclosure in Future History

Science fiction is an eminently historical genre, a 'certain type of imaginative historical tale', as Darko Suvin puts it in his *Metamorphoses of Science Fiction* (1979).[49] Edward Bellamy's *Looking Backward* (1888), set

---

[47] Arrighi, pp. 309–35.
[48] I examine the various dimensions of privatisation—the dominant form of the post-1973 new enclosures in the United States—in Chapters 2 and 3 and the growth of intellectual property rights in Chapter 5. On the destruction of public housing, see Jason Hackworth, 'Destroyed by HOPE: Public Housing, Neoliberalism and Progressive Housing Activism in the US', in *Where the Other Half Lives: Lower Income Housing in a Neoliberal World*, ed. by Sarah Glynn (London: Pluto Press, 2009), pp. 232–56. On the sale of the electromagnetic spectrum, see David Bollier, *Silent Theft: The Private Plunder of Our Common Wealth* (London: Routledge, 2003), pp. 148–53.
[49] Darko Suvin, *Metamorphoses of Science Fiction: On the Poetics and History of a Literary Genre*, 2nd edn (Oxford: Peter Lang, 2016), p. 101.

in the year 2000, and William Morris's *News from Nowhere* (1890), set in the late twenty-first century, are not about those years, but about 'collective human relationships in the 1880s', at least as Bellamy and Morris saw them. Similarly, *1984* is about George Orwell's perception of 1948, while *2001* speaks to Stanley Kubrick's view of things in 1968. 'However fantastic (in the sense of empirically unverifiable) the characters or worlds described,' Suvin writes, 'always *de nobis fabula narratur*.'[50] It follows that *Alien*'s twenty-second century, *Blade Runner*'s 2019, and *Total Recall*'s 2084 are not really predictions about these dates or periods, speculations about the future, but accounts of their own historical moment. They are the autumnal fictions of the long twentieth century; their stories are our story. Why is science fiction oriented thus, towards history? And why do Hollywood's science fictions of the late twentieth century narrate their historical moment through the phenomenon of enclosure?

Though science fiction's origins remain contentious (did the genre begin with the 1818 publication of Mary Shelley's *Frankenstein*, for instance?), most interesting for our purposes are those accounts, such as Jameson's, that attribute its emergence to Verne and Wells in the final third of the nineteenth century, the dying decades of British hegemony. This periodisation offers a suggestive contrast with the destiny of the historical novel, the writings of whose progenitor, Walter Scott, coincide with the beginning of the British-led systemic cycle of accumulation. That the historical novel and science fiction open and close the same cycle is no coincidence. As Jameson argues, drawing from Georg Lukács, the historical novel presupposed the juxtaposition between capitalist and non-capitalist zones, which distinction Scott, positioned as he was between the commercial activity of the Lowlands and the clan societies of the Highlands, could readily observe. During the nineteenth century, however, capitalism became increasingly universal, its imperial logic forcing open new markets abroad, and consequently the contrast constitutive of the historical imagination started to disappear. The historical novel underwent a double metamorphosis: on the one side, it turned into naturalism, realism evacuated of its historicity, and on the other, it became science fiction, whose speculations serve to redefine the present as the past of the future, thus to dramatise, to bring to consciousness, that waning of historicity.[51] The same spatio-temporal expansions that

---

[50] Suvin, p. 92.
[51] Jameson, 'Progress versus Utopia', pp. 149–50. For Lukács's classic discussion of the historical novel, see his *The Historical Novel*, trans. by Hannah and Stanley Mitchell (London: Penguin, 1981).

whittled away the conditions for the historical novel during the long nineteenth century prepared the ground for the emergence of science fiction at the end of it.

The third systemic cycle having given science fiction its conditions of possibility, the vicissitudes of the fourth reverberated through the genre. The economic-hegemonic crises of the long twentieth century—the signal crisis of 1973, the terminal crisis of 2007—manifested themselves, within the speculative output of the hegemon's national cinema, as aesthetic crises, moments of recomposition and renewal. Crucially for us, the difference requisite to properly historical consciousness—the contrast between capitalist and non-capitalist spaces, between Lowlands and Highlands (to recall Jameson's example)—took the diminished form, during the long twentieth century, and within the capitalist core, of the distinction between common or public property, semiautonomous from the logic of capital, on the one hand, and capitalist private property, on the other. There still remained, for much of the twentieth century—and particularly after the Great Depression, when the American public sector grew—sufficient exteriority to capital, if not for historical novels, then at least for the speculative genre charged with thematising those novels' impossibility. With the 1970s crisis, however, and with the ensuing spatio-temporal reconfiguration of the capitalist world-economy, even that began to change. The result was a *belle époque* for Hollywood science-fiction cinema, as the new enclosures initially became so much raw material for the genre's distinctive 'cognitive estrangements', before the enclosures extinguished even those remaining non-capitalist enclaves.[52] The science-fiction film started to lose its material preconditions and

---

[52] Science fiction is estranging, for Suvin, because it presents a world radically different from that obtaining in the author's milieu, and it is cognitive because it develops its estranged world with 'totalizing ("scientific") rigor' (*Metamorphoses*, pp. 15–27, 79–101). There is a vast literature on the merits and demerits of Suvin's definition. See, for just a few examples, Freedman, *Critical Theory*, pp. 16–23; China Miéville, 'Cognition as Ideology: A Dialectic of SF Theory', in *Red Planets: Marxism and Science Fiction*, ed. by Mark Bould and China Miéville (Middletown: Wesleyan University Press, 2009), pp. 231–48; Patrick Parrinder, 'Revisiting Suvin's Poetics of Science Fiction', in *Learning from Other Worlds: Estrangement, Cognition, and the Politics of Science Fiction and Utopia*, ed. by Patrick Parrinder (Liverpool: Liverpool University Press, 2000), pp. 36–50; and John Rieder, *Science Fiction and the Mass Cultural Genre System* (Middletown: Wesleyan University Press, 2017), pp. 13–31. Interestingly, Seo-Young Chu recasts 'cognitive estrangement' as an attribute of science-fictional referents, not texts, in *Do Metaphors Dream of Literal Sleep? A Science-Fictional Theory of Representation* (Cambridge, MA: Harvard University Press, 2010), pp. 3–10.

thus its critical edge. Rather than to estrange, it began to naturalise private property.

My claim in this book is not merely that the Hollywood science-fiction films of the 1980s and early 1990s sought to estrange us from the new enclosures, but that such estrangements were utopian in character. To understand why this is the case, why a science-fiction cinema critiquing enclosure might take utopian (and dystopian) form, however, we must come down from the heights of historical overview and peer instead into the genre's inner mechanism. Let us return, in particular, to Suvin's account, according to which science-fictional estrangements consist in a ceaseless perceptual shifting between the reader's observable society and the fiction's more richly constructed world, which bestows upon the reader a profounder view of their reality. Science fiction is analogical, it follows, its aesthetic quality proportional to its cognitive quality.[53] Suvin's emphasis here on the centrality of analogy to science fiction, his formulation of estrangement as an essentially analogical device, constitutes a rejoinder to those for whom the core of science fiction is, on the contrary, extrapolation, the projection and enlargement of this or that particular process into the future. In Suvin's view, extrapolation is only one kind of analogy, and a particularly bad one at that, its brute, linear abstraction reeking of technocracy, positivism, and bourgeois meliorism. 'Thus, although extrapolation was historically a convention of much SF,' Suvin suggests, 'pure extrapolation is flat, and the pretense at it masks in all significant cases the employment of other methods.'[54]

But is this necessarily the case? At one point in his discussion, Suvin begins to offer another reading of extrapolative science fiction. 'Extrapolating one feature or possibility of the author's environment may be a legitimate literary device of hyperbolization equally in anticipation-tales, other SF [...] or indeed in a number of other genres such as satire,' Suvin writes, before reiterating that the 'cognitive value' of science fiction consists in analogy, reference to the author's present, 'rather than predictions, discrete or global'.[55] As such sentences make clear, the object of Suvin's criticism is not extrapolation per se, but rather its use as futurology or forecast, which he takes to be inimical to art.[56] Suvin thus leaves open the possibility that, where it functions

---

[53] Suvin, pp. 87–92.
[54] Suvin, p. 93.
[55] Suvin, p. 95.
[56] 'Ontologically, art is not pragmatic truth nor is fiction fact. To expect from SF more than a stimulus for independent thinking, more than a system of stylized narrative devices understandable only in their mutual relationships

as a form of hyperbole, exaggerating consciously for effect, extrapolation may well have cognitive and aesthetic value.

If Suvin does not dwell on the practice of extrapolative hyperbole, or offer any examples, this is largely because (as we have just seen) his purpose in *Metamorphoses* is to establish that estrangement is primarily analogical. Pursuing the matter a little further here, however, we might venture the hypothesis that one of those 'other' science fictions in which extrapolation is 'legitimate' is the dystopia.[57] By no means necessarily futurological, extrapolation works in dystopian texts to bring into focus social, political, or economic processes that are underway in the author's (or filmmaker's) time, thereby to sharpen our awareness of them. To take one obvious example from the history of American (and British) science-fiction film, Terry Gilliam's *Brazil* (1985) extrapolates the bureaucratic machinery of the modern state, but cannot persuasively be read as a prediction that bureaucratisation will ever reach that degree. From this construal of dystopia as extrapolation two important corollaries follow. First, dystopias are particularistic: they can choose one, two, or more discrete processes to enlarge into our awareness. Second, dystopias are quantitative: their worse societies increase the problems afflicting the author's or filmmaker's society by degree. Though they imagine a society dramatically worse than the one presently existing, it remains the same *kind* of society.

If extrapolation forms one 'limit-case' of analogy, as Suvin puts it, utopias represent the analogical limit in the other direction.[58] It is their

---

within a fictional whole and not as isolated realities, leads insensibly to the demand for scientific accuracy in the extrapolated *realia*' (Suvin, pp. 41–42).

[57] 'Most direct extrapolation of our own conditions and forms—social and political but also immanently material—has been in effort or intention dystopian: atomic war, famine, overpopulation, electronic surveillance has written 1984 into millenia of possible dates,' Raymond Williams observes, in a 1978 essay, a propos science fiction's turn away from utopia ('Utopia and Science Fiction', in *Tenses of Imagination: Raymond Williams on Science Fiction, Utopia and Dystopia*, ed. by Andrew Milner (Oxford: Peter Lang, 2010), pp. 93–112 (p. 109)). Sean Seeger and Daniel Davison-Vecchione discuss the extrapolative dystopia (which they take, however, to be only one kind of dystopia) in 'Dystopian Literature and the Sociological Imagination', *Thesis Eleven*, 155 (2019), 45–63 (pp. 55–63).

[58] Suvin, pp. 93–94. If utopias are science fictional, then this complicates Jameson's periodisation of the latter, according to which (as we have seen) the first science fictions were Verne's and Wells's, written in the second half of the nineteenth century. Utopias such as More's must be seen as precursor forms, working out one particular kind of analogical estrangement. For the classic statement of this view, see Suvin, p. 76.

task to portray, not simply a better society, but a qualitatively better one, a change in kind. They must transform, not merely one or two aspects of the society in question, as do extrapolative fictions, but the entire social universe. This accounts for utopias' customary need, at the level of content, to demarcate utopian from non-utopian space: the channel separating More's Utopia from the mainland, the dream-state of Morris's narrator, the volcanic eruption blocking off 'Herland' in Charlotte Perkins Gilman's 1915 novella of that name, or space itself between Anarres and Urras in Ursula Le Guin's *The Dispossessed* (1974). It also explains, at the level of form, the primacy of description in utopian texts, which labour to construct a world anew, and which must therefore occupy themselves with minutiae that the author of a dystopia can ignore without fear of embarrassment, thus allowing the latter more space for narration—for action, conflict, resolution.[59] Inverting the particularistic and quantitative dystopia, utopias are universalistic and qualitative: they set fire to the old world, resolve to build a new one.

Crucially for us, this universalistic and qualitative character of utopian thought, its need to sweep away all that exists, entails an implicit denunciation of enclosure, since the latter constitutes the basis of the capitalist mode of production and the oppressions deriving therefrom. Utopias must identify the source of the social ills they seek to remedy, an operation carried out, paradigmatically, in Book I of More's classic text, where enclosure indeed becomes the target of sustained criticism.[60] Dystopias, on the other hand, enjoy relative freedom in selecting the object of their criticism: they can extrapolate automation, or militarisation, or natural selection, or global heating, or something else entirely—often several at one time, if they wish.[61] It follows that, where late twentieth-century Hollywood cinema seeks to criticise the new enclosures by negation, it must turn to the specifically utopian form of analogical representation particular to science fiction. And where, by contrast, it seeks to criticise them by extrapolation, it tends towards

---

[59] Jameson discusses the necessity of utopian closure in *Archaeologies of the Future: The Desire Called Utopia and Other Science Fictions* (London: Verso, 2007), pp. 38–40, 204, and the relation between narration and description in utopian and dystopian texts in *The Seeds of Time* (New York: Columbia University Press, 1994), pp. 55–57.

[60] As we shall see in Chapter 4, however, Raphael Hythloday (More's fictional adventurer, who has visited Utopia) posits greed and pride as the chief motivations behind enclosure, and thus behind the social ills he diagnoses.

[61] Thus Gregory Claeys distinguishes between political, environmental, and technological dystopias (*Dystopia: A Natural History* (Oxford: Oxford University Press, 2017), p. 5).

dystopian expression. That closer scrutiny of many such films will detect the coexistence of utopian and dystopian elements in each complicates rather than confutes this analysis, to which we shall therefore return in the following chapters.

New Hollywood and the *Novum*

The release, in 1977, of the first *Star Wars* film, directed by George Lucas, and Steven Spielberg's *Close Encounters of the Third Kind* heralded the beginning of a new wave of Hollywood science-fiction cinema—by some counts, the third. Much had changed since the first wave, in the 1930s, which saw the production of hybrid science-fiction–horror films such as *Frankenstein* (1931) and *The Invisible Ray* (1936), expressing both the interest in new scientific and technological developments (the so-called 'Machine Age') and the pessimism of the Depression.[62] The next wave of Hollywood science-fiction cinema came in the 1950s with the rise of the disaster film, interpreted most famously by Susan Sontag as responses to nuclear anxieties and the threat of dehumanisation.[63] *The Thing* (1951), *Forbidden Planet* (1956), and *Invasion of the Body Snatchers* (1956) stand as some of the most emblematic releases of the decade. Yet science fiction was not entirely absent from Hollywood in the intervening period: as J. P. Telotte notes, elements of the genre persisted in the serials of the 1930s and 1940s, such as *Flash Gordon* (1936) and *Buck Rogers* (1939).[64] Perhaps the most significant Hollywood science-fiction film of them all, Kubrick's *2001: A Space Odyssey*, was released in 1968, between the second and third waves, and served as inspiration for the aesthetic and conceptual complexities of the latter, particularly *Alien* and *Blade Runner*.[65]

Star Wars and *Close Encounters* are also two of the earliest products of the 'New Hollywood' period, which forms the industrial context of most of the films examined in this book. After the breakup of the classical studio system, in which a handful of vertically integrated

---

[62] J. P. Telotte, *Science Fiction Film* (Cambridge: Cambridge University Press, 2001), p. 90. Though it is not a Hollywood film, Fritz Lang's *Metropolis* (1927) also exerted a major influence on Hollywood science fiction.

[63] Susan Sontag, 'The Imagination of Disaster', in *Against Interpretation and Other Essays* (London: Penguin, 2009), pp. 209–25.

[64] Telotte, pp. 90–94.

[65] For a discussion of *2001*'s position vis-à-vis the second and third waves, see Carl Freedman's provocative essay 'Kubrick's *2001* and the Possibility of a Science-Fiction Cinema', *Science Fiction Studies*, 25.2 (1998), 300–18 (pp. 300–05).

companies dominated the market, film production in Hollywood became an increasingly ad hoc affair. Studios preferred to bring together specific personnel for specific projects. One result of this fragmentation, at least in the 1960s and 1970s, was the so-called 'Hollywood Renaissance', which saw the production of a range of innovative films, challenging convention, and seeming to give voice to the counterculture, or certain aspects thereof (*Bonnie and Clyde* and *The Graduate*, both released in 1967, are notable examples).[66] The tide changed again with the success of Spielberg's *Jaws*, the summer hit of 1975, opening the second phase of New Hollywood. Hollywood having suffered a financial crisis since the late 1960s, *Jaws* renewed the studios' confidence in big-budget features. Blockbusters moved to the heart of their strategy; the studios' financial picture would henceforth depend on the success of a few big hits per year. By the 1980s, this apparently quite risky approach had become viable for three reasons: first, many of the studios had been absorbed by conglomerates, which gave them sufficient resources to survive flops; second, the studios could rely increasingly on ancillary markets (video and DVD sales, action figures, theme park rides, soundtrack albums, and so on) to compensate if a blockbuster performed poorly at the box office; and, third, the studios received growing returns from overseas markets, especially in Europe.[67]

Science fiction is a genre attuned to the problematic of historical consciousness as capital's expansion begins to impede such consciousness. This explains its concern with the new enclosures since the late 1970s. But why should so many such science fictions be produced as Hollywood blockbusters, especially given the latter's generally conservative politics? Geoff King and Tanya Krzywinska suggest that science fiction is well suited to the blockbuster partly because it lends itself to the production of spectacle, partly because its content is easily repackaged as the action figures, computer games, and theme-park rides that form major sources of revenue in the New Hollywood system.[68] Christine Cornea makes a similar argument: spectacular science-fiction cinema is perfect for Hollywood's increasingly global market, while its hybridity, the ease with which science fiction can absorb elements from other genres, helps widen its appeal.[69] Such answers are plausible, I think, but incomplete

---

[66] King, pp. 11–48.

[67] King, pp. 49–84; Thomas Schatz, 'The New Hollywood', in *Film Theory Goes to the Movies*, ed. by Jim Collins, Hilary Radner, and Ava Preacher Collins (New York: Routledge, 1993), pp. 8–36.

[68] Geoff King and Tanya Krzywinska, *Science Fiction Cinema: From Outerspace to Cyberspace* (London: Wallflower, 2000), pp. 60–63.

[69] Christine Cornea, *Science Fiction Cinema: Between Fantasy and Reality*

in so far as they do not consider what we have seen Suvin describe as the essentially analogical operations of the genre. Is there a more fundamental explanation for this strange marriage between a radical and critical science-fiction cinema, one seeking to estrange us from those property-forms that have come to seem natural, and the incurious conservatism characteristic of the blockbuster?

The answer lies in an oft-quoted comment made by Steven Spielberg in an interview in 1978. 'What interests me more than anything else is the idea,' Spielberg said. 'If a person can tell me the idea in twenty-five words or less, it's going to be a good movie.'[70] For Justin Wyatt, the kind of 'high-concept' film Spielberg here evokes underpins the advertising strategies of post-classical Hollywood. High-concept texts admit of easy translation between pitch and picture, the latter being reducible to the former, and thus imply the existence of low-concept ones, whose marketing, by contrast, cannot but misrepresent the whole.[71] Crucially for us, the distinction between high and low concept maps onto that between dystopias and utopias, at least as I have defined them above. The dystopia being particularistic, premised on this or that specific change to the world, its innovations can be extracted and reproduced as pithy marketing. Take *RoboCop*'s tagline: 'Part man, part machine, all cop', and *The Truman Show*'s: 'On the air. Unaware.' Each names the film's core extrapolation: for *RoboCop*, the automation of policing, and for *The Truman Show*, the expansion of the spectacle to the point where it subsumes everyday life. On the other hand, the utopia's universality, its need to construct a whole world anew, does not admit of such condensation. (The boredom sometimes attributed to the utopian genre is a symptom of this irreducibility, each detail demanding the same readerly or viewerly attention as the last.) It follows that specifically dystopian science fiction, extrapolating discrete processes into the future, aligns quite precisely with the marketing practices dominant in the New Hollywood system.[72]

The consonance between dystopian extrapolation and high-concept cinema helps us understand, in turn, why the third phase of Hollywood

(Edinburgh: Edinburgh University Press, 2007), p. 113.
[70] Spielberg is quoted in Justin Wyatt, *High Concept: Movies and Marketing in Hollywood* (Austin: University of Texas Press, 1994), p. 13.
[71] Wyatt, pp. 10, 16–17.
[72] To be clear, this explains why dystopian science fictions of the sort produced in the 1980s and onwards have become one of Hollywood's major offerings, but not why science fictions would take predominantly dystopian form during this period in the first place. I turn to such a question near the end of Chapter 4.

science-fiction films splits off in two directions. There is, I think, a clear, almost intuitive distinction between texts such as *Star Wars* and *Close Encounters* and more explicitly political works such as *Alien*, *RoboCop*, and *Total Recall*. The first, in my view, are only superficially science fictions. They are high-concept films, in Wyatt's sense, but their organising concepts are not extrapolations or analogies. While they incorporate tropes and images common to science fiction (space travel, alien life, fantastic technology), these are not derived from real historical forces or tendencies so much as magicked into the diegetic world. The question of genesis, the origins of Wookiees or lightsabers, is of little interest to *Star Wars*, for instance. By contrast, in the second, properly dystopian and therefore science-fictional group, the genesis of the *novum* (Suvin's term, borrowed from Ernst Bloch, for the novelty responsible for estrangement) demands explanation, the validation of its cognition.[73] Unlike the monsters of *Star Wars*, the alien of *Alien* is conceived as a product of natural selection—it is the 'perfect organism', as the science officer aboard the *Nostromo* puts it—while the automation of policing in *RoboCop* is comprehensible as a response to certain definite political and economic pressures, spelled out in the film (the need for more robust policing to support construction work, thus to produce profits, for instance).[74] This second group of films are science fictions whose dystopian form happens to have been amenable to the structures of high-concept cinema. It is therefore the films of this more fundamentally science-fictional branch of spectacular New Hollywood cinema that will concern us in the following pages.

What *Star Wars* and *Alien* do have in common, however, is that both are franchises, and thus extremely valuable intellectual properties, whose potential to generate returns exceeds their initial release—a useful trait in the New Hollywood economy. Intellectual property being the enclosure that bears most insistently on the business of cultural production, we ought to note the changing relation between Hollywood itself and copyright law in the post-classical period. Significantly, the breakdown of the studio system at the end of the 1940s laid the foundations, not only for the artistic innovations of the Hollywood Renaissance, but also for successful auteurs' growing control over their creations. Shortly after the release of *Star Wars*, for instance, Lucas started up a licensing bureau that would inspect the film's fan fiction for

---

[73] Suvin, pp. 79–101.

[74] For further discussion of the specificity of science fiction's monsters, see Vivian Sobchack, *Screening Space: The American Science Fiction Film*, 2nd edn (New Brunswick: Rutgers University Press, 1987), pp. 30–38.

copyright infractions. Then, when *Battlestar Galactica* appeared in 1978, Lucas sued the television series for plagiarising *Star Wars*. 'Despite his generous use of film history,' Peter Decherney writes, noting *Star Wars*'s borrowings from the 1930s and 1940s serials, 'Lucas has always had a low tolerance for work that he thinks takes inspiration from his films.' The judge presiding over the case, Irving Hill, concluded that both texts simply drew from the standard repertory of science-fictional tropes, and Lucas—or, more precisely, Fox, which had produced *Star Wars*—could not claim ownership of the genre.[75]

Yet Hollywood has not simply invoked intellectual property law when it senses infringement; it has shaped such laws through its lobbying power. As Decherney observes, film studios had opposed United States membership of the Berne Convention, the international copyright treaty inaugurated in 1886, since the 1930s. Represented by lobbyists for the Motion Picture Association of America, however, they changed their position in the 1980s, when Berne membership seemed to offer protection from the growing problem of global film and video piracy. For quite different reasons—specifically, the prospect of securing 'moral rights', which were not enshrined in domestic copyright law—the Directors Guild of America also advocated membership, and the United States finally joined the Berne Convention a few years later, in 1989.[76] The Digital Millennium Copyright Act, passed in 1998, extended the domain of copyright still further by prohibiting even the attempt to circumvent digital copyright protection, a ban that effectively criminalised 'fair use' in certain contexts. The Act thereby exceeded the studios' longstanding ambition to secure copy protection by technical means, such as in their efforts to prevent duplication of VHS tapes with Macrovision or of DVDs with the Content Scrambling System.[77] As we shall see in Chapter 5, the expansion of intellectual property rights at the end of the twentieth century was rapid enough to capture the attention of some New Hollywood science-fiction films themselves.

---

[75] Peter Decherney, *Hollywood's Copyright Wars: From Edison to the Internet* (New York: Columbia University Press, 2012), pp. 130–33. Hill's decision, we ought to note, construes literary and cinematic genre as something generic and common, thus not to be enclosed.

[76] Decherney, pp. 114–16, 144–50.

[77] Decherney, pp. 201–11.

Anticipating Evisceration

Released in 1979, in the early years both of the second phase of New Hollywood and the third phase of Hollywood science-fiction cinema, Ridley Scott's *Alien* exemplifies the consonance of dystopian and blockbuster form posited in the previous section. *Alien*'s plot begins, as I have noted, sometime in the early twenty-second century, when British–Japanese corporation Weylan-Yutani detects a warning signal from outer space and, presuming that the signal implies alien encounter of some kind, sends one of its commercial tugs, the *Nostromo*, to investigate. The company aims to contain an alien in the *Nostromo* and bring it back to Earth for analysis, possibly to deploy it as a weapon. Of course, the process of capture is likely to kill or injure the crew, so it is important that the relevant employees remain unaware of the precise nature of their task. To keep them in the dark, Weylan-Yutani programs the *Nostromo*'s mainframe, known as 'Mother', to hide the key details from its captain. It swaps the crew's science officer for an android, Ash (Ian Holm), whose job it is to inspect the alien, but also, even more importantly, to ensure the crew's complicity. One crew member, Kane (John Hurt), gets attacked by a 'facehugger' while he inspects the derelict spacecraft from which the warning signal emanates. The crew being unsure what this alien form is, they bring Kane back aboard the *Nostromo*—a disastrous decision, though it accords with Weylan-Yutani's secret plans. Kane starts to get better, until suddenly, in one of the most famous and shocking scenes of New Hollywood's science-fiction cinema, the alien bursts through his chest. Loose aboard the *Nostromo*, the alien proceeds to hunt the rest of the crew. It kills all but Ripley (Sigourney Weaver), who, finally thwarting the company's aims, blows up the ship and its cargo, ejects the alien into outer space, and escapes in the *Nostromo*'s shuttle.

This high-concept film therefore rests on two extrapolations. The first is an almost unimaginable expansion of the sphere of commodity circulation, whose interstellar exchanges dwarf today's mere international flows of global capital. The 'commercial towing vehicle', the *Nostromo*, on which *Alien*'s action takes place, must lug 20 million tons of mineral ore through space, and is currently, as we join it at the start of the film, en route back to Earth. *Alien* wants us to know that such an extrapolation has taken place: these details appear as titles on its establishing shots, which depict the *Nostromo* floating through the universe. The second extrapolation is less obvious, shows up later in the film, and is evolutionary in character. It manifests itself in the alien, which Ash praises as 'the perfect organism', its activity 'unclouded by conscience, remorse, or delusions of morality'. *Alien*'s terror derives from the coexistence of these two extrapolations: the vast dark and empty spaces of the commercial spacecraft, months away from planet Earth, create the perfect environment for the rapacious, undiscriminating alien to hunt the humans aboard it. 'In space,' *Alien*'s marketing reminds us, 'no one can hear you scream.'

Yet we might get a still better sense of how *Alien* relates to the structures of the New Hollywood blockbuster if we compare it to the latter's urtext, *Jaws*. I want to begin here by drawing attention to Jameson's reading of *Jaws*, particularly of the shark's polysemy, which he initially gleans from the diverse allegorical readings of the film. In the critic's eyes, Jameson observes, the shark becomes an avatar of this or that psychoanalytic or historical anxiety about the Other, 'whether it be the Communist conspiracy or the Third World', or even of 'the unreality of daily life in America today, and in particular the haunting and unmentionable persistence of the organic—of birth, copulation, and death'. Jameson does not seek to refute any of these readings, but meditates instead on their coexistence, their multiplicity, which 'suggests that the vocation of the symbol—the killer shark—lies less in any single message or meaning than in its very capacity to absorb and organize all of these quite distinct anxieties together'. In the ideological operation par excellence, the film channels these fears into the biological figure of the shark and naturalises them thereby.[78] Jameson's suggestion here, that the shark is objectively and strategically polysemous, offers an explanation, in a different theoretical register, for the blockbuster's widely noted conservatism. This last consists, it follows, not primarily in the projection of specific ideologies, but in a kind of relativism, as so many diverse fears are resolved on the screen, the ideologies underpinning them undisturbed.

Let us bear *Jaws*'s ideological relativism in mind as we now turn to *Alien*, which I shall suggest narrows our interpretive options a little more than Spielberg's film does. At the start of *Alien*, there is little to suggest division or seniority. We watch the crew wake up, wearing identical clothes in identical hypersleep containers, as though they were being reborn. They sit around a circular table, a table with no head, and eat, talk, and joke together. Tracking around the table, at distance enough that always more than one individual is in view, and therefore introducing each member in the moment of their interrelation with others, Scott's camera likewise confers a kind of formal equality upon the crew. The tracking stops, however, between Parker (Yaphet Kotto)

---

[78] Fredric Jameson, 'Reification and Utopia in Mass Culture', in *Signatures of the Visible* (Abingdon: Routledge, 2007), pp. 11–46 (p. 35).

Figure 1: The prelapsarian state (*Alien*, dir. by Ridley Scott (20th Century Fox, 1979))

and Brett (Harry Dean Stanton), the *Nostromo*'s engineers, such that we are privy to Brett's gesture to Parker, this indicating that he wants the latter to broach the inequitable 'bonus situation' and claim the engineers' right to 'full shares'. With Parker's intervention, the blissful, prelapsarian state is broken; the captain, Dallas (Tom Skerritt), responds, 'You get what you're contracted for, like everybody else.' The labour contract becomes the locus of antagonism again when it transpires that the crew are unaware of their obligation to investigate the derelict spacecraft's help signal. Ash tells Parker that failure to investigate entails a forfeiture of all shares, but later, after Parker attacks Ash (Ash himself having first attacked Ripley), the crew learn that he lied, that they were not obliged, in fact. Ash lies simply to ensure that the crew follows the company's wishes. It becomes clear that the labour contract has been used, not as the basis of transparent understanding between two free individuals, but as the opposite: a form of coercion, a means of exercising class power. The contract itself is irrelevant. Its purported content merely serves as cover for the company's more sinister motives.

Class struggle rumbles on in the low-level acts of worker resistance and disobedience in the *Nostromo*. The ship having landed roughly on the unexplored moon, Parker enumerates across the intercom its various faults, and Dallas asks how long they need to mend it. 'Seventeen hours, tell 'em,' Brett mutters to Parker, but Parker claims they actually need 'at least twenty-five'. There is an element of class strategy, we see, in the negotiation between captain and engineer. This latent conflict between the manual labourers and the senior crew rears its head again when they begin to search for the alien. Ripley says that she thought Parker and Brett had fixed 'twelve module', an area in the *Nostromo* where the lights are not working. Brett replies, 'We did. I don't understand it,' and Parker suggests that the electric circuits 'must've burned out'. Ripley's tone and wording, however, make clear her suspicions that Parker and Brett have neglected their duties, and have not fixed the ship properly. Although, as Dallas reminds Ripley, 'standard procedure is to do what the hell they'—the company—'tell you to do', the interpersonal drama of *Alien* derives largely from insubordination, crew members' threats to transgress the formal division of labour, the most significant, perhaps, being Ash's decision to overrule Ripley by letting Dallas, Lambert (Veronica Cartwright), and the stricken Kane back aboard.

As for capital itself, it finds representation in *Alien* only in highly mediated form. In the first instance, it appears in the company's demands and compulsions, but these also act at a remove, as it were, as various members of the crew are relied upon to articulate Weylan-Yutani's interests. It is thus the captain, Dallas, who tries to justify the engineers' lower payment and urges the crew to comply with the company's demands. But Dallas is not a perfect spokesperson in so far as, contrary to the company's aims, he tries to kill the alien, when it is the crew who are meant to be expendable. When Ash begins to try to sabotage the crew's efforts to save themselves, we learn that he is a truer representative of the company. Unlike Dallas, Ash is fully aware of Weylan-Yutani's objectives, and he has been placed on the *Nostromo* to ensure that they are achieved, by fair means or foul. Yet arguably the ultimate instantiation of the company is the alien itself. As Jeff Gould points out, the alien boards the ship, contrary to Ripley's efforts; it accords with the company's judgement that the crew is expendable; and it entrenches divisions among the crew.[79]

It is now time to register the essential ambivalence of the alien-figure, however, which must also be read as a symbol for the working class, particularly for the *Nostromo*'s manual workers. Recall Ripley's insinuation that Parker and Brett did not complete all of the repair work in 'twelve module', which the engineers claim they had fixed. This is a crucial moment in the film's symbolic structure, where the darkness begins to evoke the workers' background resistance to the dehumanising and debilitating effects of capital accumulation. It is to this darkness that the alien belongs, not in the mundane sense that it is evil, but rather in the sense that the darkness is its body or, conversely, that it is the body of the darkness. The dark spaces of the *Nostromo* before the crew awake conjure the terrible prospect of a post-human future: as viewers,

---

[79] See Gould's piece in Jackie Byars and others, 'Symposium on *Alien*', *Science Fiction Studies*, 7 (1980), 278–304 (p. 283).

we see what the characters cannot, since, as soon as they wake up, the lights turn on.[80] The darkness of this post-human future is, of course, what the alien also threatens, and indeed achieves, in so far as it strands Ripley, cutting her loose from human society. Additionally, when we see the alien (and, until the end, we see it only partially), its body melts into the darkness of its surroundings: it lifts the silent objectivity, even naturalism, of the *mise en scène* into a symbolic realm of heightened drama and meaning. The alien is therefore the corporeal expression of the ship's *mise en scène*. It is the *Nostromo*'s dark space, the space of the manual workers, stepping forward in animal form.

This second dimension of the alien's allegory, according to which it represents a certain resistance to capital, finds expression on the screen through anamorphosis. The alien's short life is one of change; every time we see it, we notice different body parts; new and terrifying features appear. It nevertheless remains unclear whether these changes are mutations in the object itself (the alien's body is maturing) or whether it has to do with the position of the viewing subject (the different angles and distances from which we see the alien, and how it is lit, determine which parts are visible). In this impossible interpretive situation—does the shift occur in the object or the subject?—we can say only that the alien is anamorphic, that this perceptual distortion is the essence of its being. It is as if the alien takes the space of the *Nostromo*—a disciplinary space, which permits or prohibits crew members' access to particular areas on the basis of their seniority—and bends it around itself, thus posing a symbolic challenge to the architecture that maintains Weylan-Yutani's control. In so far as these doors, corridors, and barriers exert disciplinary force, keeping the crew's (and thus the company's) internal hierarchy intact, the alien exists as some absolute limit to corporate domination, to the subsumption of ever greater zones of human (and non-human) existence under the logic of capital. The alien accords with some of Weylan-Yutani's wishes, as Gould argues, but it also seems to embody what the company, and what capital, cannot control.

While these two interpretive options—the alien as capital, the alien as resistance to capital—by no means exhaust allegorical readings of the film, it is significant that *Alien* seems to reorient *Jaws*'s strategic

---

[80] For a sustained analysis of how the film's opening shots create this sense of 'post-human futurity', see Caetlin Benson-Allott, 'Dreadful Architecture: Zones of Horror in *Alien* and Lee Bontecou's Wall Sculptures', *Journal of Visual Culture*, 14 (2015), 267–78.

polysemy around the relation between capital and labour.[81] Scott's film strikes a compromise at a fundamental level between the blockbuster's need to offer points of identification for different ideologies, thus different subject positions, and the new politics inchoate in Hollywood's science fiction. What we shall now proceed to observe in *RoboCop, Total Recall, Blade Runner,* and *The Truman Show* in the next two chapters is a further refinement of the form's politics. The contradiction between capital and labour sustained in the figure of the alien becomes, in these later films, a tension between dystopia and utopia, between a world enclosed and a moment or principle incompatible with enclosure.

---

[81] See, for probably the most well-known allegorical reading of the film, Barbara Creed's interpretation of the alien as the parthenogenetic mother who threatens patriarchy and symbolises death (*The Monstrous-Feminine: Film, Feminism, Psychoanalysis* (Oxon: Routledge, 1993), pp. 16–30).

Chapter 2

Privatisation
Conceptualising Enclosure in *RoboCop* and *Total Recall*

Why it was Paul Verhoeven, and not someone else, who came to direct two of Hollywood's major political films of the late 1980s in particular, and perhaps the Reagan period in general—*RoboCop* (1987) and *Total Recall* (1990)—is difficult to ascertain, at least from his own accounts. Verhoeven came to both projects belatedly, after other directors had turned them down or given up. Orion Pictures eventually asked him to direct *RoboCop*, Verhoeven supposes, because they liked *Flesh and Blood* (1985), his first English-language film, which he had recently made with them.[1] *Total Recall* had already passed from Disney to the De Laurentiis Entertainment Group before, the latter having gone bankrupt, Arnold Schwarzenegger prompted Carolco Pictures to buy the rights and brought Verhoeven onto the project.[2] Verhoeven claims that he was keen to make science-fiction films in his early Hollywood years, not for political or satirical reasons, but because he felt that a 'futuristic' or 'over-the-top' speculative style would help conceal his unfamiliarity with American cultural mores, among other things.[3] Perhaps unsurprisingly, then, Verhoeven's own readings of what this chapter takes to be two unambiguously political films are equally resolutely apolitical. *RoboCop*

---

[1] Indra Bhose, 'Paul Verhoeven Tackles Science Fiction', trans. by Alexandra Valentine Proulx, in *Paul Verhoeven: Interviews*, ed. by Margaret Barton-Fumo (Jackson: University Press of Mississippi, 2016), pp. 47–54 (pp. 47–48).

[2] In fact, Verhoeven was the first director Ronald Shusett (who, together with Dan O'Bannon, wrote the earliest drafts of the *Total Recall* script) had wanted to make the film—back in 1981, after Shusett had seen Verhoeven's *Soldier of Orange* (1977). See David Hughes, *Tales from Development Hell: Hollywood Film-Making the Hard Way* (London: Titan, 2003), p. 67.

[3] Cornea, p. 135. In a 1991 interview, Verhoeven says, 'Politics are of no interest to me. I have no political beliefs. I find everything fascinating, especially the political beliefs of the United States' (George Hickenlooper, 'The Vitality of Existence', in *Paul Verhoeven*, pp. 57–63 (p. 59)).

is about 'the immortality of the soul', he suggests, while *Total Recall* is a philosophical film concerned with the nature of truth.[4]

At this historical moment, the latter half of the 1980s, the concept of privatisation was as new to most Americans as American mores were to Verhoeven. 'A new word—*privatization*—has entered the lexicon of federal budget making,' Stuart M. Butler declared at the start of a 1986 primer on that subject for conservative think tank The Heritage Foundation.[5] Seeking to legitimise privatisation, to paint it as an established practice, privatisation advocates stretched the term's range such that it came to encompass, not only sales of state-owned enterprise, but contracting out, voucher use, joint ventures, and franchising. Defined thus, privatisation occurred at almost all levels of American government in the 1980s. City and county managers contracted out more and more public services; Reagan privatised the National Consumer Cooperative Bank, sold off loans by the Department of Education and the Farmers Home Administration, and put the government's stake in Conrail on the stock market; and private companies began to own and manage prisons, while the number of private police officers likewise grew. In 1987, the year of *RoboCop*'s release, Reagan appointed his Commission on Privatization, whose report would recommend a more comprehensive programme than Reagan himself had attempted hitherto.

Indeed, it is principally to the *concept* of privatisation that *RoboCop* and *Total Recall* attend, I shall suggest in this chapter. *RoboCop* presents a corporation taking over provision of a range of formerly public services, while *Total Recall* imagines the enclosure of air, which is no longer an uncommodifiable 'public good'. So far has privatisation extended in these diegetic worlds that the films imagine the distinction between public and private itself breaking down. Thus *RoboCop*'s Omni Consumer Products (OCP) and *Total Recall*'s Agency combine the *modus operandi* of the profit-making company with that of the state's repressive apparatus and suggest thereby that the distinction between public and private has become anachronistic in their speculative futures. If the Reagan administration sought to familiarise American citizens with privatisation *qua* process and concept, *RoboCop* and *Total Recall* respond by defamiliarising 'public' and 'private' as categories.

From here, *RoboCop* and *Total Recall* proceed to thematise the other conceptual problems posed by expanding capital accumulation and a vanishing public sphere. Areas of our social world that were not

---

[4] Bhose, p. 50; Cornea, p. 138.
[5] Stuart M. Butler, 'Privatizing Federal Services: A Primer', *Heritage Foundation Backgrounder*, 488 (1986), 1–13 (p. 1).

primarily defined by their relation to capital must now be rethought, and that process of rethinking generates these films' main conflicts. In *RoboCop*, the privatisation of law enforcement prompts the police officers to debate their relationship to labour and capital. Are they manual workers like plumbers, say, who should be able to strike? Meanwhile, the film's drama grows out of the tension between OCP's claim to RoboCop (Peter Weller) as a commodity and the increasing evidence that he remains, on some level, a person, with memories, intentions, and emotions. In much the same way, in *Total Recall*, Douglas Quaid's (Schwarzenegger) identity dilemma—is he Vilos Cohaagen's (Ronny Cox) henchman, Hauser, or is he really a construction worker dreaming about that?—appears as a question of class affiliation. Later on, *Total Recall* codes the Schwarzenegger body as a form of property in its own right, such that Quaid and Hauser's struggle over their right to occupy that body allegorises a kind of primitive accumulation, an original claim to corporeal territory. Who was really 'here first', the film asks?

Released as they were at the end of the 1980s, *RoboCop* and *Total Recall* come at a crucial moment in the periodisation proposed in this book, according to which the 1970s economic crisis, and the new enclosures consequent thereon, prompted Hollywood's science fictions into a renewed meditation on private property. On the one hand, the most recent wave of enclosures had been underway for long enough, had penetrated the fabric of American society deeply enough, that they had become available to consciousness, as *RoboCop*'s and *Total Recall*'s explicit evocations of the phenomenon testify. On the other, the discourse of privatisation was new enough, unfamiliar enough that its status as a contested, manipulated, eminently political and ideological concept could likewise be registered. It is the combination of these two factors—the persistence of enclosure, the newness of 'privatisation'—I propose, that allowed *RoboCop* and *Total Recall* to measure the distance between the one and the other, between process and concept, and to generate two dramas of conceptualisation.

'A New Word'

The idylls of unfettered enterprise having always occupied a central place in American national identity, the United States presents itself as an outlier in most histories of privatisation.[6] Although the Great

---

[6] In a 1987 statement introducing his Commission on Privatization, Reagan noted that privatisation 'follows in the great tradition of free enterprise and

Depression and the Second World War prompted the United States government to expand the public sector—by 1953, it was the largest provider of electricity and insurance, the largest lender and borrower, and the largest landowner, to give just a few examples—state-owned companies have played only a marginal role in its economy.[7] American legislators have preferred regulation and private litigation to ownership, and thus privatisation upset the balance of economic power less in the United States than it did elsewhere.[8] The Thatcherite privatisations that wracked the United Kingdom's aerospace, gas, and telecoms industries, and that augured a wave of privatisations across the world—in France, the sale of Banque Paribas; in Japan, of Nippon Telegraph and Telephone; in Mexico, of Telefonos de Mexico—are hardly comparable to Reagan's, whose major divestiture came only at the end of his presidency, in 1987, when he sold the government's stake in Conrail, a freight rail operator, for $1.65 billion.[9] Yet closer attention both to legislation passed at the end of the twentieth century and to the increasing capaciousness of the concept of privatisation—its ambit enlarged by Reagan and others in the 1980s—suggests that the United States conforms to the picture rather more closely, that it too underwent a wave of privatisations in the 1980s, these providing the starting point for *RoboCop*'s and *Total Recall*'s depictions. It was only during the Reagan years that the theory of privatisation, on the one hand, and its practice, on the other, were consciously brought together, and privatisation migrated from the margins to the centre of American political discourse.[10]

The kinds of processes we know today as privatisations were already common in the United States in the early to mid-twentieth century. San

private ownership of property that has long been a part of American history, from the initial sale of government lands under the Northwest Ordinance to the homestead program that brought the pioneers to the American West over 100 years ago' ('Statement on the President's Commission on Privatization', 3 September 1987 <https://www.reaganlibrary.gov/archives/speech/statement-presidents-commission-privatization> [accessed 17 May 2022] (para. 1 of 6)).

[7] Nicholas Henry, 'The Contracting Conundrum in the United States: Or, Do We Really Understand Privatization?', in *Privatization or Public Enterprise Reform? International Case Studies with Implications for Public Management*, ed. by Ali Farazmand (Westport, CT: Greenwood Press, 2001), pp. 95–126 (pp. 95–96).

[8] William L. Megginson, *The Financial Economics of Privatization* (Oxford: Oxford University Press, 2005), p. 4.

[9] Megginson, pp. 15–17.

[10] Jeffrey R. Henig, 'Privatization in the United States: Theory and Practice', *Political Science Quarterly*, 10 (1989–90), 649–70 (p. 649).

Francisco franchised its rubbish collection to private companies as early as 1932. Going back further still, school boards in Vermont towns with no public or union district high school could pay for their students to study at certain schools inside or outside the state.[11] Yet such efforts were largely pragmatic: according to Jeffrey R. Henig, Milton Friedman's 1962 work *Capitalism and Freedom* (which construed the state as a monopoly and proposed the use of education vouchers) and rational choice theory (which defined citizens as consumers, voting with their feet) elaborated a theoretical framework for privatisation from the 1950s to the 1970s. Subsequent studies of fire protection in Arizona and refuse collection in New York claimed that the privatisation of these services increased their efficiency and spurred innovation. Proponents of privatisation began to redefine the term itself—making the concept as we know it today—such that it would include not only outright sales of state enterprises, but also, retrospectively, the long-established practice of contracting. They endowed privatisation with a history and legitimised it thereby.[12]

Even in 1981, when Reagan started his term, few Americans were familiar with the word 'privatisation'. Reagan did not run on an explicitly pro-privatisation platform, but when he entered office, his administration began to use the term, giving it currency, much as Thatcher was doing in the United Kingdom. Reagan considered the prospects of privatising a range of governmental assets early in his first term—park and wilderness lands, National Weather Service satellites, and Conrail, *inter alia*—and, just as importantly, continued to broaden the word's definition.[13] Thus the president's Private Sector Survey on Cost Control, established in 1982, identified several different forms of privatisation: contracting out, franchising, complete divestiture, joint venture. It noted that, while privatisation is a 'relatively new' concept, 'it has been applied successfully at state and local levels'.[14] A range of books and reports on privatisation published in the 1980s followed Reagan by defining the concept in its broad sense, with the unforeseen consequence that this

---

[11] President's Commission on Privatization, *Privatization: Toward More Effective Government* (Washington, DC: The Commission, 1988), pp. 2–3.

[12] Henig, pp. 651–58.

[13] Henig, pp. 661–62. On the origins of the term 'privatisation', see Germà Bel, 'The Coining of "Privatization" and Germany's National Socialist Party', *Journal of Economic Perspectives*, 20.3 (2006), 187–94.

[14] President's Private Sector Survey on Cost Control, *Report on Privatization* (Washington, DC: US Government Printing Office, 1983), i. In its report, the President's Commission on Privatization redefined deregulation as a kind of privatisation (*Privatization*, p. 2).

logic could work in reverse, the failure of one kind of privatisation now serving to delegitimise the others.[15]

When we look through the Reagan government's analytic frame, the United States suddenly appears as a major privatiser of the 1980s. The sale of assets, perhaps the most obvious form of privatisation, is a relatively marginal one in American cities and counties—less popular than the private construction and acquisition of facilities and contracting out. According to a 1987 survey, about 80 per cent of cities and counties had used privatisation in the last five years or planned to in the next two. Of those, 24 per cent had sold assets, 32 per cent had privatised facilities, and 99 per cent had contracted out services, with 96 per cent planning to continue contracting out over the next two years. Solid waste disposal, vehicle towing or storage, and building or grounds maintenance were the three most contracted services in the mid-1980s, while transport infrastructure, municipal buildings, and sewage works were the facilities most frequently constructed or acquired by private companies. Representing about a fifth of American cities, survey respondents together contracted out over $1 billion worth of services per year, and they intended to privatise a further $3 billion worth of facilities between 1987 and 1989. County and city executives claimed that increasing demand for services, the elimination of federal revenue sharing, infrastructure decay, and public resistance to tax rises were their main motives for privatisation at this juncture.[16]

But city and county managers were not the only ones dealing ever more with the private sector. Throughout the 1980s, federal officials also dramatically increased their outlay on professional and administrative support services, secured through 'service contracts'. Their expenditure on such contracts more than doubled between 1979 and 1989, from $23 billion to $48 billion. Spending on federal personnel in this period thus rose at a much slower rate than both federal budget and contract

---

[15] Henig, pp. 666–67. Brian J. Glenn stresses that British and American conservatives had to make privatisation 'attractive enough to elicit popular support' ('Privatisation as a Strategy in the United Kingdom, the United States, and Beyond', in *Domestic Policy Discourse in the US and the UK in the 'New World Order'*, ed. by Lori Maguire (Newcastle: Cambridge Scholars Publishing, 2010), pp. 179–205 (p. 179)).

[16] David T. Irwin, 'Privatization in America', in *The Municipal Year Book, 1988* (Washington, DC: International City Management Association, 1988), pp. 43–55 (pp. 43–46). Only cities with more than 5,000 inhabitants were invited to complete the survey. By the mid-1990s, we ought to note, the growth of local privatisation had slowed somewhat (Henry, pp. 115–16).

outlays.[17] At the turn of the century, the federal government was awarding around 180,000 contracts to 60,000 different companies per year, and more than 15 per cent of annual federal expenditures (more than $200 billion) passed into private hands through contracts. The Pentagon was the largest privatiser by such a metric: the Department of Defense accounted for three quarters of government spending on procurement contracts in this period.[18]

Parallel to the history of privatisation as process and concept is its history in legislation. Issued in 1955, Eisenhower's Bureau of the Budget Bulletin 55-4 asserted the federal government's policy not to 'start or carry on any commercial activity to provide a service or product for its own use if such a product or service can be procured from private enterprise through normal business channels'.[19] In 1966, the Office of Management and Budget released OMB Circular A-76, which reaffirmed the government's policy 'to rely on competitive private enterprise to supply the products and services it needs', and modified it in 1979 to stress that certain inherently governmental activities still ought to be provided in-house.[20] A 2003 revision tightened the criteria on what counted as inherent: now only processes requiring *'substantial* discretion in applying government authority and/or in making decisions for the government' were off-limits to privatisers.[21] This is not to mention a range of 1990s legislation that formalised the federal procurement process and recast certain rules (for instance, that federal officers must award contracts to the lowest bidder) as guidelines.[22]

The Reagan administration not only privatised assets during its tenure, but laid the groundwork of privatisations to come. We have seen that Reagan put Conrail on the stock market in 1987. He also privatised the National Consumer Cooperative Bank in 1982 and sold off loans by the Department of Education and the Farmers Home Administration in 1987.[23] Near the end of his premiership—and in the same year as *RoboCop*'s release—Reagan appointed his Commission on Privatization,

---

[17] US General Accounting Office, *Government Contractors: Are Service Contractors Performing Inherently Governmental Functions?* (Washington, DC: US General Accounting Office, 1991), pp. 48, 54.
[18] Henry, p. 99.
[19] Executive Office of the President, Bureau of the Budget, Bulletin 55-4 (1955).
[20] Executive Office of the President, Office of Management and Budget, Circular No. A-76 (1966, 1979).
[21] Executive Office of the President, Office of Management and Budget, Circular No. A-76 (2003). The italics are mine.
[22] Henry, pp. 110–11.
[23] President's Commission on Privatization, pp. 3–4.

whose 1988 report recommended a range of future measures. Local and federal government had long intended to privatise their services, the commissioners noted, but these wishes had 'not been applied effectively'.[24] The report advocated privatising low-income housing, federal loan programmes, education, and healthcare (among others), sometimes in piecemeal fashion, through the use of vouchers, and sometimes more comprehensively, as in their recommendation that the Naval Petroleum Reserves be completely privatised. The commissioners identified other areas—air traffic control, the postal service, and urban mass transit—where a combination of contracting out and asset sales might be desirable.[25]

Some of the Commission's recommendations have now been fulfilled. In 1997, the government sold its 78 per cent stake in the Elk Hills oil field for $3.65 billion—the largest privatisation in American history, according to the Department of Energy. This was another public asset sold at highly profitable rates, kick-starting capital: Elk Hills was valued on the basis that it would cost $4.50 to extract a barrel of oil, but Occidental Petroleum, its new owner, gleefully drew barrels for a third of that.[26] In the late 1980s, conservatives set up think tanks favourable to school vouchers. The first true effort to use vouchers followed in 1990, when the Milwaukee Parental Choice Program allowed select students to go to schools other than the ones they had been assigned.[27] Jeb Bush enacted America's first state-wide voucher programme in 1999. By 2018, 64 voucher or voucher-like programmes operated across 30 states and the District of Columbia, their main beneficiary being religious schools.[28] The privatisation of the United States Postal Service, another of the Commission's recommendations, has likewise been incremental. In their report, the commissioners foresaw the resistance such measures would provoke, and the struggle between privatisers and postal unions continues today.[29]

Most relevant to *RoboCop* are the twin privatisations of prison and policing. Private companies began to own and manage prisons in the 1980s. Now, in the twenty-first century, the private sector builds the

[24] President's Commission on Privatization, p. 129.
[25] President's Commission on Privatization, p. xv.
[26] Alexander Cockburn, 'Al Gore's Teapot Dome', *The Nation*, 17 July 2000, p. 10.
[27] Glenn, pp. 190–93.
[28] Joanne Barkan, 'Death by a Thousand Cuts: The Story of Privatising Public Education in the USA', *Soundings*, 70 (2018), 97–116 (pp. 102, 107–08).
[29] See Martha Ecker, 'Efforts to Privatize the United States Postal Service', *Labor Studies Journal*, 43 (2018), 173–88.

majority of new American prisons, their population growing by 77 per cent between 1999 and 2015. America's two largest prison companies, GEO Group and CoreCivic, have seen their revenues increase by more than 86 per cent since 2006. They also incarcerate about 65 per cent of Immigration and Customs Enforcement detainees.[30] Policing, meanwhile, is an increasingly hybrid system in the United States, as private law enforcement has grown dramatically since 1970. By 2000, private officers outnumbered public police approximately three to one, and the events of September 11, 2001, spurred their expansion still further. Public and private officers patrol together and share information. Public police also contract out a range of services, including 911 dispatching, vehicle towing, and crime laboratory analysis.[31] Though some small towns contract out full police services, more common is the use of private police to supplement the public force in high-crime areas.[32]

Plumber or Police Officer?

'Take a close look at the track record of this company and you'll see that we've gambled in markets usually regarded as nonprofit: hospitals, prisons, space exploration,' crows Dick Jones (Ronny Cox), the senior vice president of OCP, at the beginning of Verhoeven's *RoboCop*. Behind Jones, on an array of television screens, 'marine', 'data', and 'energy' appear—other 'nonprofit' areas, it would seem, into which OCP has heroically ventured. Jones is speaking before the company's executives, to whom he is about to unveil his enforcement droid, ED-209, a huge machine armed with automatic guns and rocket launchers. As Jones informs us, OCP have won a contract to manage Detroit's police department; the purpose of ED-209 is thus 'urban pacification', fighting the city's rampant crime. OCP is not doing so out of the good of its heart, of course: in order to raze Old Detroit and build the gentrified Delta City in its place, the former's rampant crime must be curtailed.

---

[30] Lauren-Brooke Eisen, *Inside Private Prisons: An American Dilemma in the Age of Mass Incarceration* (New York: Columbia University Press, 2018), pp. 29–32.

[31] Karena Rahall, 'The Siren is Calling: Economic and Ideological Trends toward Privatization of Public Police Forces', *University of Miami Law Review*, 68 (2018), 633–75 (pp. 647–49). As Wilbur R. Miller emphasises, private policing came before public forces in the United States. The former can be traced back to groups such as slave patrols, park police, and associations for the prevention of horse theft (*A History of Private Policing in the United States* (London: Bloomsbury, 2019), pp. 51–56).

[32] Miller, p. 58.

Unfortunately for Jones, the ED-209 droid intended for that purpose malfunctions, gunning down one of the executives in the meeting.

Jones's mishap opens the door for Bob Morton (Miguel Ferrer), who works as part of Security Concepts (seemingly a department within OCP), to propose his 'RoboCop' programme as a contingency. The advantage of Morton's scheme is that it keeps organic components in the police officer, who is therefore a cyborg, apparently less likely to fail than a pure machine such as ED-209. The 'Old Man' (Dan O'Herlihy), OCP's chairman, gives Morton permission to take his plans forward. All that is needed is for a police officer to die or, as Morton puts it, to 'volunteer' for the programme. Alex Murphy (Peter Weller) is the unwitting participant, but Morton directs his scientists to remove Murphy's entire body, leaving only (we presume) the brain. And since Murphy's memory is also to be wiped, it seems that RoboCop is a cyborg in a merely formal sense. Very little live human material remains.

RoboCop begins to fight crime in Detroit until one day, quite incomprehensibly, he dreams. In the dream, RoboCop relives Murphy's death at the hands of Clarence Boddicker (Kurtwood Smith) and his gang. How RoboCop is able to dream remains unclear to OCP (and to us), but these visions of Boddicker change him: RoboCop deviates from OCP's priorities and turns his attention to the gang. Teaming up with Murphy's old partner, Anne Lewis (Nancy Allen), while the rest of the police department are on strike, protesting OCP's takeover, RoboCop hunts the gang down and kills them at an abandoned steel mill. By now, RoboCop has learnt that the Boddicker gang is in cahoots with Jones, who earlier sent Boddicker to kill Morton. Their alliance being proven, RoboCop returns to OCP's headquarters and concludes the film by shooting Jones.

RoboCop thus asserts a connection between the corporation, operating in the formal economy, and the criminals, moving in its shadows. But just as important, for our purposes, is the film's equation of the corporation with government, such that OCP becomes the afterimage of the American state in an era of privatisation. As Edward Neumeier, the film's screenwriter, points out, OCP's boardroom was designed so as to resemble the Reagan White House.[33] The Old Man was modelled

---

[33] Neumeier is quoted in Milo Sweedler, 'Class Warfare in the *RoboCop* Films', *Jump Cut*, 56 (2014–15) <https://www.ejumpcut.org/archive/jc56.2014-2015/SweedlerRobocop/index.html> [accessed 17 May 2022] (pp. 1–2 (p. 1)). Steven Best adds that the executives going behind the Old Man's back recall Oliver North's and Richard Secord's takeover, apparently unbeknownst to Reagan, in the Iran–Contra affair ('*RoboCop*: In the Detritus of Hi-Technology', *Jump Cut*, 34 (1989) <http://www.ejumpcut.org/archive/

on Reagan himself, who really was an 'old man'—the oldest, at the time, to become president of the United States (inaugurated a week shy of his 70th birthday). Several of the services named by Jones as so many successful OCP expeditions into 'nonprofit' areas are those that Reagan also deemed to be subject to undue governmental interference.[34] Later on in the film, when Jones tells Boddicker to destroy RoboCop and Boddicker responds that they will need military-grade weapons, Jones reassures him that 'we practically are the military'. In *RoboCop*, the bureaucratic officials of old have become executives and CEOs, the political class manifest as the capitalist class, the public realm collapsed into the private.[35]

The boardroom scene also serves to establish what is no longer visible when, capital having subsumed everything under itself, we see the world through only those categories that are proper to it. Such is the purpose of ED-209's protracted violence, which does not kill Kinney (Kevin Page) as much as brutalise him. Unable to detect that Kinney—whom, for purposes of demonstration, Jones instructs to point a pistol at ED-209—has put the weapon down, the machine discharges its cannons into him for nearly 15 seconds. In this period, Verhoeven cuts from a close-up of the two weapons; to a medium shot of Kinney's chest, erupting with blood and flesh; back to an extreme close-up of the left cannon, which continues to pump metal into Kinney; and then to a close-up of the rapidly disintegrating body—already a corpse—from behind, as the exit wounds multiply. Verhoeven continues to alternate between cannons and body, the latter now surely emptied of consciousness but

onlinessays/JC34folder/RobocopBest.html> [accessed 17 May 2022] (para. 1 of 49)).

[34] Jeffords, p. 108. Irvin Kirshner's *RoboCop 2* (1990) imagines OCP taking over not merely individual public services, but the city itself. We learn that the Detroit administration owes OCP more than $37 million, and that, if the city defaults, OCP has the right to foreclose all public assets. The producers of Nuke—a highly popular, highly addictive drug—offer to settle the city's debts to OCP in return for legal immunity, and the mayor agrees. The choice confronting the mayor is not between private or public provision of the city's core amenities, but rather between which private organisation will take control of Detroit.

[35] Michael Robertson also draws the link between *RoboCop*, privatisation, and enclosure in 'Property and Privatisation in *RoboCop*', *International Journal of Law in Context*, 4 (2008), 217–35. Moving beyond Robertson's focus on the film's satire of actually existing privatisations (policing and intellectual property rights, principally), the present chapter suggests that *RoboCop* criticises privatisation as a *concept* that Reagan (and others) redefined in order to legitimise the new enclosures.

staggering backwards, zombie-like, and collapsing on the model of Delta City. Kinney's flesh writhes for a few more seconds yet, the ammunition churning through his legs. Gruesome this spectacle may be, but it fails to move the Old Man. 'Dick, I'm very disappointed,' he says. 'We're scheduled to begin construction in six months. Your "temporary setback" could cost us 50 million dollars in interest payments alone.' The film's point is hard to miss: the brutalisation of a human body is irrelevant to the logic of the balance sheet.

It is worth pausing here to consider *RoboCop*'s reputed technophobia, apparent not just in ED-209's malfunction, but in the news story about the president's 'Star Wars Peace Platform', which has lost power, and in RoboCop's own failures. Surveying these moments, Steven Best criticises the film for dwelling only on the dangers of technology, for overlooking its emancipatory potential. But I would suggest that *RoboCop*'s portrayal of backfiring machines is less a comment on technology per se, technology in the abstract, more a critique of the application of technological solutions to social problems.[36] For instance, because OCP sees crime as a productivity issue, delaying their construction of Delta City, automated policing—Jones's '24-hour-a-day police officer', who need not eat or sleep—seems an apt solution. Yet ED-209 is clearly too heavily armed for, as Jones puts it, 'urban pacification', and the botched demonstration illustrates this. The film's satirical play on 'peace' recurs in the abovementioned Star Wars Peace Platform (punning on the nickname for Reagan's Strategic Defense Initiative), which juxtaposes 'peace' with 'war' and implies that the tools used for waging the latter might not be appropriate for achieving the former. As for RoboCop's own failure, his abandonment of his police duties so he can seek revenge, this is less a comment on technology per se than it is a utopian assertion of the primacy of the human subject in a world increasingly dominated by capital (an aspect of the film to which we shall return shortly). It follows that the figure of RoboCop too must be read as an allegory for specifically capitalist technology, not technology as such.

With private capital encroaching on the police department and the public/private dichotomy breaking down, *RoboCop*'s police officers must reconceptualise their place in the capitalist system. The dilemma

[36] Best, para. 41 of 49. There is in fact a hesitation in Best's essay, which indeed reads *RoboCop* as technophobic, and concludes with this judgement, but at other moments observes, as I do here, that the film criticises 'technicism' in particular—that is, the view that technology can solve social problems. *Pace* Best, I would argue that the film's criticisms of technicism, a specific historical conception of technology, do not necessarily imply scepticism of the possibility of humans' non-alienated relationship to technology.

Figure 2: Supply and demand (*RoboCop*, dir. by Paul Verhoeven (Orion Pictures, 1987))

asserts itself at the beginning of the film, before the boardroom scene, when Murphy enters the police station and informs Sargent Warren Reid (Robert DoQui) of his transfer to Metro West from Metro South. 'We work for a living down here, Murphy,' Reid replies, his comment recalling the critical injuries of Frank Fredrickson, another Detroit police officer, which were just reported in the film. In Reid's comment, 'work' means something more than work: it means a state of precariousness, even peril, beyond what other labourers experience. A few moments later, as the camera carries us into the locker room, we learn that the police officers are contemplating striking, largely in response to the threat of privatisation. Reid puts his foot down: 'I don't wanna hear any more talk about a strike,' he says. 'We're not plumbers; we're police officers. And police officers don't strike.' Thus Reid again implies that police officers exceed the status of ordinary manual labour. In the end, the dual threats of privatisation and automation, as well as the mortal danger of their job, compel the officers to walk out, rejecting both Reid's warning and his definition of wage labour. The strike is nothing less than an affirmation by the police officers that they are not qualitatively different to plumbers.

RoboCop extends its dramatisation of privatisation to the figure of the free, competitive market, in whose name the state carried out many such privatisations (the state itself, we recall, having been framed as a kind of monopoly by Friedman). As one member of the Boddicker gang asserts, there 'ain't no better way of stealing than free enterprise'.

What he means by this we see later, when Boddicker negotiates with Sal (Lee de Broux), a capitalist who runs a cocaine factory. At first, the two discuss freely, sending each other signals, feeling out the equilibrium price. 'I don't think I wanna pay you that, Sal,' Boddicker starts, before Sal asserts his prerogative, as seller, to set his price. Boddicker returns that he is 'the guy in Old Detroit', and that if Sal wants entry to that market, he is going to have to give Boddicker a 'volume discount'. Sal again declines. Boddicker unveils a gift for Sal—a briefcase stuffed with cash, which might lubricate the deal—but Sal remains unmoved. He notes that Boddicker's heavy connections and reputation for killing cops mean many of Sal's associates 'would love to see a guy like me put a guy like you out of business'. If Sal leaves it unclear whether he intends to oust Boddicker by competitive means, through the free action of the marketplace, or by force, Boddicker's bellicose response pushes him towards the second option, and suddenly each exchanger finds himself surrounded by guns. Boddicker and Sal's initial price signals turn out to be the first in a series of escalating threats, as the real determinants of their exchange come into view: firepower, connections, bribery, and physical access to markets. By dramatising a criminal, informal, thus nominally unregulated market that is nonetheless highly coercive, even oligopolistic, *RoboCop* suggests that the neoliberal dream of free, unfettered enterprise must remain just that.

If Boddicker and Sal impute a certain violence to the free market, RoboCop goes further and rejects commodity exchange *tout court*. When he returns to 548 Primrose Lane, Murphy's old house, RoboCop finds it up for sale. A cheery estate agent on a screen just inside the front door greets him and prompts him to 'take a stroll through [his] new home'. Walking from room to room, RoboCop recalls Murphy's family life: his son watching television, the taking of a family photo, his wife telling him she loves him. At the end of the tour, the virtual agent asks, 'Why don't you make me an offer?' RoboCop punches the screen, shattering it. To the request for a price signal, again, we have a violent, even symbolic response, an assertion of the impropriety of the price mechanism when applied to something as meaningful, as intimate, as a home. It is no accident that this rejection of the logic of exchange occurs only once RoboCop has started acting autonomously, Murphy's subjectivity having irrupted into the machine, since such re-emergence challenges the transcendental basis of commodity exchange, which presupposes precisely the demarcation of active, exchanging subjects from their passive, exchanged property. 'You're our product, and we can't very well have our products turning against us, can we?' says Dick Jones, seeing that RoboCop himself has become the ultimate category error: a subjectivised object, a walking, talking, avenging commodity.

In this irruption of subjectivity, it need scarcely be noted, consists *RoboCop*'s utopianism. Unlike all other forms of private property, RoboCop resists his appropriation, fights back against his owner, and thus establishes a contrast with the rest of the film's diegetic world, in which the public sphere is dragged steadily into the jaws of the private. It might be argued that the film's denouement undermines such utopianism in so far as it reminds us of the continuing limits on RoboCop's freedom, thus on his status as subject: since his programming ('Directive 4') prohibits RoboCop from arresting any officer of the company, the Old Man must fire Jones before RoboCop—literalising the metaphor—can shoot him. Does the film not then conclude with a reassertion of capital's domination, its subsumption of everything under itself? Yet the firing is not *RoboCop*'s final action, in fact. Jones having fallen through the window, the Old Man proceeds to ask RoboCop what his name is. The latter responds, 'Murphy,' such that the film actually shows, in its final moments, both the durability of corporate domination, the persistence of OCP's ownership and control of RoboCop, *and* RoboCop's contrary affirmation of subjecthood. The point is the contiguity of these two events: Verhoeven wants to reiterate the utopian and dystopian dimensions of his film at once, since each acquires its charge by contrast with the other. *RoboCop* is not a utopia or a dystopia but, I would submit, a utopian dystopia, in which the contrast between the two serves to bring to the fore the contradiction between the logic of private property and, in this case, RoboCop's existence as property that 'turns against' its owner.

Why *RoboCop* and many of the other Hollywood science-fiction films released in the last third of the twentieth century opt to perpetuate this tension, this contrast between private property and its negation—between dystopia and utopia—I shall examine in Chapter 4. Suffice it to note for now that the limits to *RoboCop*'s utopianism lie elsewhere: not in its depiction of the survival of the big, bad corporation, but rather in its use of the police department as the privileged site of labour struggle (perhaps, because the officers are threatened by automation, as an evocation of Detroit's deindustrialisation in particular). It is as if the film's condemnation of the private sphere, in which the logic of capital is preponderant, seems to tip over into an overly positive evaluation of the public, such that what is public becomes good *a priori*. This is why the powerful objections to the use of policing as an allegory for labour—put most bluntly, that policing fabricates a social order that dominates the labourer[37]—must appear irrelevant to *RoboCop*, for which a public police force is distinct, morally, from a private one.[38] If free enterprise is a form of theft, then the public police officer suddenly appears, no longer as an agent tasked to secure capitalism's reproduction, but as the investigator par excellence into corporate malfeasance.

Rebel or Henchman?

Verhoeven's next feature film, *Total Recall*, takes us to the year 2084, where industrialist Vilos Cohaagen rules over the human settlements on Mars. Cohaagen can wield absolute power over his subjects as long as he continues to export terbinium ore back to Earth; as such, he crushes the riots periodically organised by the followers of Kuato (Marshall Bell), a mysterious underground insurgent. Cohaagen has almost complete control over the Martian population, who must pay him for even the air that they breathe; yet as long as he cannot locate Kuato, the insurgent movement remains alive, and with it the threat to his power. Cohaagen hatches a plan: he creates a fictional identity, 'Douglas Quaid', and programmes one of his henchmen, Hauser, to act and behave like Quaid back on Earth. Quaid is settled in a mundane job, married to a woman, and given a memory implant to believe that this has always been his life, that he was always a construction worker on Earth. Next, having gone to great lengths to turn Hauser into Quaid, Cohaagen plans to convince Quaid that he was, in fact, Hauser—to turn the whole thing around again by telling Quaid that he used to work for an intelligence agency on Mars. The difference this time is that Quaid thinks he is Cohaagen's antagonist, so he joins Kuato's rebel

---

[37] At the heart of policing, Mark Neocleous writes, 'is the need to "compel people to labour and honest industry" [...] and hence to drive out what from the perspective of capital appear to be modes of life that are either useless or antithetical to accumulation (and usually both). The police power involves a set of apparatuses and technologies not only fabricating social order in general, but the law of labour in particular' (*A Critical Theory of Police Power: The Fabrication of Social Order*, 2nd edn (London: Verso, 2021), p. 22).

[38] *RoboCop 3* (1993), directed by Fred Dekker, complicates things somewhat. While it continues to raise the public over the private (the public police officers here are unequivocally good, the private militarised police just as clearly bad), it also wants to assert the superiority of American manufacture over Japanese, this being the purpose of RoboCop's battle with the robotic samurai. For further discussion of the 'Japan panic' widespread in Hollywood cinema in the 1980s and early 1990s, see Chapter 5.

forces. Believing that he is fighting Cohaagen, not abetting him, Quaid leads Cohaagen right to Kuato, who is promptly killed. The resistance defeated, Cohaagen prepares to reimplant Quaid's old memory, to get his friend Hauser back.

Only when the mission seems to have succeeded does it go wrong. Quaid refuses to return to his life as Hauser and frees himself and his partner, Melina (Rachel Ticotin), who helped him fight Cohaagen. Shortly before his death, Kuato told Quaid to start the terbinium reactor, supposedly built by aliens deep in a mine. Remembering this, Quaid and Melina hasten to the mine, find the reactor, and set it off. Cohaagen's secret, it turns out, is that the reactor would melt Mars's icy core, releasing air and triggering a seismic event in which Mars generates its own atmosphere. Cohaagen dies trying to prevent Quaid and Melina from starting the reactor, so he does not witness the downfall of his regime and the liberation of the human populace on Mars, who can now emerge from their protective domes and explore the planet unaided. Surveying the newly habitable landscape of Mars, Quaid wonders whether this extraordinary chain of events was all a dream.

But the twist that Verhoeven applies to this story is that it may well have been. At the beginning of *Total Recall*, before the action really gets underway, we learn that Quaid is obsessed with the idea of going to Mars, much to the displeasure of his wife, Lori (Sharon Stone). Against his co-worker's advice, Quaid decides to go to Rekall, a company that sells memories of spectacular vacations on Earth and other planets. Quaid buys memories of a trip in which he is a secret agent trying to save Mars, and where his sexual interest is a demure and wanton brunette. Of course, this is exactly the plot of the rest of the film: Quaid works undercover as a spy, fights the Martian administration, meets his love interest (the demure and wanton brunette Melina), and frees the citizens of Mars. We cannot be sure whether Quaid's heroics are fictional memories implanted at Rekall or whether they really happened, Quaid's true existence as a former secret agent prompting him to pick that fantasy in the first place.

Total Recall's is a complicated plot, playful and parodic. But if we bracket for the moment the narrative indeterminacy—the irresolvable question about what is real in this fictional world—we can see more easily that it requires, as its background, an advanced system of enclosure. The conflict that motivates the film is Cohaagen's private ownership of means of subsistence, specifically air, and thus *Total Recall*'s resolution must depend on Quaid's redistributing it, which he does by starting the reactor. This is another textbook example of science-fictional extrapolation: ideas, food, land, and water having been enclosed in reality, all that is left for *Total Recall* to imagine is control over the most basic means of survival—oxygen. Mars is an apt site for Verhoeven's thought experiment, since air is no longer automatically a 'public good' (in the parlance of academic economics) there: the air, finite in quantity, is potentially depletable, and Mars's inhabitants can be excluded from it (as, for instance, when Cohaagen switches off the supply to Venusville).

But does the public/private binary still hold on Mars in 2084? How does *Total Recall* present the relation between the two spheres? While Cohaagen is the 'administrator' of Mars and implements martial law during a period of unrest, he behaves as a chief executive: his position depends on the successful commodification of Mars's environment, in particular its reserves of terbinium ore. (As Linda Mizejewski notes, Cohaagen's Afrikaner name and his mining industry recall South Africa specifically.[39]) Meanwhile, it is never clear what 'the Agency', mentioned several times in the film, actually is—whether it is an arm of the state or a branch of a company. Possible references, on the pink notes Quaid retrieves from a briefcase, to a 'federal' bank on Mars, and on Quaid's television, to Northern and Southern 'blocs' on Earth, suggest that some sort of state or super-state system lingers in the background. Mars, the film implies, is just one of several 'Federal Colonies' (this logo appearing on the screen behind Quaid and Cohaagen when the two finally meet). In general, however, the public/private distinction seems to have become anachronistic in *Total Recall*'s diegetic world, where the state's disciplinary function shades into the corporation's profit-making, and where the commodification of air is now as effective a means of control as the Agency's repressive apparatus. As if to emphasise the relation between the two, when Cohaagen determines to punish the Venusville insurrectionists, he must pull out his officers before he can turn off the air supply—or, rather, withdraw it from the market.

This background of deepened enclosure enters into the foreground of *Total Recall* in the guise of Quaid's identity crisis, which is also essentially a drama of class affiliation (and thus recalls the police officers' arguments over striking in *RoboCop*). 'I've been playing for the wrong team,' Hauser says to Quaid in his first video communication. 'All I can do now is make up for it.' Yet herein lies *Total Recall*'s most devilish paradox, since each of Quaid's potential identities—one as a spy, working for Cohaagen on Mars, the other as a construction worker on Earth—is determined by the relations of production obtaining on the opposite planet. To put it as

---

[39] Linda Mizejewski, 'Total Recoil: The Schwarzenegger Body on Postmodern Mars', *Post Script*, 12.3 (1993), 25–34 (p. 28).

simply as possible, if what we see for the majority of the film is Quaid's Rekall simulation, in which he appears to be a secret agent, this is only because he is in fact a labourer, the drudgery of whose life has prompted him to go to Rekall. If, on the other hand, the events we see are real, and Quaid's initial existence as a construction worker is a simulation (Cohaagen having wiped his memory and settled him as such), then that 'simulation' arose only because Quaid is really Cohaagen's spy. It is because Quaid is a terrestrial labourer that he appears as a Martian spy; it is because he is a Martian spy that he appears as a terrestrial labourer. Each relationship to production generates the simulation of its opposite.

That Quaid's identity crisis is, at heart, the uncertainty of his relationship to capital and labour sharpens and intensifies Quail's dual crises in 'We Can Remember It for You Wholesale' (1966), the Philip K. Dick short story from which Ronald Shusett and Dan O'Bannon (and later Gary Goldman) adapted *Total Recall*'s script. In Dick's narrative, Quail begins as a lowly clerk—a *'miserable little salaried employee'* at the West Coast Emigration Bureau[40]—who can only dream of visiting Mars. When Quail goes to Rekal for a memory implant, however, it transpires that he was actually an assassin working for the terrestrial government. This distinction is similar to Quaid's one between construction worker and spy, though Dick leaves the government's relation to capital relatively ambiguous. *Total Recall*'s elaboration of the Agency's involvement in commodification and enclosure and its hints at its relation to the state on Earth are, then, particular to the adaptation. The film differs, too, in its excision of what, in Dick's tale, is Quail's second fantasy, according to which, as a nine-year-old, he prevented an alien invasion of Earth by impressing the aliens with his warmth and humanity. This fantasy also turns out to be true: Quail really did stop the aliens, who have agreed not to invade Earth as long as Quail is alive. If Quail's first fantasy thus revolves around his relationship to capital (is he really a miserable salaried employee, too lowly to go to Mars?), his second one replaces it with the antagonism between humans and aliens, such that Quail becomes a defender of humanity as such, not merely of one its classes. *Total Recall*'s scriptwriters not only removed from their source text the crisis centred on human universalism in favour of the one revolving around capital and labour, but they also sharpened and elaborated that aspect of the crisis.

Equally, while *Total Recall* frames Quaid's identity crisis as an equivocation between two class positions, near the end of the film, this crisis

---

[40] Philip K. Dick, 'We Can Remember It for You Wholesale', in *Selected Stories of Philip K. Dick* (Boston: Houghton Mifflin Harcourt, 2013), pp. 325–45 (p. 325).

opens out into a property dispute between Quaid and Hauser. When Cohaagen captures Quaid and explains his elaborate plan, which just about seems to have come off, and Quaid continues to disbelieve him, Cohaagen starts a videotape, filmed before Quaid's settlement on Earth, in which Hauser speaks to the future occupant of his body. Hauser informs Quaid that Quaid is going to have to forfeit the body, which Hauser sees as a kind of property: 'That's my body you've got there, and I want it back.' Then Hauser turns to a racist idiom: 'Sorry to be an Indian giver, but I was here first.' The phrase 'Indian giver', we should note, dates back at least as far as the mid-eighteenth century, and expresses the coloniser's confusion at the Native American's expectation that their gift-giving be reciprocated.[41] Hauser does not really think of his body as a gift in the above-defined sense, of course: he uses the phrase 'Indian giver' as a kind of joke. His point is not to frame the body as a gift, but the opposite: by using the white coloniser's racist term, to disavow the logic of the gift, inimical as it is to the coloniser's regime of private property. His next claim—'I was here first'—complicates things further, not least because such grounds for ownership are antithetical to colonisation, whose agents could not have been 'here first'. What Hauser is doing, it seems, is pastiching Indigenous claims to property and land. The effect is that of a coloniser gloating, mocking the arguments of the colonised, whom they appear to have defeated.

Until now, I have attempted to read *Total Recall* through its critique of the Reaganite enclosures in particular, yet Hauser's turn of phrase here suggests that the film also looks back to the original enclosures of North America, the dispossession of the Indigenous population. While it is perhaps a stretch to read *Total Recall*'s aliens as an allegory for Native Americans in particular, the former conjure the scene of displaced indigeneity nonetheless.[42] The official line, promulgated by

---

[41] 'The opposite of "Indian giver",' Lewis Hyde suggests, 'would be something like "white man keeper" (or maybe "capitalist"), that is, a person whose instinct is to remove property from circulation, to put it in a warehouse or museum (or, more to the point for capitalism, to lay it aside to be used for production)' (*The Gift: How the Creative Spirit Transforms the World* (Edinburgh: Canongate, 2012), p. 4). On this view, Cohaagen is the ultimate 'white man keeper': it is not this or that object or artefact that he withdraws from circulation, but the air itself, whose scarcity he maintains by closing off the reactor (and also, later, the supply to Venusville).

[42] The narrative function of the aliens is then starkly different in *Total Recall* and 'We Can Remember It for You Wholesale'. Where, in *Total Recall*, the aliens prove, unwittingly, the saviours of Venusville's inhabitants, in Dick's short story they pose an existential threat to humanity.

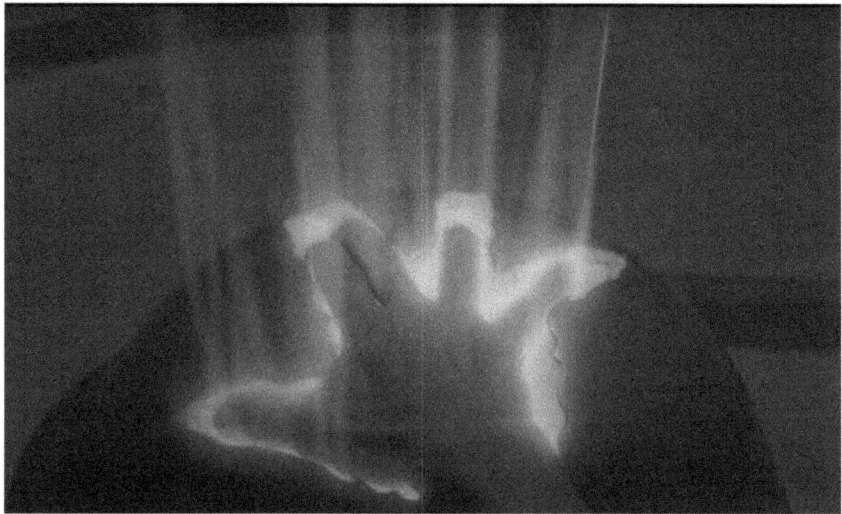

Figure 3: Proof of prior occupation (*Total Recall*, dir. by Paul Verhoeven (TriStar Pictures, 1990))

Cohaagen early in the film, in a television broadcast where he is asked about the possibility of alien artefacts on Mars, is that the aliens did not exist. 'I wish I could find some nice alien artefacts,' he jokes. 'Our tourist industry could use a boost.' Later, when Dr Edgemar (Roy Brocksmith) is trying to convince Quaid that he is dreaming, Edgemar warns him that, should he refuse to return to reality, he will 'even have fantasies about alien civilisations', as per his request at Rekall. Melina too is incredulous: 'Aliens? Are you sure about this?' she asks as Quaid takes her to the reactor. Quaid and Melina's discovery of the reactor, and their subsequent activation of it, is then nothing less than a confirmation that the aliens did exist, that an alien population lived on the land that Cohaagen has commodified—in short, that Mars once had its own Martians. The film's utopianism consists, not only in the reactor's generation of a new atmosphere, which makes air physically uncommodifiable, permanently common, but in this proof of a native population's prior occupation of the land. It is they, not the colonising forces, who were 'here first'.

Yet this affirmation is double-edged. We have just seen that Hauser's invocation of the 'Indian gift' functions to distinguish Cohaagen's regime from the alternative forms of property that it supplants and mocks. On the one hand, the perennially breathable atmosphere might itself, in this context, be construed as a gift, and thus reinforce *Total Recall*'s characterisation of the aliens as an absent Indigenous group. On the other hand, precisely because of the aliens' absence, their gift does not seem to demand reciprocation or recognition. If anything, the gift opens up new frontiers, if not for enclosure, then at least for colonisation, as humans can now cross Mars unencumbered by space suits and breathing apparatuses. *Total Recall* gives the aliens existence precisely in and through their 'improvement' of Mars, whose clouds and sunshine will presumably mean that humans can cultivate it in a manner not unlike they do on Earth. This renders another historical irony, in so far as the claim that Indigenous populations do not—indeed, cannot—improve the land as effectively as the coloniser has served as a major pretext for the theft of their land, in North America and elsewhere.

The film's final moment, where the sun breaks through the clouds and, drenching Mars in light, turns the whole screen white, therefore carries a double signification. It might mean that Quaid's dream has come to an end, since he is presently being lobotomised back at Rekall.[43] But the blanket whiteness would also seem to represent Mars as a *tabula rasa*, or, more precisely, *terra nullius*: land declared empty by the coloniser, and thus deemed available for settlement and cultivation. *Total Recall* closes with a reminder that the aliens might be a figment of Quaid's imagination, something he has paid to have simulated at Rekall, and that, even if they are real, their gift might have simply opened up new ways for humans to colonise and exploit the land. So it is that, as we saw also in *RoboCop*, *Total Recall* sustains the tension between utopia and dystopia. Perhaps the new atmosphere means the end of corporate domination on Mars, but perhaps it does not. The point is the persistence of the two possibilities, the utopianism of the one throwing into relief the dystopianism of the other and vice versa. This is a structure that we will now find repeated in *Blade Runner* and *The Truman Show* in Chapter 3, before we consider the reasons for the emergence of such a structure, the historical situation from which it arises, in Chapter 4.

---

[43] Verhoeven was committed to making a film that, in his own words, 'had two levels, and that both levels, throughout, would always be consistent, and that you could never say, "Now we are in a dream," or, "Now we are in reality"' (*Imagining 'Total Recall'*, dir. by Jeffrey Schwarz (Artisan Entertainment, 2001)).

Chapter 3

Urbanisation
Images of Los Angeles in *Blade Runner* and *The Truman Show*

It has been little noted that urbanism holds a central place in Guy Debord's *The Society of the Spectacle* (1967). 'While all the technical forces of capitalism contribute toward various forms of separation,' Debord writes there, 'urbanism provides the material foundation for those forces and prepares the ground for their deployment. It is the very *technology of separation*.'[1] Capital's concentration of the proletariat in the city—a situation Debord sees as latently revolutionary—is what makes such a technology useful, indispensable even, to the bourgeoisie. Yet while his target is urbanism as such, not this or that particular urbanist philosophy, the detail of Debord's claims points particularly towards architectural modernism, whose monofunctional zoning practices might indeed be considered a form of *'authoritarian decision making* which abstractly converts the environment into an environment of abstraction'. In the next paragraph, again recalling us to the dilemmas of modernism, Debord criticises the 'dictatorship of the automobile', which 'has left its mark on the landscape with the dominance of freeways, which

---

[1] Guy Debord, *Society of the Spectacle*, trans. by Ken Knabb (London: Rebel Press, 2004), § 171. That Debord reserves much space in his classic text for a critique of urbanism ought to be no surprise. Since the mid-1950s, the Situationists had elaborated their own practice of 'Unitary Urbanism', which was concerned less to design new blueprints, more to provoke city dwellers into conscious engagement with their surroundings. For an outline of Unitary Urbanism, see Situationist International, 'Editorial Notes: Unitary Urbanism at the End of the 1950s', trans. by Paul Hammond (1959) <https://www.cddc.vt.edu/sionline/si/unitary.html> [accessed 17 May 2022] (14 paras); and for a discussion of the conflicting urbanisms within the Situationist International, see Brian Elliott, 'Debord, Constant, and the Politics of Situationist Urbanism', *Radical Philosophy Review*, 12.1/2 (2009), 249–72.

tear up old urban centres and promote an ever-wider dispersal'.² The development of malls, or 'distribution factories', ensues. By these means and others modernist urbanism does the spectacle's work, provides its 'material foundation', and produces a new internal separation where the external, physical separation of proletarians from one another is no longer possible.

Had Debord written his critique of the spectacle 30 years later, at the end of the twentieth century, might he not have felt compelled to add a sentence or two about the privatisation of the cityscape, which has proceeded apace since 1970? By no means unique to postmodernity, privatisation is nonetheless integral to its reorganisation of urban space.³ This chapter focuses on Los Angeles—the postmodern metropolis par excellence—where Business Improvement Districts, corporate plazas, malls, and gated communities have all served as prominent means of privatisation. What is characteristic about the first three examples, we ought to note, is not merely that they make public space private, but that they do so while continuing to pass themselves off as public. They enfold public space within themselves, so to speak, and subordinate the kinds of activity one would expect to be permissible there—protesting, leafleting, rough sleeping, and so on—to the caprices of their owners. Through such mechanisms, postmodern cities exacerbate the subject's dissociation from their environment and perpetuate the counterrevolutionary function of urbanism as such.

The postmodern city is still more spectacular than the modern one, then. Its zealous privatisation of public space turns the city into so many images, as places that one could previously enter, inhabit, and use become available merely as things to be looked at. Privatisation cleaves into the objectivity of the built environment itself the distinction between the (public) spaces *from* which one looks, such as pavements or greens, and the (private) places *on* which one looks, and which exist, for most of us, as spectacles.⁴ In her study of the California Plaza—one of the new private spaces I shall discuss in this chapter—Marina Peterson notes that photography is prohibited on the plaza because management fears that users might profit from selling pictures of the private buildings. 'This

---

² Debord, *Society of the Spectacle*, §§ 173, 174.
³ For an overview, see Nan Ellin, *Postmodern Urbanism*, 2nd edn (New York: Princeton Architectural Press, 1999), pp. 167–73.
⁴ John David Rhodes argues that houses embody the same 'to-be-looked-at-ness' that Laura Mulvey so influentially discerned in Hollywood's portrayal of women (*Spectacle of Property: The House in American Film* (Minneapolis: University of Minnesota Press, 2017), p. 12). Mulvey's classic essay is 'Visual Pleasure and Narrative Cinema', *Screen*, 16.3 (1975), 6–18.

should be understood in the context of Los Angeles,' Peterson continues, 'in which every place is a possible movie or commercial photography location.'⁵ What is suggestive in Peterson's account is that management conceives of its private property as immanently spectacular, even cinematic. Jameson posits that our postmodern 'appetite' for architecture is in fact a displaced desire for photography, for the image,⁶ but the foregoing discussion suggests a slightly different relation: we desire buildings because, as members of the public, we may engage them *only* as images. They exist to us solely as abstractions fizzing up the optic nerve. What we desire is not to see, but rather to break into, trespass on, nose around private space. It is in this sense that the postmodern city is spectacular, exceeding even the alienation of the modernist city, on whose form Debord already found the spectacle assiduously at work.

The last chapter suggested that *RoboCop* and *Total Recall* approach privatisation as a concept. This one argues that *Blade Runner* and *The Truman Show* conceive of Los Angeles as an image: a static, petrified, alienated structure external to the subject, who must regard it as they would a photograph. Such is already the implication of *Blade Runner*'s opening sequence, where an establishing shot of a dark, dystopian Los Angeles in 2019 cuts to an extreme close-up of a blue eye, on whose surface soaring industrial flares shimmer, and then back to the city, which is now a little closer. *Blade Runner*'s slow, staggered zoom in contrasts with *The Truman Show*'s rapid zoom out: during the credits of the (diegetic) 'Truman Show',⁷ the camera withdraws from Seahaven (a television set in Hollywood) until it shows the whole world floating in space, as though the shot were taken from the moon, this recalling the first famous photographs of Earth as a 'blue marble'. Crucially, the internal organisation of 'The Truman Show'—in which an artificial moon (known as the 'Lunar room') serves as the show's control centre, and the Seahaven set becomes its Earth—mirrors such a structure. Through this equivalence the film suggests that the world itself is more than the sum of its objects, that it now exists in some meaningful sense as an image.

That *Blade Runner* and *The Truman Show* comprehend the increasingly alienated, and therefore increasingly spectacular, character of the postmodern metropolis is this chapter's first claim. Its second is that

---

⁵ Marina Peterson, 'Patrolling the Plaza: Privatized Public Space and the Neoliberal State in Downtown Los Angeles', *Urban Anthropology and Study of Cultural Systems and World Economic Development*, 35.4 (2006), 355–86 (p. 381, n. 5).

⁶ Jameson, *Postmodernism*, p. 99.

⁷ I will place the name of the diegetic television show in quotation marks, to distinguish it from Weir's film.

these films' utopianism consists in their protagonists' ability to escape the urban image. Because he is a blade runner, Rick Deckard (Harrison Ford), Scott's reimagined hardboiled detective, gains access to the city in its totality, public and private spaces alike. The blade runner is in fact one of the few constituents of this dystopia whose movement through the metropolis remains relatively unimpeded. Deckard becomes the privileged, well-nigh utopian viewer of the urban image, someone who rises above the city (most emblematically in the Spinner, the flying police car) and surveys it in its totality, the implication being that most other people in *Blade Runner*'s world are not subjects at all, but objects, 'little people', anthropic shadows cast by capital accumulation. *The Truman Show* presents the opposite situation: now Truman Burbank (Jim Carrey) is the object, part of the image itself, and everyone else, the millions around the globe who watch him, subjects. In this context, Truman's rejection of the show, his decision to leave the set, constitutes the film's utopian moment.

Privatising Los Angeles

Before we turn to *Blade Runner* and *The Truman Show*, however, let us consider Los Angeles itself, whose privatisation exemplifies the increasing enclosure of urban life. The period between the release of these films—that is, between 1982 and 1998—witnessed a rapid expansion of gated communities.[8] Energised by the 1980s real-estate boom, developers seized on the considerable land available for master-planned communities, the demand for such enclaves fuelled by California's deep wealth inequality and white fear and racism.[9] Crucially for us, many of the gated communities were built so as to subsume public spaces, such that greens, roads, lakes, beaches, and pools once held in common found themselves guarded by the new gates. Some such communities have also claimed public money through 'municipal incorporation', a process by which the community sets up services exclusive to its inhabitants (private police and fire departments, for instance), but contrives to finance them in part through taxes paid outside its walls.[10] The expansion of private recreational facilities more generally has drained taxpayer support for the

---

[8] Miller, p. 73.
[9] Setha M. Low, 'Incorporation and Gated Communities in the Greater Metro-Los Angeles Region as a Model of Privatization of Residential Communities', *Home Cultures*, 5.1 (2008), 85–108 (pp. 91, 95–96).
[10] Low, pp. 98–103.

existing public ones and forced many into closure. *De facto* privatisations of this kind divide the public into enclaves, separate the rich from the poor, and entrench racialised exclusions.[11]

The Business Improvement Districts (BIDs) sprouting up across the United States likewise permit their constituents greater control over both their own and others' tax payments. BIDs function by charging property owners situated within them a fee, which pays for services, such as sanitation, street renovation, and security, to the benefit of the district alone. The political power of big capital congealed in the BID makes the latter an effective means of obtaining public funding; BIDs have thus been used to gain extra police resources and direct subsidies, as well as to encourage pro-business laws.[12] In the context of Los Angeles in particular, BIDs have formed a pillar of downtown 'revitalisation' projects. Their explicit function is to make downtown 'safe and clean' (safe from whom and cleansed of what?), but developers have seized on the perceptions of danger underlying that function: the ostensible appeal of the BIDs lies in their claim to preserve, in sanitised form, the 'excitements' and 'edginess' of downtown Los Angeles, these thrills no longer being available in the gated suburbs.[13] To keep things from getting too exciting, however, all Los Angeles BIDs employ their own private security services. One such district, the Downtown Center BID, established a 'BID Academy', where the LAPD trains its private police force, known as the 'Purple Patrol'. Combining security with entertainment, these officers cheerfully distribute guidebooks to tourists and other visitors.[14]

This privatised subdual of social conflict also finds expression in the city's malls, which have increasingly come to serve as a substitute for public space. Protesting, leafleting, panhandling, and rough sleeping are banned in most American shopping centres. Hence, while contemporary malls are often designed so as to recall an ideal, old-fashioned downtown environment, the politics of their space is at odds with public sphere,

---

[11] Margaret Kohn, *Brave New Neighborhoods: The Privatization of Public Space* (New York: Routledge, 2004), pp. 7–9.

[12] Kohn, pp. 86–88.

[13] Nadine Marquardt and Henning Füller, 'Spillover of the Private City: BIDs as a Pivot of Social Control in Downtown Los Angeles', *European Urban and Regional Studies*, 19.2 (2012), 153–66 (pp. 156–57). On the role of BIDs in disrupting homeless encampments on Skid Row, and thereby perpetuating white supremacy at the level of the built environment, see Andrea Gibbons, *City of Segregation: 100 Years of Struggle for Housing in Los Angeles* (London: Verso, 2018), pp. 125–75.

[14] Marquardt and Füller, pp. 158–60.

or at least romantic liberal conceptions thereof.[15] The mall demonstrates how defensive architecture and militarised security can be softened, made quaint or invisible. Steven Flusty gives as one of his chief examples of such 'quaintified' Los Angeles space an open-air shopping centre called (without a trace of irony) 'The Commons', whose Italian hilltown aesthetic is virtually paradigmatic of postmodern urbanism, and whose quaintness belies a highly exclusionary code of conduct, prohibiting free expression and other 'disruptive' behaviours.[16] Meanwhile, the development of new shopping centres in poorer inner-city sites since the 1980s has proceeded only on condition that such centres employ sophisticated surveillance and policing systems.[17] In the mall, the apparent freedom and equality of the marketplace, that 'very Eden of the innate rights of man',[18] coincides with its opposite, commodity exchange sustained by a vast infrastructure of closed-circuit cameras, alarm systems, and security guards.

We can observe the same relationship between the privatisation of space and intensified discipline in the plazas of downtown Los Angeles. Springing up around the central business district since the 1970s, many new plazas arose through collaboration between the Los Angeles Community Redevelopment Agency, a public body, and developers in the private sector. In principle the two parties shared equal responsibility for the projects; in reality the balance of power tilted in favour of the developers, who enjoyed bonuses for work the private sector would likely have undertaken anyway.[19] The exclusionary mechanisms we have already observed in the mall operate just as efficiently in these plazas, which are only nominally public, and which tailor their appeal to the middle-class professionals working in their environs. Street vendors, musicians, and the homeless are typically unwelcome in such spaces.

---

[15] Kohn, pp. 74–81.

[16] Steven Flusty, 'The Banality of Interdiction: Surveillance, Control, and the Displacement of Diversity', *International Journal of Urban and Regional Research*, 25.3 (2001), 658–64 (p. 662).

[17] Mike Davis, *City of Quartz: Excavating the Future in Los Angeles*, 2nd edn (London: Verso, 2006), p. 242. On private policing in malls, see Miller, pp. 71–72.

[18] Marx, *Capital*, I, 280.

[19] Anastasia Loukaitou-Sideris, 'Privatisation of Public Open Space: The Los Angeles Experience', *The Town Planning Review*, 64.2 (1993), 139–67 (pp. 145–51). 'To cash starved urban officials,' Paul Goldberger suggests, 'allowing public places to become a function of private enterprise is a fair price to pay: they see the alternative as having no new public places at all' ('The Rise of the Private City', in *Breaking Away: The Future of Cities*, ed. by Julia Vitullo-Martin (New York: Twentieth Century Fund Press, 1996), pp. 135–47 (p. 144)).

Security guards escort some people away based on the appearance of their clothing.[20] In her discussion of the California Plaza, Peterson notes that security guards ask anyone they deem to be panhandling too insistently to leave. They also follow around, with intimidating proximity, those who look unkempt.[21]

It is worth pausing here to remark on the peculiar character of such privatised 'public' spaces. Unlike the gated community, which serves as an enclosure in the most literal sense, shielding the private realm from the public, the BID, the mall, and the plaza enfold public space within themselves: they offer themselves up as public spaces while subordinating activity to their owner's prejudices. Yet this enfolding creates its own opportunities for dissent. Peterson relates an occasion when the Service Employees International Union picketed the California Plaza. They chose that particular plaza because its security guards were not members of a union and earned only minimum wage. Leading the march, in fact, was a former California Plaza guard who had been trying to unionise the workforce and was subsequently transferred. Picketing is not permitted in the plaza; however, the security guards working that day did not stop it, and some even joined the protest. As Peterson proceeds to note, the plaza's very privateness is what makes it an appealing site for agitation: disturbing white-collar workers at lunch is a particularly effective means of bringing management to negotiations.[22]

While private policing has grown in Los Angeles, and indeed across the United States, relative to public policing since 1970, it is worth noting that the latter has likewise expanded in absolute terms.[23] The LAPD employed more officers and increased its powers through the late twentieth century. In the 1970s, Mayor Bradley endowed the LAPD with greater powers to fight drug dealing and gangs (these two being deliberately and unhelpfully conflated) so as to promote the city as a safe place for international capital. Reagan's war on drugs served in turn as a lucrative means of funding for Los Angeles, as mid-1980s legislation allowed cities to make more money through narcotics, property, and cash seizures. The revenue gained thereby was used to expand and further militarise the LAPD,[24] and proved especially valuable in an era of fiscal constraint (made worse in California

---

[20] Loukaitou-Sideris, p. 154.
[21] Peterson, p. 373.
[22] Peterson, pp. 375–76.
[23] Mike Davis notes that, between 1980 and 1990, the city's fragmented and defensive suburban geography tripled demand for security services (*City of Quartz*, pp. 249–50).
[24] Max Felker-Kantor, *Policing Los Angeles: Race, Resistance, and the Rise of the LAPD* (Chapel Hill: University of North Carolina Press, 2018), pp. 200–01.

specifically through the passing of Proposition 13, capping property taxes, in 1978), the result of which, as we saw in the last chapter, was to compel a raft of privatisations at city level.

Depicting Los Angeles

That the expansion of public and private policing served ultimately to secure Los Angeles for the investment of overaccumulated capital, or at least to give the impression of such security, should come as no surprise. As David Harvey argues, capital has always looked to the city as a means of absorbing its surplus at moments of crisis. Harvey notes that Baron Georges-Eugène Haussmann's boulevards, constructed in Paris in the 1850s and 1860s, helped resolve the 1848 economic crisis, while Robert Moses put idle capital to work expanding New York's suburbs and rebuilding its infrastructure after the Second World War.[25] Los Angeles knew its own postwar suburbanisation, driven in the 1950s and 1960s by merchant building and home mortgage industries. By the 1970s, however, developable coastal land had diminished, and control of the remnants fell to the few companies large enough to bank it and build new outlying cities altogether.[26] Offshore investment expedited the building boom of the 1970s, with a significant amount of downtown highrise construction completed between 1975 and 1985.[27] These projects, as well as the new skyscrapers, plazas, malls, and gated communities noted above, share the same vocation: they offer so many spatial fixes for overaccumulated capital.

What I want to add is that the metropolitan transformations here documented by Harvey produce a concomitant shift in the city dweller, who must adjust their sensorium, their movement, their very being to the strange new world rising around them. Take the flâneur, who could most often be found in the glass-roofed, marble-panelled arcades built in Paris in the first half of the nineteenth century. In Walter Benjamin's account, the construction of the arcades gave flânerie its raison d'être: it allowed the 'man of the crowd' to walk at their leisure, enchanted by the phantasmagoria of gaslit commodities, and observe those around them.[28] When Haussmann later destroyed some of the arcades and

---

[25] David Harvey, 'The Right to the City', *New Left Review*, 53 (2008), 23–40 (pp. 25–29).
[26] Davis, pp. 130–31.
[27] Davis, pp. 189–90.
[28] Walter Benjamin, *Charles Baudelaire: A Lyric Poet in the Era of High Capitalism*,

reorganised the city around boulevards, he estranged the flâneur from the urban fabric. The Second Empire's urban innovations 'turned the genial ambulatory philosopher of the July Monarchy into a key figure of loss', an expression of the new city's anomie.[29] The flâneur retreated to the bazaars and department stores, the vestiges of their beloved *intérieur*.

Crucially for us, the suburbs sprawling outwards at the end of the Second World War generated their own social types as surely as the Parisian arcades and boulevards had a century before. Among these we find the hardboiled private detective, the sharp-witted, cynical perambulator of mid-century Los Angeles, and the flâneur's distant relative. As Benjamin notes, the flâneur was already an 'unwilling detective' whose peregrinations led them to a crime;[30] the hardboiled detective is accordingly a flâneur who can persist in their craft, in their loitering, philosophising, and observation, only by professionalising it. Hence we tend to find the hardboiled hero depicted as either a self-employed detective, such as Philip Marlowe ('I'm just a small businessman in a very messy business, but I like to follow through on a sale,' he affirms in *Murder, My Sweet* (1944)),[31] or another professional, like Walter Neff, the insurance salesman in *Double Indemnity* (1944). The automobile is to Marlowe and Neff what the arcade was to the flâneur: it allows them to observe, incognito, the crowds surrounding them. Yet their professional status also facilitates their entry into the private enclaves themselves. Marlowe often finds himself amid the grandeur of Los Angeles's stately homes, while Neff's role selling insurance requires some knowledge of private affairs and gains him admission to the Dietrichson household.

The hardboiled detective belongs to mid-century Los Angeles, with its clear demarcation of public and private, scandal smouldering in the suburbs. So what happens to this figure, how must they adapt, when the city changes yet again, when it absorbs yet more surplus capital, especially through the process of privatisation, as in postmodern Los Angeles? I would like to claim that the blade runner's significance

---

trans. by Harry Zohn (London: Verso, 1983), p. 36.
[29] Priscilla Parkhurst Ferguson, *Paris as Revolution: Writing the Nineteenth-Century City* (Berkeley: University of California Press, 1994), p. 81.
[30] Benjamin, pp. 40–41. On the relationship between the flâneur and the hardboiled detective, see Petra Nolan, *Hardboiled Heroes, Deadly Dames: Modernity and 1940s Film Noir* (Saarbrucken: VDM Verlag, 2008).
[31] There remains an ambivalence here, we ought to note, for Marlowe wishes to 'follow through' on the 'sale' (that is, persist in his investigation) primarily because he failed to protect his client, Lindsay Marriott. The language of business thus supplies the apparent justification for a task really carried out because of a personal debt.

emerges from this context: Deckard is the product of an effort to theorise the optimal observer of just such a city.[32] At the beginning of *Blade Runner*, Deckard returns to work, briefly and reluctantly, for the LAPD. His job is to kill, or 'retire', a group of 'Replicants', androids produced to serve as slaves, who have escaped their offworld colony and returned to Earth. The Replicants face a distinctively human crisis: they have risked their journey so as to confront their maker—a man called Eldon Tyrell (Joe Turkel), the CEO of the company that produced them—and, through his intervention, to overcome death. The Replicants are almost identical to humans; the Voigt-Kampff empathy test administered by blade runners is the sole means of distinguishing them. The Replicants must therefore die young, lest they become too emotionally capable for the test to work. Deckard falls in love with one Replicant, Rachael (Sean Young), and escapes death at the hands of another, Roy Batty (Rutger Hauer), but eventually he succeeds, exorcising from Earth—at least for now—the twin spectres of posthumanity and simulacra.

In *Blade Runner*'s sprawling Los Angeles, a city oversaturated with surplus product, each parcel of private space seems to have exceeded itself, each room, building, and surface sullied by the detritus of another. Neon colours the streets, searchlights penetrate J. F. Sebastian's (William Sanderson) block, steam pours from vents, noise murmurs through walls, advertising sprawls itself across skyscrapers, and rain drips through ceilings. This aesthetic of excess is not so much negated as raised to a higher power in the emptiness of the other flats in Sebastian's building, where emptiness compounds upon emptiness: space overflows its own boundaries, as though space itself were somehow in excess. One might remark the same of the Tyrell building, in which space seems superabundant, the echoes of human voices suggesting an even greater room than what we can see. Tyrell's consumption of space is as excellent an indicator of the company's wealth in the film as its owl is in Philip K. Dick's *Do Androids Dream of Electric Sheep?* (1968), the novel on which *Blade Runner* is loosely based.

This kind of city—one divided into parcels, each overflowing with surplus—is precisely the sort of place in which the blade runner feels at

---

[32] In a sense, the blade runner is an effort to imagine the properly postmodern subject, adapted to the specificity of postmodern space, the actuality of whom Jameson denies: 'I am proposing the notion that we are here in the presence of something like a mutation in built space itself. My implication is that we ourselves, the human subjects who happen into this new space, have not kept pace with that evolution: there has been a mutation in the object unaccompanied as yet by any equivalent mutation in the subject' (*Postmodernism*, p. 38).

home. Endowed with police privileges, the blade runner can enter the private spaces off limits to the 'little people', Captain Bryant's (M. Emmet Walsh) term for the largely non-white subjects thronging in the streets.[33] Deckard exploits this privileged position vis-à-vis property rights and privacy often in the course of his investigation, during which he enters the Tyrell building, Zhora's (Joanna Cassidy) dressing room, Leon's (Brion James) apartment, and Sebastian's block. Put simply, the cop is the chief role in *Blade Runner* because, unlike other humans, they can make exceptional movement through an enclosed and congested metropolis. Only the police officer can tie the city's various enclaves together; to them alone is Scott's sprawling Los Angeles available as a coherent, navigable whole. The flying police car, the Spinner drifting above the masses, emblematises perfectly this difference between the hyper-mobile blade runner, to whom the urban form offers little resistance, and the little people funnelled through the streets.

The socially symbolic function of the blade runner, who thematises the act of moving through an increasingly privatised and militarised city, recurs in other 1980s Hollywood science fictions. We might interpret Schwarzenegger's thumping stride as a device for drawing attention to the process of urban movement itself, as the Terminator chases Sarah Connor (Linda Hamilton) and Kyle Reese (Michael Biehn) through Bunker Hill and Santa Monica. *The Running Man* (1987) exploits Schwarzenegger's physique for the same purpose. What Ben Richards, the convict played by Schwarzenegger, must navigate here is an abandoned part of Los Angeles, 400 blocks destroyed by an earthquake in 1997. This space divides into quadrants through which several 'stalkers' pursue, and attempt to kill, Richards and his comrades. The film's dystopianism lies in its portrayal of surveillance, incarceration, and militarised policing, an immense repressive apparatus whose brutalities the entertainment industry both conceals and makes spectacular. Against this background, Richards's ability to move through a derelict Los Angeles, defeating the heavily armed stalkers as he goes, acquires a utopian charge. His exceptionality and heroism lie precisely in his ability to traverse militarised urban space.

Where *Blade Runner* surpasses *The Terminator* (1984) and *The Running Man*, however, is in the extent to which it comprehends the postmodern city itself as a spectacle. It is no coincidence that, while indulging in his motorised flânerie, floating through Los Angeles airspace in Gaff's (Edward James Olmos) Spinner, Deckard sees the city through lens flare,

---

[33] For a brief discussion of *Blade Runner*'s representation of race, see Chapter 5.

Figure 4: Ocular mechanics (*Blade Runner*, dir. by Ridley Scott (Warner Bros., 1982))

as though the vehicle itself were an organ of vision and Deckard its retina, bombarded by light. The neon draping the streets in red, green, and blue serves a similar purpose: we get the feeling that it lights the city so in the hope that the latter will be filmed, and Scott has simply obliged. Neon turns a sign, a functional component of the urban fabric, into a backlight (or a diegetic fill light, perhaps, for the glowing umbrella shafts), and treats the city as a composition, as something that is already, immanently, image. The steam and smoke blowing through the streets exist to be illuminated, to trap stray light, to give it depth and shape. The conception of urban space as an image also underlies the Esper machine, which navigates the pictures of Leon's apartment as though its user, Deckard, were actually there, nosing around private space in the manner of a Marlowe or a Neff. *Blade Runner*'s Los Angeles has the same ontological status as the Replicants' memories, which are themselves reducible to photographs. The city is an object from which the subject has been alienated, and which consequently renders itself as an image.

More than this, *Blade Runner* prompts us to think of the eye itself as a kind of object, a fleshy orb extrinsic to the subject. I have already suggested that the Spinner represents a great eye opened wide to the phantasmagoria of the postmodern city. But more literally, the film demands that we apprehend the materiality and spatiality of the eyeball itself. Prior to Rachael's test, Tyrell reduces the metaphysical disclosure of the Voigt-Kampff machine to the level of ocular mechanics: 'Capillary dilation of the so-called blush response, fluctuation of the pupil, involuntary dilation of the iris,' he says by way of greeting. At other moments the eye becomes an emitter of light, as in the many instances where we see light reflected on the back of Replicant eyeballs, and also on the back of the eyes of Tyrell's owl, this just moments before Roy crushes the blood out of Tyrell's own eyes. The Voigt-Kampff machine mimics the thing it measures: its camera looks like an eye, its pupil a red light. The Replicant manufacturer whom Roy and Leon confront, Chew (James Hong), happens to be a producer of eyes (Chew works at 'Eye World', this branch of Replicant production seemingly outsourced). We see Chew put an eye under a microscope through which he then peers, eyeball scrutinising eyeball. The eye is here explicitly an object, something remarkable to look at in its own right, quite as much as it is the source of vision.

It is through such objectifications, crucially, that *Blade Runner* evokes the obsolescence of the hardboiled detective, the 'private eye'. To solve their crimes, the blade runner requires not a human but a mechanical eye—that of the Voigt-Kampff machine—the irony being that humans must now rely on machines to distinguish themselves from machines. Compounding this irony, the director's cut of *Blade Runner* intimates more strongly than the others that Deckard is himself a Replicant: this version includes Deckard's unicorn dream, which gives Gaff's model unicorn greater significance, since it suggests that he knows of Deckard's dreams, and therefore that Deckard might be an android. Here, then, two machines separate humanity from its self-recognition. In this respect *Blade Runner* goes further than *The Terminator*, in which dogs can still sniff out the cyborg, such that the power of discrimination remains—precariously, thanks to canine companionship—at only one remove from humanity.[34]

So far, we have tended to construe science fiction as a work of extrapolation, *RoboCop* and *Total Recall* enlarging the Reaganite privatisations, *Blade Runner* accelerating urban overaccumulation. But it would be equally accurate to describe the latter's distinctive generic process, the means by which it turns noir science fictional, as one of reduction.[35] What is notable about *Blade Runner* in this respect is that it elides noir's focal classes, the middle and upper strata of Los Angeles, who, departing

---

[34] Though *The Terminator* foregrounds the materiality of vision much as *Blade Runner* does (for example, when the Terminator excises his own eyeball), smell holds an equally prominent place in James Cameron's film. When pointing out how difficult humans find it to detect Terminators, Reese draws attention to their 'sweat' and 'bad breath', not merely their looks. Humans cannot smell the difference, but the difference nevertheless resides in smell, hence why dogs sniff out Terminators right away.

[35] Jameson theorises 'world-reduction' as a third kind of science-fictional estrangement in 'World-Reduction in Le Guin: The Emergence of Utopian Narrative', *Science Fiction Studies*, 2.3 (1975), 221–30 (pp. 223–24).

for their offworld colonies, take with them the scandals that once formed Chandler's and Cain's raw material.[36] Their sensibilities withdrawn, the ornamented and 'quaintified' architecture designed to please them can likewise vanish. The absence of noir's focal classes thus expresses itself in the pervasiveness of noir in the most literal and reified sense: in the darkness, the grime and miasma of Scott's metropolis. For Davis, hardboiled literature and film acted as an antidote to turn-of-the-century boosterism and cultivated a 'populist' anti-myth of Los Angeles.[37] *Blade Runner* perceives the end of that Los Angeles but perpetuates the critique. It shows us the infrastructure of discipline, exploitation, and oppression on which the bungalows and mansions, the manicured lawns and sweeping drives, in short, the whole middle- and upper-class suburban idyll rests.

We might gain a still clearer sense of *Blade Runner*'s politics by contrasting it with another film set in Los Angeles: Kathryn Bigelow's *Strange Days* (1995), which borrows much aesthetically from *Blade Runner* while carefully defusing its most radical implications. Produced in the wake of the 1992 Los Angeles riots, *Strange Days* centres on two police officers' murder of a Black man, which happens to be captured on a headset (known as a 'SQUID') that records the wearer's sensations. Lenny Nero (Ralph Fiennes) is the noir hero of *Strange Days*, but he lacks the blade runner's novelty: Nero's observational skills remain hardboiled, as when he infers from a customer's clothes that the latter works as an attorney for the entertainment industry. For his part, Nero enjoys fictional SQUID tapes but draws the line at snuff recordings; he distinguishes between good images, which respect their distance from reality, and bad ones, which do not. The image is thus the place of fiction in *Strange Days*, and not a basic ontological feature of the object-world, as in *Blade Runner*. Most significantly, despite occasional critiques of LAPD racism and violence—largely articulated by Lornette Mason (Angela Bassett) and Jeriko One (Glenn Plummer)—*Strange Days* places faith in righteous police officers to weed out the racist ones, as Commissioner Strickland (Josef Sommer) arrests the murderous cops in the film's ending. The apparently utopian conclusion, with crowds celebrating the

---

[36] For an enumeration of the social types that populate Chandler's narratives, see Fredric Jameson, *Raymond Chandler: The Detections of Totality* (London: Verso, 2016), pp. 42–48.

[37] Davis goes as far as to describe 1940s film noir as a 'Marxist *cinema manqué*, a shrewdly oblique strategy for an otherwise subversive realism' (*City of Quartz*, p. 41). It is worth noting, as Davis himself remarks, that much film noir sets itself in downtown Los Angeles, and thus shifts the genre's focus from the middle classes to gangsters and corruption.

new millennium, reinforces rather than subverts such a reading, since the new year comes as 'justice' is done and the bad cops die.[38]

The twist is then that while *Strange Days* ends with rupture, the beginning of a new millennium—a moment whose import is the subject of great conjecture—the film's thrust is more or less anti-utopian. The new year's jubilation coinciding narratively with the arrest and death of two white supremacist officers, the new era is one in which the police is merely less tolerant of its aberrations. The difference with *Blade Runner* is illuminating, since the latter eschews millenarian ecstasies, its social structure locked firmly in place, and yet orients itself towards utopia. *Blade Runner*'s utopianism is not temporal, consisting in a break or rupture, but spatial. It belongs to the nature of the blade runner themselves, since they are the only figure to whom the fragmented, privatised, militarised metropolis appears unified, exists as a navigable totality. It might be objected that the blade runner remains a cop; but, unlike *Strange Days*, *Blade Runner* gives us no sense that their morality changes their social function or that Deckard is, or was, a particularly virtuous cop himself. Ultimately, *Strange Days* borrows *Blade Runner*'s iconography and themes without comprehending the underlying social dilemmas to which they respond. *Strange Days* depicts a world, *Blade Runner* a system. A world can be reformed, a system only overthrown.

Picture-Perfect Urbanism

Peter Weir's *The Truman Show* is closer to *Blade Runner*, conceptually, than *Strange Days* is. The film introduces us to Truman Burbank, an ordinary man unaware that he is the star of the world's biggest reality television programme. The show's premise is simple: using thousands of cameras, it depicts Truman's normal, day-to-day existence on Seahaven Island, which is, of course, unbeknownst to Truman, a giant Hollywood set. We join the show in its 30th year, as Truman's urge to leave Seahaven grows. His neighbours and cohabitants, who are actors on the show, try to dissuade him, though it seems his departure might be impossible anyway: the director, Christof (Ed Harris), had Truman's father drown in front of Truman when he was a boy, such that he now fears water.

---

[38] The 10,000 extras celebrating new year in this scene did so under the watch of 50 off-duty and a dozen on-duty police (Romi Stepovich, '*Strange Days*: A Case History of Production and Distribution Practices in Hollywood', in *The Cinema of Kathryn Bigelow: Hollywood Transgressor*, ed. by Deborah Jermyn and Sean Redmond (London: Wallflower, 2003), pp. 144–58 (pp. 152–54)).

Truman's desires to escape and his suspicions about the nature of his reality continue to grow, however, until one night he leaves his house, boards a boat, and sets sail. When Christof finds Truman, he throws a huge artificial thunderstorm at him, recreating the conditions in which his father perished, but Truman persists. Truman reaches the outer limits of the set, a blue wall with puffy clouds. He walks along the edge of the water, ascends a short flight of stairs, and resisting Christof's efforts to convince him otherwise, steps out of the set, much to the delight of the show's many viewers.

The Truman Show was shot largely on location in Seaside, a small beach town on the Florida panhandle.[39] What is notable about this choice, at least for our purposes, is that Seaside was built on private land, passed down to developer Robert Davis from his grandfather. Davis then hired Andrés Duany and Elizabeth Plater-Zyberk to plan his 80-acre town, the construction of which began in 1981. Not bound by existing zoning codes, Duany and Plater-Zyberk determined to turn Seaside into a 'New Urbanist' neighbourhood, the first self-contained community constructed according to New Urbanist principles. (The Seaside Institute describes the town as a 'living laboratory'.)[40] Stressing, at least in their theory, the importance of sustainable communal design, New Urbanists have sought to develop neighbourhoods that combine mixed-use and mixed-income development, open spaces, neotraditional aesthetics, front porches, pavements, and a central civic space. Land use is important for New Urbanists, who reserve particular ire for modernist zoning practices, which, in their view, generate segmented and decentralised urban growth and feed suburban anomie.[41] Following these principles, Seaside comprises small lots, narrow streets, mid-block walkways, and shops surrounding a green. Straight roads fan out from the centre and facilitate a short walk from house to post office, restaurant, or marketplace.[42]

---

[39] According to Douglas A. Cunningham, the film turned several façades of Seaside buildings into those of Seahaven's offices and shot some house interiors in a local warehouse, though most of Truman's own house is indeed a real Seaside property ('A Theme Park Built for One: The New Urbanism vs. Disney Design in *The Truman Show*', *Critical Survey*, 17.1 (2005), 109–30 (p. 129, n. 30)).

[40] Seaside Institute, 'Our Mission' [n.d.] <https://www.seasideinstitute.org/mission> [accessed 17 May 2022].

[41] Here I draw from Jill Grant's overview of the origins and principles of New Urbanism in *Planning the Good Community: New Urbanism in Theory and Practice* (London: Routledge, 2006), pp. 45–78.

[42] For a description and evaluation of Seaside, see Grant, pp. 82–84.

Of particular interest to us, given the last section's focus on movement, is the New Urbanist valorisation of walking. Ratified in 1996, the 'Charter of the New Urbanism' proposes that 'networks of streets' be 'designed to encourage walking, reduce the number and length of automobile trips, and conserve energy'.[43] The five-minute walk (the so-called 'pedestrian shed') is thus one of the conceptual foundations of New Urbanism, an elementary unit of its design. The town centre and key shops and amenities all ought to be accessible within five walking minutes, or roughly a quarter of a mile, New Urbanists suggest, else residents are liable to jump into their cars. The charter imagines its pedestrian as an observer—a flâneur, even—whom the urban environment should stimulate: 'Streets and squares should be safe, comfortable, and interesting to the pedestrian,' it advises.[44] The five-minute stroll should not be a means to an end, on this view, but a pleasurable activity in its own right.

Yet despite their emphasis on community, and on the latter's material supports—parks, playgrounds, churches, and so on—New Urbanist neighbourhoods have proven fertile ground for privatisation.[45] Their open

---

[43] Congress for the New Urbanism, 'Charter of the New Urbanism' (1996) <https://www.cnu.org/who-we-are/charter-new-urbanism> [accessed 17 May 2022] (§ 12).

[44] Congress for the New Urbanism, § 23.

[45] Judged by New Urbanism's own standards, its experiment has failed. Soaring prices have made houses unaffordable to all but the wealthy. Most people strolling around Seaside today are in fact tourists, the 'neighbourhood' having become a luxurious resort with only a handful of permanent residents—17, to be precise, as of December 2012 (Jennifer Parker, 'Seaside, About the Community and the Building of the Seaside Research Portal' [n.d.] <https://seaside.library.nd.edu/essays/the-community-and-building-the-portal> [accessed 17 May 2022]). These shortcomings trouble Cunningham's claim that Seaside has 'one fundamental difference' to Disney's neotraditional style, since the latter tries to erase diversity while New Urbanism seeks to 'promote and enable diversity of class and race' ('Theme Park', p. 119). As such, in Cunningham's view, it is Disney urbanism, not Seaside New Urbanism, that serves as the object of *The Truman Show*'s critique. However, while New Urbanist literature indeed waxes lyrical about remedying race and class segregations, there is yet no evidence that its practice achieves that, as Cunningham is himself aware. Most New Urbanist towns are more expensive than comparable developments, and proponents of New Urbanism use rising prices as a way of appealing to investors (Grant, p. 99). Virtuous promulgations mean little in this context. See, for a brief critique of the movement's utopianism, David Harvey, *Spaces of Hope* (Berkeley: University of California Press, 2000), pp. 169–73.

spaces, town halls, and streets are often technically private property and give their owners power to enforce the kinds of prohibitions we have already seen at work in other enfolded areas, such as the plaza and the mall. In some cases, the residents' association owns amenities and makes them accessible to residents alone; in others, these sites are not even open to the whole community. Margaret Kohn notes that the recreational facilities in Haile Plantation—a New Urbanist neighbourhood in Florida—require residents' membership of an exclusive club, and its town hall asks civic groups, nonprofits, and individuals to pay to use it.[46] While New Urbanism derives its appeal from the 'semiotics of community', and proclaims the importance of the public sphere, the politics of its space is antithetical to community in any meaningful sense.

The Truman Show's critique of New Urbanism in particular, and commodification in general, begins with its representation of product placement. At various moments, Truman's wife, Meryl Burbank (Laura Linney), delivers the patter for the 'Chef's Pal' knife, the 'Elk Rotary' lawnmower, and the 'Mococoa' hot drink. Truman's close friend Marlon (Noah Emmerich) grins cheesily as he sips 'Penn Pavel's Beer'. Two old men stop Truman in front of an advertising board with, first, 'Kaiser Chicken' and, later, 'Carleton—Fine Colonial Homes' pasted on it. But these are only the most obvious cases: it turns out that everything on the set, from the actors' clothes to their food and homes, is for sale. On one level, this quite literal commodification of everything serves as a critique of New Urbanism, many of whose towns are completely private, and swaddle themselves in the semiotics of the public sphere the better to conceal that fact. But we could also go further, for the enfolding of public space within private property rights is, as we have seen, intrinsic to postmodern urbanism, fundamental to its BIDs, malls, and plazas. The film's polemical target therefore exceeds New Urbanism: *The Truman Show* makes visible the manipulation of appearances that legitimises a range of contemporaneous privatisations of public space.

These commodities are explicitly images, 'The Truman Show' in essence one long commercial. The show's viewers look at Truman's food, furniture, and car—indeed, everything in the frame—as though they were flâneurs gazing through the arcade window, intoxicated by the commodity. For the most part, the film audience is sutured into their perspective: we see Truman from the same angles, under the same lighting, across the same cuts, either side of the same credit sequence, as the television viewers do. Yet at certain moments *The Truman Show* subverts the style of the advertisement, the commodity's visual grammar,

---

[46] Kohn, pp. 126–33.

Figure 5: 'No artificial sweeteners!' (*The Truman Show*, dir. by Peter Weir (Paramount Pictures, 1998))

and, in doing so, disrupts that identification. When the camera zooms in to Meryl's face, when she grins broadly, reaches behind her, and presents, in full view of the camera, the new hot chocolate she wants us to buy, the abrupt, exaggerated shift to advertising form foregrounds that form itself, its distinctive style, and jolts us out of the flâneur's gaze. Truman is confused by his wife's behaviour—they are quarrelling—and asks frustratedly, 'What the hell are you talking about? Who are you talking to?' In this moment we cease to identify with the show's audience, for whom Meryl's gesture is intended, and find ourselves sutured into Truman's point of view. We see the advertisement, and Meryl's behaviour, as Truman does: it seems forced, dissonant, out of place.

Yet there is a paradox here, for Truman fails to understand his wife's actions, her role vis-à-vis the spectacle, and looks upon it with bafflement only because he is himself so thoroughly integrated into that spectacle. Truman's relationship to images is therefore the inverse of Deckard's. As we have already noted, Deckard is a utopian figure because he exists outside the image: he sees the metropolis as a spectacle yet floats above it, escapes its gravity, in the Spinner. Bryant's distinction between cop and little person is in the final analysis one between subject and object, observer and observed. Truman, however, is immersed in the image, part of its content, and has no idea his world is a huge television set. In his role as a blade runner, Deckard gains access to Los Angeles in its totality—the city opens up to him, private and public spaces alike—while Truman is detached from, indeed completely unaware of, the greater Los Angeles metropolitan region to which he belongs. As a result, sealed off from context and history, Truman experiences life as the sum of its contingent, individual events. His father's return is interpretable only as some kind of a miracle, an eventuality with which he kept faith but whose underlying determinations (Christof's efforts to keep Truman on the set, to boost ratings, and so on) remain inscrutable to him. The film constructs Truman as a figure for whom totality is completely inaccessible.

Truman's self-contained world thus acts a kind of New Urbanist laboratory (to recall the Seaside Institute's suggestive term), where broader social forces, conceived as so many variables, appear to have been arrested. For New Urbanists, better design can remedy the class and race antagonisms characteristic of the postwar suburb.[47] But this solution is a superficial one: well-kept greens, picket fences, and wrap-around porches have offered little defence against the storm of rising house prices and white fear and racism. Though he shows little concern for the race or class composition of Seahaven, Christof bears strong affinities with the New Urbanist designer—the host of 'Tru-Talk', Mike Michaelson (Harry Shearer), actually calls Christof a 'designer and architect'—since it is his job, essentially, to manage the *appearance* of daily events, down to the very words the actors speak to Truman, in real time. Christof has absolute control, in other words, but what he controls is only surface, artifice, simulation. Christof's 'design' remains bound to the dictates of an overarching media environment ruled by the iron fist of capital. Thus, when Christof fails to convince Truman to remain on the set, we see, not Christof, but one of the network's executives demanding that they 'cease transmission'.

What might this suggest about *The Truman Show*'s politics, and thus about its utopianism? I want to conclude here by suggesting that the conflicting views on Truman's exit, dramatised within the film itself, are implicitly political. That they are so Christof already signals for us when he chides Truman's schoolmate, Lauren Garland (Natascha McElhone), for trying to reveal the truth to Truman. In accusing Lauren of 'thrust[ing herself] and [her] politics into

---

[47] Grant, pp. 67–68.

the limelight', Christof betrays that his contrary view on Truman's existence is similarly political. Allegorically, Christof represents an essentially reformist politics that knows only surface and that limits its mode of action accordingly to tweaks and adjustments. His plea to Truman that 'there's no more truth out there than there is in the world I created for you' grafts Seahaven's ontology, where everything is explicitly surface, onto the society beyond it. In rejecting such appeals, Truman acquires the opposite political charge, becomes the locus of the film's utopia. Truman's exit is not mere escapism. Rather, as the black doorway suggests, his is a head-on confrontation with the unknown, or, to put that another way, an escape from the objective escapism of Seahaven itself. This doorway's mysteriousness contrasts with the routine established at Truman's own front door, a site of supreme certainty: every morning, leaving the house for work, he repeats his catchphrase—'Good morning! And in case I don't see you, good afternoon, good evening, and good night'—to the family living opposite. The phrase's conditional mood ('in case I don't see you') is something of a joke in this context, where virtually everything in Truman's life is choreographed. But when Truman stands at the dark door and utters the line one last time, its conditionality becomes genuinely conditional. Truman hopes to join a world where, unlike Seahaven, circumstances do indeed elude individual control.

Paradoxically, however, the film concludes with the suggestion that it is Christof who is right. When Truman leaves and the show ends, its audience remains in thrall to the spectacle: in the film's concluding shot, having celebrated Truman's escape from the world of images, the two security guards reach for the television guide, and thus unwittingly prove Christof's point: there is no more truth outside Seahaven than inside it. What matters as regards the film's utopianism, however, is not the accuracy of Truman's appraisal vis-à-vis Christof's, but rather Truman's determination, his sincere desire and hope to leave behind such a world. Looked at thus, *The Truman Show*'s politics mirror those of *Blade Runner*, whose Los Angeles appears unsusceptible to radical change, things destined to continue as they are. The Replicants' creeping authenticity threatens human norms and the integrity of the Voigt-Kampff test, but their motive, for the time being at least, is merely the prolongation of individual lives. For both films, crucially, this background of dystopian continuity is what foregrounds their utopian discontinuities: Deckard's ability to rise above images, Truman's decision to walk away from them. It is precisely because they are set against such a backdrop that these attributes become utopian, and that utopianism becomes magnified. The utopian and dystopian elements of these texts are not opposed, not forces of light beating back darkness, or optimism scolding pessimism. The two are in fact related, dialectical twins, dystopia serving negatively to define and make legible the utopian breach in reality—a structure we have already observed in *RoboCop* and *Total Recall*, in the previous chapter.

Is this conclusion—that dystopia might entertain a predominantly complementary, not contrary, relationship to utopia—a surprising one? Is such complementarity a quirk of the films we happen to have looked at so far here, or have we seen it before, in other utopian texts? Is it an innovation attributable to late-twentieth-century Hollywood directors, or a fundamental feature of all utopias, or somewhere between the two? What is the history of the utopian dystopia, in short, and what are its determinants? These questions place us at the threshold of genre theory, whose comprehension of utopian texts must of necessity remain partial, incomplete, until it engages in the same breath capital's dispossession of proletarian life, as we shall see in the next chapter.

Part 2

Dystopia after Dystopia

Chapter 4

Expropriation
Marx, Utopia, and the Limits of Political Economy

It is only in Part Eight of the first volume of *Capital* that Marx confronts the question of capital's 'primitive accumulation': the process by which labourers become separate from their means of subsistence, dependent on wages, and subordinate to the class that pays those wages. The function of Part Eight within Marx's analysis of capital—and especially the question why it leaves unexamined ongoing forms of dispossession, the kind that detain us in this book—will be our focus shortly. What I would like to note in opening is the sheer variety of materials that Marx marshals in Part Eight, the better to understand capitalism's origins. Marx cites, among a great many other things, Jean-Jacques Rousseau's *Discourse on Political Economy* (1755), the Spiritualist William Howitt's account of the Christian colonial system (in *Colonisation and Christianity* (1838)), Dr Julian Hunter's reports on public health (these already having proven central to the argument in Part Seven, particularly Chapter 25), the Trade Union Act and the Criminal Law Amendment Act (both of 1871) passed under Victoria, and Thomas Macaulay's *History of England* (1848), which Marx quotes only because Macaulay is a 'systematic falsifier of history' and therefore 'minimizes facts of this kind'—namely, regarding the existence of free peasant proprietors—'as much as possible'.[1]

Yet perhaps Marx's reference, twice in Part Eight, to Thomas More's *Utopia* (1516) is the most curious, not least because Marx seems to treat this eminently ambiguous, playful text as a straightforward chronicle of conditions in England in the sixteenth century, when enclosure and the criminalisation of vagabondage set the wheels of capital accumulation in motion. Marx's reading of *Utopia* as chronicle rather than fiction manifests itself in his reduction of character to author: in one of his footnotes, Marx refers to the traveller who describes Utopia, Raphael

---

[1] Marx, *Capital*, I, 877, n. 1.

Hythloday, as 'Thomas More'. Such a conflation would seem problematic not least because More names another character in *Utopia*, one largely opposed to Utopian custom, after himself. (The latter's relationship to the author, and by extension More's agreement with his own utopian vision, has proven an enduring object of scholarly debate.[2]) Additionally, when we look closely at Marx's citations in Part Eight, we see that he quotes from only Book I of *Utopia*, in which Hythloday confronts the 'problem of counsel', and seems to ignore Book II, where the main descriptions of Utopia lie. Does Marx's brief, partial treatment of *Utopia* as a historical document not overlook the essentially speculative character of the utopian form? Does it not ignore those very things that make More's text a challenging, utopian work of fiction?

We might write this off as yet another instance of the old Marx's curmudgeonly utopophobia, part of his aversion to the utopian socialists of his own time. In doing so, however, this chapter suggests, we would miss the point of More's text itself, indeed of the utopian genre as such.[3] If, following More, properly utopian fiction rests its visions on common property, it does so to show, by contrast, the depredations of capitalism's enclosed world, and thus to criticise the institution of private property. These criticisms are primary to utopianism. Even where the utopian restricts themselves to describing their utopia, their new set of social arrangements, the old ones—the real object of study—linger, the negative from whose shadow the positive's light flows. It is as if all utopias imply their own Book I, their own condemnation of private property, this critical moment being definitive, constitutive of the genre as such. That More explicitly provides the critique gives Marx's reading the appearance of an evasion, but in fact the opposite is true: in Book I of *Utopia*, Marx finds himself at the heart of the utopian form. More's

---

[2] The proposition in question is stated most baldly by Karl Kautsky, whose 1888 study of *Utopia* takes Hythloday to be 'the mouthpiece of More's opinions' (*Thomas More and His Utopia*, trans. by H. J. Stenning (Whitefish: Kessinger, 2003), p. 97). For a clarification of the main terms of this debate and a signal intervention in it, see Quentin Skinner, 'Sir Thomas More's *Utopia* and the Language of Renaissance Humanism', in *The Languages of Political Theory in Early Modern Europe*, ed. by Anthony Pagden (Cambridge: Cambridge University Press, 1987), pp. 123–58.

[3] This chapter focuses on utopian literature alone, but it must be noted that certain social theories and intentional communities are also often considered utopian. For the classic statement of this position, see Lyman Tower Sargent, 'The Three Faces of Utopianism Revisited', *Utopian Studies*, 5.1 (1994), 1–37. For an opposing view, according to which utopias are 'verbal constructions' first and foremost, see Suvin, pp. 51–77.

utility to Marx's analysis of primitive accumulation proceeds from the utopia's militant, historical, critical core.

Around three and a half centuries separate *Utopia* from *Capital*, and we must wait another century still for the utopian dystopias examined in our previous chapters. But more important than the sheer stretch of time, the passing of which in itself tells us nothing, is the change in perspective that commodities have wrought in their producers during that period. Unlike More, who witnessed the transition between two distinct social systems, and was useful to Marx for that very reason, today's observer is afforded no such contrast. The new enclosures—privatising public services, parcelling up the cityscape, destroying social housing, consuming reservoir and forest—further commodify a world in which, to recall Lukács's phrase, the commodity is already the universal, determining category, and colours the totality of our existence.[4] They paint on the dull, existing greyness only a thicker coat of grey. This chapter's reading of Marx and More, and the reasons for the latter's engagement with the former, thus leaves us poised to comprehend the dystopian turn of our own time. If More's *Utopia* represents the beginning of utopian criticism, I will conclude, the utopian dystopias of the late twentieth century mark its end, an extreme adaptation beyond which the form is no longer recognisable as utopian at all. The examination of such an extreme, and the necessarily anti-utopian Hollywood dystopias that come after it, is the purpose of Part 2 of this book.

So-Called 'Primitive Accumulation'

What is Marx's focus, the object of his critique, in *Capital*? Is it the reified social relation that forms the book's title—capital—or the scholarly discipline named in the subtitle: *A Critique of Political Economy*? Does Marx take aim at the wrongs perpetrated by the capitalist system, or is his chief concern the distortion of that system supplied in the works of Adam Smith, David Ricardo, and the other political economists? Is it the thing that detains him, in short, or its conceptualisation? The answer is both: Marx's study of the various moments of capital accumulation—the process by which value increases itself, becomes surplus-value, and returns to the capitalist through the sale of their commodities—is at one and the same time a critique of the categories through which the

---

[4] Georg Lukács, *History and Class Consciousness: Studies in Marxist Dialectics*, trans. by Rodney Livingstone (Cambridge, MA: MIT Press, 1971), p. 86.

political economists misconstrue that process.⁵ Thus, to take just one example, in Chapter 19 of Volume 1 of *Capital*, Marx notes that the classical political economists define wages as the 'value of labour', and that this phrase is meaningless. It is not labour that the capitalist buys, but labour-power—not the concrete work tasks, but the capacity for work—such that wages, on average, represent the value of labour-power, not the value of labour.

As Marx adds, however, it is not entirely fair to impute the political economists' imprecision to muddled thinking, as though each had simply made an error in their analysis. In fact, their misapprehension arises from the peculiar character of the phenomenon they are studying, capitalism itself, which does indeed make it seem as though the capitalist purchases, not labour-power, the capacity for work, but labour. The wage appears to compensate the worker for the whole day's work, thus for the labour tasks actually performed, rather than for what Marx calls 'necessary labour', which represents the value of the labourer's means of subsistence, and which might be completed after only half the working day. The other half of the day, in this case, is 'surplus labour', labour generating surplus-value, and is not compensated in wages (else it would not be 'surplus'). The wage-form, and with it the political economists' insistence that it represents the whole value of labour, conceals the decisive role of exploitation, of unpaid or surplus labour, in the production of surplus-value. 'That in their appearance things are often presented in an inverted way is something fairly familiar in every science,' Marx suggests, 'apart from political economy.'⁶

It is in this sense that Marx's critique in *Capital* might be characterised as immanent: it takes, as it finds them, the categories through which its object has typically been understood, and shows, first, that such categories fail to correspond to the object, and second (arguably the more difficult task) how the object itself induces that failure. The method of such immanent critique, I want to begin by suggesting, is key to understanding Marx's analysis of primitive accumulation in Part Eight of Volume 1. On a first reading, it seems as though these chapters seek simply to write a more accurate history of primitive accumulation than did the political economists, who, where they dealt with the

⁵ 'The work I am presently concerned with,' Marx writes in an 1858 letter, 'is a *Critique of Economic Categories* or, if you like, a critical exposé of the system of bourgeois economy. It is at once an exposé and, by the same token, a critique of the system' (Letter to Ferdinand Lassalle, 22 February 1858, in *Marx–Engels Collected Works*, 50 vols (London: Lawrence and Wishart, 1975–2004), XL (1983), 268–71 (p. 270)).

⁶ Marx, *Capital*, I, 677.

matter at all, brushed over the violence constitutive of capitalism. In his study of their work, Michael Perelman identifies James Steuart, the eighteenth-century Scottish economist, as one of the few to acknowledge such brutalities. Most others, such as Adam Smith and David Ricardo, entertain a certain cognitive dissonance, and trumpet their commitment to *laissez-faire* in their writings while, in practice, advocating that the state intervene to make labour dependent on capital.[7] It would thus seem that Part Eight of *Capital* intends simply to remind us of the 'blood and fire' that such accounts omit. Marx recalls, in England, the enclosure of common land, the dissolution of the bands of feudal retainers, the passing of laws against vagabondage, the Reformation, and the Glorious Revolution; in Scotland, the Highland Clearances; and in the imperial context, enslavement, plunder, and conquest. The forms of primitive accumulation that Marx details are diverse: he counts taxation, public debt, and protectionism as means of expropriation, setting the stage for capital accumulation proper.[8]

Yet the characterisation of Marx's method offered above implies that this framing, this understanding of Marx's purposes in Part Eight, is inaccurate. Marx is not conjuring, out of thin air, a new category for the analysis of capitalism, which he then names 'primitive accumulation'. His task is rather to take this category, present already in the writings of the political economists, and subject it to immanent critique.[9] It is significant that, in the first and second German editions of *Capital*, Marx uses the title '*Die sogenannte ursprüngliche Akkumulation*', or '*So-Called* Primitive Accumulation' (my emphasis), this being the framing that Marx's translators have preserved in Part Eight of the English versions of the text. Marx thereby stresses, from the outset, that the concept 'primitive accumulation' precedes *Capital*, and hints that it forms the object of his critique. Additionally, Marx calls the first section of

---

[7] Michael Perelman, *The Invention of Capitalism: Classical Political Economy and the Secret History of Primitive Accumulation* (Durham, NC: Duke University Press, 2000).

[8] Marx, *Capital*, I, 873–940.

[9] In his analysis of primitive accumulation, 'Marx began by taking the categories of classical political economy as he found them. By investigating them more fully, he was able to invest the typically static, undialectical categories of classical political economy with a dynamic, dialectical quality,' Perelman argues (*The Invention of Capitalism*, p. 36). 'If *Capital* is read as anything other than an immanent critique,' Moishe Postone warns, 'the result is a reading that interprets Marx as affirming that which he attempts to criticise' (*Time, Labor, and Social Domination: A Reinterpretation of Marx's Critical Theory* (Cambridge: Cambridge University Press, 1993), p. 142).

Chapter 24 (later to become Chapter 26 in the English editions) '*Das Geheimnis der ursprünglichen Akkumulation*', or 'The Secret of Primitive Accumulation'. In the opening paragraph of this chapter, he proceeds to equate 'primitive accumulation' with 'the "previous accumulation" of Adam Smith'—that is, Marx introduces the concept as Smith's.[10] The 'secret' of primitive accumulation is then the bloody revolution expunged by the neutral, naturalising, ultimately euphemistic and exculpatory implications of Smith's sentence: 'The accumulation of stock must, in the nature of things, be previous to the division of labour.'[11] In the manner of immanent critique, Marx takes a concept used to explain capitalism's origin and 'convict[s] it of its own inadequacy'.[12]

As we have already seen, however, the categories of political economy are not mere errors or mistakes, thought gone awry. Rather, they arise from capitalism itself, which projects, from its structure, certain 'forms of appearance' that deceive us as to the essence of that structure. So where does this specific misapprehension, Smith's notion that capitalism derives from a prior 'accumulation of stock', come from? It is this question that the opening lines of Chapter 26—quoted earlier, but now requiring further explication—seek to answer:

> We have seen how money is transformed into capital, how surplus-value is made through capital, and how more capital is made

[10] Marx, *Capital*, I, 873. The French edition of *Capital*, the last to be published in Marx's lifetime, drops the 'so-called', a point William Clare Roberts notes in order to suggest that primitive accumulation *is*, in fact, a 'Marxist concept', Marx himself having revised the text for the French edition ('What Was Primitive Accumulation? Reconstructing the Origin of a Critical Concept', *European Journal of Political Theory*, 19.4 (2020), 532–52 (p. 548, n. 1)). This tweak to the framing of Marx's critique does not change the fundamental character of that critique, however. In the French edition, as in the previous German ones, Marx proceeds to suggest that 'primitive accumulation plays roughly the same role in political economy as original sin does in theology', a phrase that again, at the beginning of the section on primitive accumulation, imputes the concept to the political economists preceding Marx (for the French, see Karl Marx, 'Chapitre XXVI: Le secret de l'accumulation primitive' (1872) <https://www.marxists.org/francais/marx/works/1867/Capital-I/kmcapI-26.htm> [accessed 17 May 2022] (para. 2 of 14)).

[11] Adam Smith, *The Wealth of Nations: Books I–III* (London: Penguin, 1999), pp. 371–72.

[12] The phrase is Adorno's; see his *Introduction to Dialectics*, ed. by Christoph Ziermann, trans. by Nicholas Walker (Cambridge: Polity, 2017), p. 8. Marx's account of 'primitive accumulation' has been the subject of much critical commentary; for an overview, see Nichols, pp. 62–70.

from surplus-value. But the accumulation of capital presupposes surplus-value; surplus-value presupposes capitalist production; capitalist production presupposes the availability of considerable masses of capital and labour-power in the hands of commodity producers. The whole movement, therefore, seems to turn around in a never-ending circle, which we can only get out of by assuming a primitive accumulation [...] which precedes capitalist accumulation [...][13]

Marx does not introduce the concept as an objective process that he has discovered in history.[14] Primitive accumulation makes its first appearance in Part Eight as an assumption, and—more than that—an assumption based on the way the accumulation of capital 'seems', not the way it *is*. In other words, capital leaves us no trace of its origins in the bloody, fiery expropriation of the peasantry: if we retrace the course of the logic of accumulation in the hope of finding such an origin, we end up where we started. Our efforts to escape this circle must take the form of an assumption, and the content of that assumption is that capital has somehow gravitated to one pole of society, where it now appears as accumulated stock, and free labourers to the other. The self-renewing character of capital, turning over in a 'never-ending circle', reproducing

---

[13] Marx, *Capital*, I, 873.
[14] According to Nichols's reading, by contrast, Marx's project in Part Eight is to describe the 'agentic intervention' that establishes capitalism. Since this agency cannot be capital itself, and since, further, for Marx, immanent critique is the mode of analysis adequate to capital, Part Eight must depart from this immanence in favour of a different, 'empirical–descriptive' approach (*Theft is Property!*, pp. 58–59). But is it not precisely Marx's point, in the above-quoted paragraph, the first of Part Eight, that 'so-called primitive accumulation' is a conceptual reflection of capital itself, which, in its ceaseless metamorphosis, erases its origin? Does not capital therefore remain the ultimate object of critique? Such a reading does not require the rather implausible assumption that, in composing the final chapters of his book, Marx abandoned the method that had served him well for the rest of it. It also answers Nichols's subsequent concern that Marx's description, focusing as it does on the English experience, cannot constitute a general, context-independent, 'conceptual–analytic' theory of capitalism's origins (*Theft is Property!*, p. 68). On the contrary, the non-correspondence of the particular account, the violence of the English enclosures, with the political economists' vague notion of some prior accumulation of stock is precisely Marx's point in Part Eight. The gap between particular, 'empirical–descriptive' and general, 'conceptual–analytic' is the point of the critique, not its blind spot.

its foundations as it goes, elides the violence of its origin and permits the Smithian exoneration. It is capital's erasure of this violence, reified in political economy as the concept 'primitive accumulation', that Marx is concerned to criticise in Part Eight.[15]

Wolves, Sheep, and Hares

We begin with this analysis of the object of Part Eight because it is in relation to that object, the critique of the category 'primitive accumulation', that Marx's threefold citation of Thomas More must be understood. The first one occurs in the body of the text, near the beginning of Part Eight, when Marx suggests that 'comparison between the writings of Chancellor Fortescue and Thomas More reveals the gulf between the fifteenth and sixteenth centuries'—that is, before and during the revolution in property relations that established the capitalist mode of production. In this sentence, More stands as the authoritative chronicler of a period, a source of documentary evidence. (Marx has just remarked that while some such 'old chroniclers' exaggerate their complaints about enclosure, 'they faithfully reflect the impression made on contemporaries by the revolution in the relations of production', the exaggeration therefore making their chronicles more useful, not less.) Marx's periodisation here seems to suggest that fifteenth-century feudalism gives way rapidly to the capitalism of the sixteenth: there is a 'gulf' between Fortescue and More. However, a closer look reveals that things are less clear, since, on the previous page, Marx speaks of a 'prelude' to the 'revolution that laid the foundation of the capitalist mode of production', and dates this prelude to 'the last third of the fifteenth century and the first few decades of the sixteenth'.[16] The prelude is therefore almost exactly coterminous with More's life, which began in February 1478 and ended on Henry VIII's chopping block in July 1535.

---

[15] The immanent character of Marx's critique in *Capital* goes some way to answering the common complaint that Part Eight ignores ongoing, continuous, persistent forms of expropriation. Marx is not trying to write a full-blown history of expropriation; what history he does write serves strictly to undermine the Smithian exoneration. See, for one prominent example of this criticism, Silvia Federici, *Caliban and the Witch: Women, the Body, and Primitive Accumulation* (Brooklyn: Autonomedia, 2004), p. 12. This is also the misreading of Harvey's that I note in Chapter 1, in my discussion of his concept of 'accumulation by dispossession'.

[16] Marx, *Capital*, I, 878–79.

Why did Marx see fit to place More's life in the prelude to the revolution in property relations, but speak of his writings as documents of that revolution itself? It is not especially unusual for the Marx of *Capital* to treat literature so. As S. S. Prawer observes, *Capital* sometimes cites literature as documentary evidence of the history of a given period (*The Odyssey* supplies Marx with evidence of the ancient division of labour) while, at other times, invoking it as a form of anticipation (Shakespeare's Dogberry pre-empts some political economists' style of argumentation).[17] Though it seems that Marx calls on More as a chronicler, *Utopia* serves him just as much as a form of anticipation, I would suggest. This is partly because Marx goes on to cite *Utopia* in the context of Elizabeth's 1572 Act for the Punishment of Vagabonds—More's book was published over half a century earlier—and partly because the enclosure movement evoked in *Utopia* was, in More's time, incipient, and would accelerate, reaching its acme in the years 1750 to 1830, such that Hythloday's complaints seem quite prescient. More might have lived the transitional moment, the gap between the two worlds, but, being an acute observer, he grasped the significance of the new forces stirring in the English countryside.

We will consider *Capital*'s second and third mentions of More, and what they reveal about *Utopia*'s role in its argument, more closely in a moment, but first I must stress the centrality of enclosure to *Utopia* itself. As I have already mentioned, *Utopia* comprises two books: the first narrates the meeting of Thomas More, Peter Giles (a character given the name of More's friend), and Raphael Hythloday (a fictional adventurer who travelled with Amerigo Vespucci), whose conversation focuses on the question of advising rulers, and the second renders Hythloday's description of Utopia, an island on which Hythloday eventually settled.[18] Accordingly, it is in Book I that we find the English enclosures treated in most detail. Hythloday argues there that the decline of self-provisioning consequent on enclosure is responsible for much crime in England. The expropriated having sold their household effects, and having exhausted, in their wanderings, the money raised thereby, 'what alternative do they have but to steal and be hanged [...] or continue their travels and beg?' Hythloday asks.[19] Later in the discussion, Hythloday remarks that, were he to advocate Plato's vision in the *Republic* or the social practices of

[17] S. S. Prawer, *Karl Marx and World Literature* (London: Verso, 2011), pp. 334–37.
[18] We ought to note that *Utopia* also includes *parerga*—including several letters between More and his fellow Renaissance humanists, commendatory poetry, and a map of Utopia—added by Peter Giles and Erasmus to the first few editions of the text.
[19] Thomas More, *Utopia*, trans. by Dominic Baker-Smith (London: Penguin, 2012), pp. 33–34.

Utopia, his ideas 'would seem outlandish here because the rule is private ownership of property while there all things are held in common'. Hythloday concludes that a society founded on private property is by nature unjust and inimical to happiness.[20] Comments on the merits of common ownership then continue through Book II.

Marx's second reference to More is his first explicitly to *Utopia*. In a footnote in Chapter 27 of *Capital*, Volume 1 ('The Expropriation of the Agricultural Population from the Land'), Marx recites Hythloday's satirical remark that, in England, sheep 'have now, so it's claimed, begun to be so voracious and fierce that they swallow up people'.[21] This is the sentence in Book I that introduces *Utopia*'s criticisms of the English enclosures, which turned much arable land into pasture, swelled the ranks of sheep, and herded humans into towns, depopulating the countryside. Leaving aside the content of the citation, briefly, it is interesting that Marx here attributes the line to Thomas More himself, the author, not Hythloday. Prawer observes Marx's tendency to do this with a range of literary texts, though close attention to the context of Marx's argument reveals that Marx is indeed conscious of the distinction 'and expects his readers to be aware of it too'.[22] The classic example of such conflation, where Marx makes a character its author's ventriloquist, is *Timon of Athens* (1623), whose citation in the *Grundrisse* (1858) does indeed equate Timon with Shakespeare, as Prawer duly notes.[23] In our own case, Marx's conflation appears to indicate, once more, that More exists for him simply as a chronicler, whose insight into sixteenth-century England might be teased from *Utopia*'s fictional envelope.

Yet I want to suggest that the sheep metaphor also entertains an anticipatory, rather than merely documentary, relationship to Marx's argument. Hythloday imputes the greed (in his view) of the enclosers to the sheep themselves, which become 'voracious and fierce', and begin to consume humans as ravenously as humans consume mutton and wool. The image of monstrous sheep thus captures the strangeness of a new world in which livestock, the traditional object of direct human domination, incarnates in its flesh and wool capital's powers of

---

[20] More, pp. 50–53.
[21] More, p. 33; Marx, *Capital*, I, 880, n. 4 (Marx cites the original English translation, by Ralph Robinson, another sixteenth-century humanist).
[22] Prawer, p. 414.
[23] 'The equation of the incompatible, as Shakespeare nicely defined money' (Karl Marx, *Grundrisse: Foundations of the Critique of Political Economy*, trans. by Martin Nicolaus (London: Penguin, 1993), p. 163).

impersonal domination, henceforth to enchain humanity.[24] In this lies the similarity but also the difference between More's figure and Marx's depiction, earlier in Volume 1, of capital as having a 'werewolf-like hunger for surplus labour'.[25] Marx's trope animates and animalises capital, suggests that it obeys its own instincts, not the wishes of those whose labour-power it consumes. Just as a werewolf is the animal form of a human, Marx implies, so capital is the alien form of humanity. But perhaps Hythloday's figure is still more unsettling, for here it is a docile ruminant that turns into a monster. The reversal is double: not only has the animal world conquered the human, but it is the meekest creature that seems hungriest.

In *Utopia* we also encounter the rudiments of the method that Marx would later formalise as the properly materialist approach to social analysis, according to which political, cultural, and legal phenomena ought to be grounded in their corresponding relations of production.[26] Perhaps it is because of this foreshadowing that Marx finds the following passage amenable to his purposes in Chapter 28, where he discusses Elizabeth's Act for the Punishment of Vagabonds (which prescribes flogging, branding, and execution for unlicensed beggars). The passage, spoken by Hythloday, and copied into a footnote by Marx, comes shortly after the sheep metaphor:

> Consequently, just so that one insatiable glutton, a grim plague to his native land, can merge fields and enclose thousands of hectares within a single boundary, the workers of the countryside are thrown out. Some are stripped of their possessions, whether they are cheated by fraud or intimidated by force or, simply,

---

[24] Roberts argues that the concept of impersonal domination implicit in Marx's analysis of fetishism describes the domination of individuals by society as such, by the entire network of social relationships, rather than (as in feudalism, say) by other specific individuals: 'Because the domination of market society is impersonal, the specific individuals on whom one is dependent are of no import; what remains the same, no matter who one's customers and competitors are, is the relationship of all-round dependence on one another's production and consumption' (*Marx's Inferno*, p. 93). In this, Roberts suggests, Marx's criticisms draw their potency from the republican tradition, for which 'arbitrary, incontestable will' is the source of domination. For a reading of Marx's concept of alienation as an attempt to theorise impersonal domination, see Postone, pp. 158–66.

[25] Marx, *Capital*, I, 353.

[26] For the classic statement of this thesis, see Karl Marx, *A Contribution to the Critique of Political Economy*, trans. by N. I. Stone (Chicago: Kerr & Company, 1904), pp. 11–13.

> worn down by wrongs and forced to sell them. So, one way or another, it turns out that these unhappy people have to leave—men, women, husbands, wives, orphans, widows, parents with small children, a company more numerous than rich since rural occupations require many hands—all these, as I say, have to leave their known and familiar homes without finding any place to take them in. They are evicted so briskly that all their household effects, which wouldn't fetch much even if they were able to wait for a buyer, are sold off for next to nothing. Since such a small sum is soon used up in the course of their wanderings, what alternative do they have but to steal and be hanged—according to the forms of law, naturally—or to continue their travels and beg? But in that case they are liable to be thrust into prison as vagrants since no one will employ them, although they are all too willing to work: since there are no crops to be sown there is no call for their particular skills.[27]

Hythloday's argument, we recall, begins with an observation on the ravenousness of English sheep. Here it proceeds from particular to general, from appearance to essence, and lays bare the shifting property relations that manifest themselves as voracious livestock. In doing so, Hythloday places the category 'crime' itself under pressure and reveals its relationship to its social ground, namely the abrogation of common right—the peasants' rights of herbage, turbary, and piscary in the commons. It is this process itself that must be challenged, Hythloday implies in proto-materialist fashion: hanging is insufficient, and treats the symptom rather than the cause. Not only rhetorically, but methodologically—by its suggestion that relations of production exert a determining influence on law—Hythloday's comment resonates with Marx's project.[28]

---

[27] More, pp. 33–34; Marx, *Capital*, I, 898, n. 2.

[28] In the preface to his *A Contribution to the Critique of Political Economy* (1859), Marx notes that his early articles on wood theft in the Rhineland prompted him to turn to economic matters and from there to elaborate his materialist conception of history (*Contribution*, p. 10). That is to say, the very same issue at stake in Hythloday's passage, the social determinants of crime, is what led Marx, too, to the realisation that criminality itself must be understood by its relation to the economic conditions of the time. The young Marx picked up where Hythloday leaves off. For a discussion of Marx's articles and their relation to enclosure, see Peter Linebaugh, 'Karl Marx, the Theft of Wood, and Working-Class Composition', in *Stop, Thief! The Commons, Enclosures, and Resistance* (Oakland: PM Press, 2014), pp. 43–64.

Yet, if Hythloday's critique anticipates certain aspects of Marx's critique of capitalism, the Marxist perspective also makes visible Hythloday's (and perhaps More's) limitations. Situated on the threshold of two worlds, two distinct economic orders, Hythloday cannot make the final step and place these property relations in the context of capital accumulation, at least by name. Thus we find Hythloday attributing enclosure to a moral weakness: greed (and, as we find out at the end of Book II, pride).[29] In this respect his discussion foreshadows, not the Marxist, but the political-economic account of primitive accumulation—the very thing that Marx criticises, as we have seen—according to which capitalism springs from an 'original sin', the moral failing of the 'lazy rascals, spending their substance, and more, in riotous living'.[30] Hythloday reverses the political economist's terms—he charges the rich, not the poor, with indolence[31]—but the basic structure, locating a mode of production in seemingly timeless human qualities, persists. This is not to mention that the society Hythloday recommends to Giles and More shows great disdain for laziness. In Utopia, 'there is never any opportunity to waste time or be idle'.[32]

As we move into Book II, the Utopian emphasis on productivity further undermines the nascent communism we might have thought we detected in the Utopians' use of common property and Hythloday's

---

[29] In Jameson's reading, *Utopia* operates in the space 'between a proto-economic diagnosis of society', manifest in Hythloday's criticisms of money and enclosure, 'and one that remains ethical in the immemorial religious framework of the hierarchy of virtues and vices', from which derive Hythloday's criticisms of greed and pride, these corresponding to two different 'forms of class consciousness' and thus the two different epochs between which More finds himself ('Of Islands and Trenches: Neutralization and the Production of Utopian Discourse', in *The Ideologies of Theory* (London: Verso, 2008), pp. 387–414 (pp. 404–05)).

[30] Marx, *Capital*, I, 873.

[31] 'For when everyone is entitled to draw to claw together as much as he can get for himself, then, no matter how great the resources available, a small number end up dividing the whole lot among themselves, and the remainder are stuck in poverty. The usual outcome is that each group merits the fate of the other, since the former are grabbing, dishonest and unproductive and the latter brings more profit to the community than to themselves' (More, p. 52). Eric Nelson suggests that More's critique of private property derives from the Greek ethical framework, as exemplified by the thought of Plato and Aristotle, and deliberately opposes Roman conceptions of justice ('Greek Nonsense in More's *Utopia*', *The Historical Journal*, 44.4 (2001), 889–917 (pp. 895–96)).

[32] More, p. 73.

critique of enclosure. In a striking passage on the problem of overpopulation, Hythloday tells More and Giles that the Utopians permit themselves to colonise 'the neighbouring mainland, wherever the native population has redundant and untilled land'. If the natives accept the Utopian settlement, they integrate their communities:

> Freely sharing the same way of life and the same rules of conduct, the two groups easily bond together, much to their mutual profit. For by their enterprise the Utopians make that land which previously seemed poor and barren yield plenty for all. But all those who refuse to live under their laws the Utopians drive out of the territory that they claim, making war on those who resist. For they view it as an entirely just cause for war when those who possess a territory leave it idle and unproductive, denying use and possession to others who, by the law of nature, ought to be fed by it.[33]

For one thing, there is no contradiction between the Utopians' colonial expansion and the principles of commoning, since commons have themselves served as instruments of expropriation, as we saw in the context of the colonisation of North America in Chapter 1. For another, the importance the Utopians attach to productivity pre-empts the role that 'improvement' literature would play in justifying enclosures in England and abroad.[34] In particular, the Utopian ethos according to which productive labourers enjoy a natural right to cultivate unused land anticipates John Locke's argument, in his *Second Treatise of Government* (1689), that bodily exertion, the toil of labour, makes things private property. Thus 'the Hare that any one is hunting, is thought his who pursues her during the Chase', provided that sufficient sustenance remains for others.[35] This goes not merely for game and fruit, but for land itself, which the tiller, the cultivator, or the planter, simply by their work, 'does, as it were, Inclose [...] from the common'. Combining the

---

[33] More, p. 68–69.

[34] For an overview of the relation between More's *Utopia* and the colonisation of America, see Antonis Balasopoulos, 'Unworldly Worldliness: America and the Trajectories of Utopian Expansionism', *Utopian Studies*, 15.2 (2004), 3–35 (pp. 3–8).

[35] John Locke, 'Second Treatise of Government', in *Second Treatise of Government and A Letter Concerning Toleration* (Oxford: Oxford University Press, 2016), pp. 1–120 (§ 30). For Locke, it is because humans own their bodies and their labour that whatever raw material they 'mix' that labour with becomes their property too.

doctrines of original sin and primitive accumulation, Locke suggests that humans have a duty to improve the land through their labour:

> God, when he gave the World in common to all Mankind, commanded Man also to labour, and the Penury of his Condition required it of him. God and his Reason commanded him to subdue the Earth, *i.e.* improve it for the Benefit of Life, and therein lay out something that was his own, his Labour. He that in Obedience to this Command of God, subdued, tilled and sowed any part of it, thereby annexed to it something that was his *Property*, which another had no Title to, nor could without Injury take from him.[36]

The Lockean injunction to improve agricultural yield, thereby to enclose the Earth, arose organically from the discourse of the seventeenth-century agricultural improvers, who often invoked 'improvement', and reached for their Bibles, in their efforts to abrogate traditional rights.[37] *Utopia* is then a crucible in which the raw materials of both pro- and anti-enclosure arguments combine. It anticipates both the political economic justifications of enclosure and the Marxist critique of those justifications, an ambivalence that must complicate its status as a utopian text.

Differences in Degree and Kind

At the beginning of Part Eight, Marx seems to depict the political economists' accounts of primitive accumulation as utopian in their own right. 'In the tender annals of political economy,' he observes, 'the idyllic reigns from time immemorial.'[38] Erasing the 'notorious' role of robbery, enslavement, and murder in capitalism's genesis, the political economists compose a 'nursery tale' according to which capital arises from the human proclivity for barter and exchange, the double coincidence of wants. That Marx begins his critique with this wry remark is appropriate, I want to propose, because utopias proper are efforts to thematise the tragedy of dispossession, the very thing occluded by the political economists. Utopian imaginings serve principally as a pretext for this thematisation: they project a brighter future, based on

---

[36] Locke, § 32.
[37] Neal Wood, *John Locke and Agrarian Capitalism* (Berkeley: University of California Press, 1984), pp. 57–71.
[38] Marx, *Capital*, I, 874.

common property, to emphasise the ills of enclosed private property.[39] Utopian speculation, the sprawling elaborations on questions as diverse as utopian rulers, raiment, criminality, and currency, is pretext and vehicle for a critique of the present and of the property relations that undergird its oppressions.

It is unnecessary that other utopias make this critique as explicitly as More does. The critique is more often implicit in the positive vision itself: it is as if all utopias carry their own Book I, their own condemnation of the existing state of affairs, within themselves. As readers of such material, it becomes our task to make these repressed criticisms of enclosure speak, which are not adornments on the utopian form but the genre's basic function and purpose.[40] It follows that Marx's use of More as an anticipatory document—his bracketing off the utopianism of Book II in favour of Book I—is, strictly speaking, no violation of utopian exegesis. Marx intuits (or, less charitably, stumbles upon) the entire raison d'être of the form, which is precisely to explore the violence of a process that Adam Smith could comprehend only as a 'previous accumulation of stock'. The mental operation that Marx performs, and that I have quoted above, where he follows the circuits of capital accumulation in search of a founding moment, is an integral part of the utopian method, which requires such a moment, such an 'original sin', to oppose. In *Utopia*, Book I does not serve as mere prefatory material for Book II; it does not illuminate social problems

---

[39] As Jameson notes, 'the attempt to establish positive criteria of the desirable society characterizes liberal political theory from Locke to Rawls, rather than the diagnostic interventions of the Utopians, which, like those of the great revolutionaries, always aim at the alleviation and elimination of the sources of exploitation and suffering, rather than at the composition of blueprints for bourgeois comfort' (*Archaeologies*, p. 12).

[40] The understanding of utopia outlined here extends Jameson's influential statement of the form's purpose: namely, 'to bring home [...] our constitutional inability to imagine Utopia itself, and this, not owing to any individual failure of imagination but as the result of the systemic, cultural, and ideological closure of which we are all in one way or another prisoners' ('Progress versus Utopia', p. 153). Such, Jameson seems to suggest, is the utopia's specific means of accomplishing the larger science-fictional enterprise of thematising our inability to think the future (a point I invoked in Chapter 1). What I am proposing here is that the utopia *also* concerns itself with the chief cause of the waning of historicity, this last being the basis for science fiction's 'multiple mock futures'. Utopia is not simply one way of making us aware of the failure of our collective imagination; it is also, and perhaps more importantly, an enquiry into the very conditions that bring about that failure. That is its *differentia specifica*.

in order to support the Utopians' solution. In fact, Book II offers a utopian vision whose goodness retrospectively justifies the critical work of Book I.

If utopias are principally critiques of past and present property relations, and only secondarily blueprints for the future, this implies definite evaluative criteria, which we can then employ to distinguish the properly utopian from material merely vestigially or superficially so. The clearer the utopian's denunciation of private property, the firmer their sense that common ownership of the means of production lays the foundation of a better world, the more genuinely utopian they are. For a utopian text to break with what exists, to escape the stinking effluvia of the capitalist system, its author must comprehend that enclosed property forms the foundation of modern, impersonal domination, and that any meaningfully better society, guarantor of its inhabitants' freedom, must dismantle it first. The utopia expresses what the political economists, with few exceptions, could not. It aestheticises their lacunae. Thus, where ostensibly utopian texts impute capital's violence to individual weaknesses, or even human nature, as did those economists, the surer we might be that they are not utopian at all, and serve as so many speculative sanctifications of the world as it is.

I have already examined More's text from this perspective and observed that, despite its critique of property relations, *Utopia* grounds enclosure in greed and pride, and also formulates justifications for colonial expropriations. Let us now turn to the utopian literature written in Marx's wake, at the end of the nineteenth century, for three further examples, whose divergence on the property question is conspicuous. The utopianism of Edward Bellamy's *Looking Backward*, published in 1888, consists in the supersession of the 'private capitalism' of the nineteenth-century United States by 'public capitalism' (to use the author's own words).[41] Bellamy's utopia thus takes shape as a giant monopoly, with all production and distribution administered by the state, this being, in his view, the terminus of the centralisation of capital. *Looking Backward* renders the heroic expropriation of the expropriators, the moment of revolution envisaged by Marx near the end of Part Eight, unnecessary: the normal development of capitalist production suffices to transform capital into national stock. America's fully nationalised mode of production entails that the common fund, and thus most property, is likewise nationalised, but Bellamy adds that private property survives in 'personal possessions'—a phrase that seems to beg the question, for what

---

[41] See Bellamy's preface to *Equality* (Frankfurt: Outlook, 2019), p. 3.

then counts as personal possessions?[42] Are not such possessions defined at least in part by their being private property? *Looking Backward* suggests that the source of our social problems is not private property per se but its deployment in an antagonistic and competitive economic system.

The task of William Morris's *News from Nowhere*—published in 1890, a direct response to Bellamy—is to overcome these limits, to articulate a more profound utopianism, a clean break with capital. Where the transition from private to public capitalism occurs seamlessly in Bellamy, Morris devotes much time to the messy, uncertain struggle by which the people come to share what their masters once enclosed.[43] Crucially, in Morris's narrative, British society passes through a stage of State Socialism, where—the workers having forced the capitalists to reduce their hours, fix a minimum wage, and regulate the price of necessities—the government establishes its own factories and markets. Yet this State Socialism (or rather, 'public capitalism') does not succeed: the year 1952, just before the Great Change, 'was one of the worst of these times', since 'the partial, inefficient government factories, which were terribly jobbed, all but broke down'.[44] In the wake of the revolution, by contrast, Morris's utopians 'flocked into the country villages, and, so to say, flung themselves upon the freed land like a wild beast upon his prey', and abolish private property entirely.[45] *News from Nowhere* comprehends that English capitalism rests on the enclosure of open fields. Its depictions supersede what Morris characterises in his review of *Looking Backward* as Bellamy's 'half-change'.[46]

---

[42] Edward Bellamy, *Looking Backward: 2000–1887* (Oxford: Oxford University Press, 2007), p. 123.

[43] Williams avers that 'the crucial insertion of the *transition* to utopia, which is not discovered, come across, or projected—not even, except at the simplest conventional level, dreamed—but fought for', is the strongest aspect of *News from Nowhere* ('Utopia and Science Fiction', p. 103).

[44] William Morris, *News from Nowhere: Or, An Epoch of Rest* (Oxford: Oxford University Press, 2003), p. 94.

[45] Morris, *News from Nowhere*, p. 61. It transpires that such events are in fact the visions of Morris's dreaming protagonist (who, in the tradition of *Utopia*, is a fictionalised version of the author himself), such that the revolutionary blood is still to be spilled: this too is a critique of *Looking Backward*, whose narrator sleeps for 113 years and simply wakens into the era of public capitalism.

[46] For Morris, Bellamy's temperament 'may be called the unmixed modern one, unhistoric and unartistic; it makes its owner (if a Socialist) perfectly satisfied with modern civilization, if only the injustice, misery, and waste of class society could be got rid of; which half-change seems possible to him' ('*Looking Backward*' (1889) <https://www.marxists.org/archive/morris/

Our third example comes from another of Bellamy's and Morris's contemporaries, H. G. Wells, whose *A Modern Utopia* (1905) purports to supersede the uniform utopias, devoid of individuality, preceding it. Though these utopias, such as More's, are the narrator's chief target (Bellamy and Morris begin to challenge their homogeneity, according to the narrator), his critique also extends to the political economists. Political economy rests on unsubstantiated assumptions, he suggests at one point, and ought to be grounded in the study of physics, geography, and sociology.[47] Part of the narrator's solution, as he projects it onto his utopians, is the use of energy credits as currency. These would be exchangeable with local authorities (which serve as the 'universal landowner', and thus run the 'common generating stations') for a certain amount of energy, for private or commercial use.[48] Additionally, though the modern utopia therefore prohibits private property in land and natural resources, it admits it in business and personal possessions, the latter seen as prerequisites of freedom.[49] From even this circumscribed domain of private property flows, however, the deluge of capitalist ills: Wells's modern utopia has crises, surplus populations, gendered wealth inequality, wages, profits, and eugenics, to name but a few. Whatever the narrator's claim to have produced a utopia, his world preserves the capitalist system. That world is, in large part, anti-utopian.

This might seem a harsh judgement on Wells, who does appear to think of himself as having produced a utopia. Fortunately, however, Wells can count on the support of a significant tendency in utopian studies, for which even pro-capitalist visions may be considered utopian. This argument for capaciousness finds its classic expression in Ruth Levitas's *The Concept of Utopia* (1990), whose objections we ought now to confront, if only to defend the principle of defining utopias in terms of content and form, and thus discriminating between utopian and anti-utopian texts, as I have done here. Levitas's position is that any such definition, extracting from its corpus a genuinely utopian content, form,

works/1889/commonweal/06-bellamy.htm> [accessed 17 May 2022] (para. 4 of 12)). Contrast this with Morris's appraisal of More, who, looking at nascent capitalism, 'saw deeper into its root-causes than any other man of his own day, and left us little to add to his views on this point except a reasonable hope that those "causes" will yield to a better form of society before long' ('Foreword to Thomas More's *Utopia*' (1893) <https://www.marxists.org/archive/morris/works/1893/utopia.htm> [accessed 17 May 2022] (para. 3 of 8)).

[47] H. G. Wells, *A Modern Utopia* (London: Penguin, 2005), pp. 62–63.
[48] Wells, pp. 57–58.
[49] Wells, pp. 63–70.

or function, excludes utopian material and obscures differences between utopian texts.[50] Definitions of utopia thus ought to be 'analytic' rather than 'descriptive'; they ought to embrace the richness and variety of utopian expressions, rather than identify a set of common traits, which are then taken to constitute utopianism proper. One of the advantages the analytic holds over the descriptive, Levitas proposes, is that it frees us from politics: no longer can we assign the label 'utopian' solely to those future-bearing images that appeal to our individual tastes.[51] Levitas thereby cloisters the academic study of utopia, separates it from the noisy, normative business of choosing which utopia is better than another, or what counts as being more utopian than something else. Levitas's argument is at odds with my own, not only because I place limits on the range of authentically utopian expression, but also—this being virtually an axiom of Marxist cultural criticism—because I hold the 'analytic' dimension to be inextricable from 'normative' political questions. My position is that the latter should—in fact, in all cases, whether we are conscious of it or not, *do*—guide the former.

Levitas's own attempt at definition—utopia consists in 'desire for a better way of being'—seems to dodge the perils of content, form, or functional approaches.[52] Rather than focusing on the intrinsic properties of utopian expression (which would entail admitting content or form constraints) or on the latter's effects (its function), this definition directs our gaze to the motivations behind utopianism: the desire impelling the vision, calling it into existence, is what makes it utopian. Levitas's quiet, simple definition nonetheless threatens to upset traditional conceptualisations of the field. Does it not challenge More's place at the centre of the utopian canon, to take one particularly significant example? We cannot say with certainty that *Utopia* bears witness to More's desire for a better way of being; the text is notoriously, paradigmatically unclear in this respect. As we have already seen, More includes a character with his name in the narrative, but this character objects to the Utopian way of life. Raphael's surname, Hythloday, means 'distributor of nonsense' in Greek.[53] How seriously are we to take his discourse? This is not the place to answer such questions; we need only observe that their existence renders More's desire opaque.

[50] Ruth Levitas, *The Concept of Utopia* (Oxford: Peter Lang, 2011), pp. 4–6.
[51] Levitas, *Concept of Utopia*, p. 230.
[52] Levitas, *Concept of Utopia*, pp. 228–29.
[53] As Nelson adds, the name 'More' is itself a pun, playing on the Latin for 'foolish' (*morus*), such that much of *Utopia* sees the 'distributor of nonsense' debating the merits of a 'no-place' (*ou-topia*) with a fool ('Greek Nonsense', pp. 890–91).

Hence the fundamental problem with Levitas's capacious definition: it cannot tell us anything about actual utopian texts or practices. Construed as a particular kind of desire, utopia is displaced from the object of study to the fluttering chambers of the utopian heart. It has no necessary relationship to, no determinate correlation with, the form or content of what the utopian represents in their activity. As Levitas writes, 'if utopia is the repository of desire, we should be wary of suggesting that one mode of its expression is better or more properly utopian than any other'.[54] But Levitas avoids definitions in such terms at the cost of forfeiting knowledge about the fundaments of utopian practice, which are decisions about form and content. The argument for capaciousness allows her to claim, for instance, that the British neoliberal and conservative right are both essentially utopian. On such a view, it is enough that the right envisages changes to society that they deem beneficial, such as lower taxes or more fervent flag-waving.[55] Yet this constitutes a reference to content (here, to substantive aspects of their policy) and an implicit admission that such content is what stamps their politics as utopian. Levitas's interpretations are therefore at odds with the conclusions of her definitional work.

Just as importantly (and as I have already intimated), Levitas's effort to eliminate politics from the domain of utopian studies, to discard 'evaluative' definitions in favour of capacious ones, is itself political. The stipulation that utopias desire merely 'better' ways of being obscures the difference between a change in degree (or quantity, or 'half-change', to recall Morris's criticism of Bellamy) and a change in kind (or quality). The neoliberal visions that Levitas deems utopian are examples of the former: they desire simply a freer market, a more competitive individual, a thinner commons. In *A Modern Utopia*, the narrator explicitly enjoins us to reject qualitative distinctions (the extremes of 'Socialism' and 'Individualism') in favour of adjustments, tweaks, increments—a sure sign of anti-utopianism.[56] The utopia of *Utopia*, however, represents (aside from the occasional invocation of 'improvement' discourse) a change in kind, from nascent capitalism to some sort of communism, and *News from Nowhere* goes even further. The category 'better' pertains only to degree, such that every political change becomes reform, and communism loses

---

[54] Levitas, *Concept of Utopia*, p. 230. It would be perfectly reasonable to suggest that one can discern desire in form and content, that specific desires express themselves in certain styles, tropes, and images, but then one must also concede that definitions in terms of form and content are indeed legitimate.
[55] Levitas, *Concept of Utopia*, pp. 214–19.
[56] Wells, pp. 51, 67.

its radical, epoch-making character. Erasing differences in kind, Levitas's analytic definition consecrates the gradualist anti-utopian ideology against which her stated politics rails.[57] By contrast, the principle I have elaborated above, according to which utopias must sweep away the source of social ills, implies that the properly utopian society is one so opposed to the norm that it appears as a difference in kind alone.

The distinction between degree and kind is then not only epistemologically but politically necessary. My argument in this chapter proceeds from it, for a truly utopian text, breaking with what exists, must render a difference in kind, and thus must reject capitalist property relations. The positive future serves, sometimes explicitly, sometimes implicitly, to criticise the framework of property rights within which capital accumulates. Virtually codifying such a process in its division into Books I and II, More's *Utopia* becomes a model for all utopias that follow and opens up the possibility that criticism, not prescription or prognostication, is the essence of utopian thought.[58]

---

[57] 'I am a socialist by inheritance and by conviction, as well as a sociologist by training,' Levitas remarks in a more recent book. She proceeds to argue that 'capitalism doesn't work, which is why the utopian exploration of alternatives is necessary' (*Utopia as Method: The Imaginary Reconstruction of Society* (London: Macmillan, 2013), p. 216). That utopia is a historically specific response to the oppressions of an equally historically specific mode of production, capitalism, is precisely my argument here. Nonetheless, in this same text, Levitas reaffirms her commitment to the anti-utopian definitional work of *The Concept of Utopia*, and continues to describe British right-wing politics as utopian, which severs the bond between utopia and anticapitalism. Levitas's work is opposed to itself; as such, it is inevitable that it is also partly at odds with my contentions here.

[58] Though my argument here is not an empirical one, it finds ample validation in the wealth of utopian materials that do indeed envisage community of property. According to Gregory Claeys, by the end of the eighteenth century, 'the term "utopian" was clearly identified with communal property-holding' (*Utopia: The History of an Idea* (London: Thames & Hudson, 2020), p. 90). Jameson likewise affirms that the abolition of property and money, the Utopians' solutions to the social ills More portrays in Book I, 'runs through the Utopian tradition like a red thread, now aggressively affirmed on the surface, now tacitly presupposed in milder forms or disguises' (*Archaeologies*, p. 20). Jameson's identification here of a characteristic utopian content marks a shift from his strictly formalistic construal of the genre in the 'Progress versus Utopia' essay. The first part of *Archaeologies*, 'The Desire Called Utopia', also revises the familiar Jamesonian proposition that utopias are valuable in so far as they fail; see *Archaeologies*, pp. 178–81, and Jameson's prior discussions, in that book, of utopian science and wish-fulfilment.

The Utopian Dystopia

A full account of the twin histories of enclosure and utopia exceeds the scope of this chapter, indeed of this book. The foregoing discussion of More's *Utopia* and Marx's *Capital*, and of the theory of utopian fiction emerging from their intersection, serves primarily to help answer the questions posed at the end of the previous chapter, concluding my readings of *Blade Runner* and *The Truman Show*. There I asked: what is the relationship between utopia and dystopia, and why do they combine in Hollywood's speculative production of the late twentieth century? Are the two to be considered antitheses, or are they complementary forms, halves of a broken whole? What is the nature, what is the history of the utopian dystopia?

That the 1980s witnessed the emergence of a new kind of dystopia—a critical, revolutionary, utopian dystopia—is the argument of Tom Moylan's classic account of the period in *Scraps of the Untainted Sky* (2000). Referring principally to the work of Kim Stanley Robinson, Octavia Butler, and Marge Piercy, Moylan reads their 'critical dystopias' as so many responses to the increasing anti-utopianism of the Western world: the destruction of welfare systems, the environment, and labour protections (to give just a few examples) carried out by neoconservatives and neoliberals since Reagan's and Thatcher's fateful elections. The twentieth century had already seen its first (largely anti-utopian) wave of dystopian culture in the wake of the Second World War, but the post-1980 dystopias differ, first, in their critical function, turning against the objective anti-utopia surrounding them, and second, in their utopianism. As Moylan himself puts it, the critical dystopias 'tend to express an emancipatory, militant, critical utopian position'.[59] In light of Moylan's work, we might recast our motivating questions thus: to what degree are the utopian dystopias examined in previous chapters consonant with such an account?

I want to begin by looking at Moylan's effort to articulate text with context, since this holds the key to our understanding of the subgenre's socio-political function. As we have just seen, Moylan grounds the emergence of the critical dystopia in the drift of human affairs, which he describes as 'dystopian' itself.[60] Moylan thus implies that 'utopia' and

---

[59] Tom Moylan, *Scraps of the Untainted Sky: Science Fiction, Utopia, Dystopia* (New York: Routledge, 2018), p. 199. For an overview of the shifting thematic concerns of American and British dystopian writing across the twentieth century, see Claeys, *Dystopia*, pp. 494–96.

[60] For instance, speaking of Reagan's and George H. W. Bush's presidencies, Moylan claims that 'the situation became increasingly dystopian as the celebration of Utopia became a mark of triumph for Anti-Utopia'. Moylan

'dystopia' are both generic *and* sociological categories, cultural forms and the social ground or infrastructure from which those forms arise. Fictional dystopias exist, Moylan seems to suggest, because reality has become increasingly dystopian, because reality is itself the concrete inversion of utopia. But could we not just as easily propose that the causation runs the other way? Do we not perceive reality as 'dystopian' (rather than simply as 'bad' or 'oppressive') only because it resembles the depictions we have already come across in dystopian literature and film? Dystopian fiction having coloured our perception of the processes that prompted their composition, causes blur with effects, and we end up with Moylan's tautological equation of dystopias with dystopias. Any effort to ground utopian or dystopian texts that uses those terms in the description of the ground itself does not suffice to explain their emergence. The mediation buckles; its levels collapse.

Even if we read Moylan's use of 'dystopia' as metaphorical, a way of expressing merely that things have got worse, neoliberalism having slashed the safety net of the postwar 'class compromise', this by no means solves the problem. To claim that the depiction of a worse state of affairs derives from a real worsening of society is to identify, on some level, the cause with the referent, to make referent cause and cause referent. Such is insufficient as an understanding of the dystopia's history, since it assumes what it is supposed to explain, namely *why* bad times give rise to a genre devoted to depicting bad times, a claim genre theory cannot treat as self-evident.[61] Applied to the utopia, this argument is clearly problematic, because utopias do not spring from especially good times; referent and cause are non-identical. More's *Utopia* responds to the fencing off of English fields, the lords' betrayal of the feudal compact, and the rise of a whole new kind of wrongdoing, abstract, objectified,

> then proceeds to draw our attention to income inequality, increasing homelessness and unemployment, attacks on oppressed social groups, the erosion of public services, and the deterioration of the environment—this all amounting to 'the triumph of transnational capital and right-wing ideology' (*Scraps*, pp. 183–84). The Third Way iteration of neoliberalism did little to improve things, and often made it worse, Moylan observes, such that (as of 2000, the book's publication date) 'the world continues to drift toward Anti-Utopia' (*Scraps*, p. 186).

[61] Moylan observes, at another moment, that the co-optation of utopian symbols by capitalism itself means that criticism must be dystopian (*Scraps*, p. 187). As an alternative way of grounding the genre, this too strikes me as inadequate. For one thing, it assumes that all criticism is either utopian or dystopian; it subsumes criticism under those terms. For another, as the second half of this book will show, the culture industry has proven particularly adept at co-opting dystopia as well.

and impersonal, as evoked by Hythloday's sheep metaphor. From *Utopia* down to the present, the history of utopian production tracks not the beneficence of capitalism at a given moment but, much more precisely, the size of the dominion of private property.

Having noted the utopia's preoccupation with property rights, I would like to propose an alternative explanation for the emergence of the utopian dystopia in the 1980s, when the time is again ripe for a critique of enclosure. The (critical) dystopian turn occurring at this moment arises from the character of the new enclosures themselves, which, being driven by capital, resolving its crisis of overaccumulation, intervene in an already advanced state of commodification. As we saw, More lived in the gap between the two orders, feudal and capitalist, and this allowed him to document the specificity of the latter's nascent form—hence Marx's praise. But the observer of today's enclosures perceives no such contrast. They dwell in no gap, perch on no cusp. What they experience is not the emergence of reification but the tightening of its grip. Crucially, by subordinating ever vaster zones of the world to capital, it is the new enclosures themselves that make such contrast increasingly unavailable.

I want to argue that it is this precise context, that of the new enclosures, and not some real-life neoliberal dystopianism, to which the utopian dystopia (Moylan's 'critical dystopia') responds. By placing its utopian elements against the dystopian backdrop, the utopian dystopia emphasises those elements, throws them into relief.[62] Such texts thus contrive to thematise, within the confines of a work of art, two different historical logics, one founded on private property, the other congruent only with communal property. They reconstruct, within their diegesis, and for the benefit of their alienated viewer, a distinction in kind, a qualitative distinction. Take *Blade Runner*: here, I have argued, it is Deckard's free movement around the city, his ability to navigate between different spaces, different properties, that bears the film's utopian charge. This movement is of course unavailable to most of us in the modern city, which presents itself as an immense accumulation of locked doors. The principle underlying Deckard's movement belongs in a utopia, a fictional world premised on common property, shared space, but it has been torn from that context and placed instead in a deeply enclosed city. Such is

---

[62] The persistence of More's utopian structure, albeit with its elements reordered or inverted, and charged with different functions, might profitably be understood as a kind of generic sedimentation, as per Jameson's discussion in *The Political Unconscious: Narrative as a Socially Symbolic Act* (Abingdon: Routledge, 2002), pp. 122–32.

the utopian essence of the critical dystopia—a utopian moment to whose emphasis the whole dystopian backdrop is devoted. It follows that what Moylan calls the 'critical dystopia' is the old utopia adapted for a new round of enclosure. Its criticism is directed towards, not the excesses of the capitalist system or moments of particular capitalist egregiousness (as if excess and egregiousness were not an intrinsic feature of that system), but, like all utopias, the institution of private property as such, which it shows to be incompatible with human freedom. The utopia and the dystopia are not here contrary tendencies, pulling against each other, but complements, the latter serving to amplify the principles underlying the former.

Perhaps most importantly, the different ways Moylan and I contextualise the utopian dystopia generate divergent views on particular dystopias' politics. We can see this in Moylan's dismissal of what he regards as *The Truman Show*'s 'resigned, closed, anticritical, pseudo-dystopian sensibility', a conclusion markedly at odds with my own in the previous chapter.[63] Moylan recalls Peter Fitting's article, 'Unmasking the Real? Critique and Utopia in Recent SF Films' (2003), where Fitting argues that, although *The Truman Show*'s denouement shows Truman escaping into the real world, this real world is no less false, no less artificial, than Seahaven. For Fitting, therefore, 'the film reaffirms rather than critiques the present, suggesting by means of [Truman's] escape that the only real "utopia" is our own world, thus negating the utopian project itself'.[64] 'Wrong life cannot be lived rightly,' Adorno once wrote;[65] and implicitly, on Fitting's view, *The Truman Show* would only have succeeded had Truman stepped into the right life, the utopia. Yet what such a reading misses is that the sheer depth of the dystopian background, the impossibility of escaping it, serves all the better to emphasise the film's utopian moment, the instant of decision, where Truman chooses to leave the realm of images. That this choice is doomed, a false choice, is precisely the point: the choice itself, in abstraction, belongs to another context, one where the image is again an incidental aspect of society, something one could indeed walk away from, and not, as in the Debordian analysis, its structuring feature,

---

[63] Moylan, pp. 193–94.
[64] Peter Fitting, 'Unmasking the Real? Critique and Utopia in Recent SF Films', in *Dark Horizons: Fiction and the Dystopian Imagination*, ed. by Raffaella Baccolini and Tom Moylan (London: Routledge, 2003), pp. 155–66 (pp. 157–59).
[65] Theodor Adorno, *Minima Moralia: Reflections on a Damaged Life*, trans. by E. F. N. Jephcott (London: Verso, 2005), § 18.

pervading everything.[66] Fitting's and Moylan's implicit requirement that the film create for Truman a genuinely contrastive society, a utopia, into which to flee makes sense only if we regard the utopian dystopia as principally an effort at imaginative construction. But if we take the view argued in this chapter, that utopia is first and foremost a critique of enclosure, one that takes speculative form, we need not demand that utopia actually appear. What matters (*pace* Fitting) is not the existence of a positive image, but the quality of the text's critique of property relations, the raison d'être of the utopian form.

From our perspective, *The Truman Show* is notable precisely because it *is* one of the last genuinely utopian Hollywood dystopias. The utopian dystopia is a fragile form, and it vanished for the same reason that it had emerged. With hindsight we can see that the 1980s was a critical decade: long enough after the inception of the new enclosures (in the 1970s) for them to be registered as a distinctive feature of American society, but not so long that they had eliminated the surviving non-capitalist zones, whose existence attests to the possibility of change and the reality of alternatives. That is, although the epochal contrast of More's day, the transition between two socio-economic systems, had disappeared long ago, there still remained a distinction between the vast tracts of our world that were subordinated to capital and the enclaves that were not. The new enclosures—further commodifying reservoir, forest, shelter, knowledge—have eroded even that, however. The very enclosures that motivated utopian criticism came, later on, to attenuate such criticism, such that, by the late 1990s, Hollywood dystopias had lost their utopian edge.

---

[66] Debord, *Society of the Spectacle*, § 4.

Chapter 5

Innovation
Intellectual Property in *The Matrix*, *The Island*, and *District 9*

'If the future is technological, and if technology has become Japanised, then the syllogism suggests that the future is now Japanese too. The postmodern era will be the Pacific era.' This summation, by David Morley and Kevin Robins, of the American attitude towards Japan during the 1980s, when the latter seemed to threaten the former's political, cultural, and economic dominance, offers a more or less accurate insight into the prognostications of the American cyberpunk novels and films produced during that decade.[1] In the realm of science-fiction cinema, *Blade Runner* remains the most prominent example of such 'techno-Orientalism', projecting 'Japan panic' onto its dystopian future: the film codes many of its Angelenos as Asian, sustains them on a sushi diet, and employs other stereotypically Japanese iconography, such as whiteface make up and origami, as several critics have observed.[2] We might also add that this particular kind of futuristic Orientalism predates cyberpunk proper. Recall that the corporation in *Alien* (released three years before *Blade Runner*) is named 'Weylan-Yutani', a coupling devised by Ron Cobb, one of the film's designers. Cobb later noted that he had 'wanted to imply that poor old England is back on its feet and has united with the Japanese, who have taken over the building of spaceships the same way they have now with cars and super-tankers'.[3] Ridley Scott's evident attachment to techno-Orientalist style would culminate in 1989 with *Black Rain*, in

---

[1] David Morley and Kevin Robins, *Spaces of Identity: Global Media, Electronic Landscapes and Cultural Boundaries* (London: Routledge, 1995), p. 168.

[2] See Lisa Nakamura, *Cybertypes: Race, Ethnicity, and Identity on the Internet* (London: Routledge, 2002), pp. 62–64; Timothy Yu, 'Oriental Cities, Postmodern Futures: *Naked Lunch*, *Blade Runner*, and *Neuromancer*', *MELUS*, 33.4 (2008), 45–71 (pp. 52–59); and Edward K. Chan, 'Race in the *Blade Runner* Cycle and the Demographic Dystopia', *Science Fiction Film and Television*, 13.1 (2020), 59–76 (pp. 61–68).

[3] See Cobb's discussion in 'The Authorized Portfolio of Crew Insignias from

which Japanese detective Masahiro Matsumoto (Ken Takakura), sitting in an Osaka nightclub with his two American colleagues, takes a moment to remind them of the new status quo: 'Now, music and movies are all America is good for. We make the machines. We build the future.'[4]

It was 1995 when Morley and Robins published the abovementioned reflections on the United States' confrontation with Japan, and yet even then, as they conclude by noting, change was in the air. The Japanese economy had started to splutter, and the high-profile acquisitions of Columbia Pictures by Sony in 1989 and of MCA-Universal by Matsushita in 1990 had not yet shown financial reward.[5] Today, we can see that 1995 was a key year in the struggle between the United States and Japan for another reason: on 1 January, the Agreement on Trade-Related Aspects of Intellectual Property Rights (TRIPs) came into effect, representing the outcome of negotiations that had begun, formally, in 1986, with the inception of the Uruguay Round of the General Agreement on Tariffs and Trade. Shaped not just by the United States but also by European nations and Japan, TRIPs laid down a strong, enforceable legal framework for much international intellectual property exchange in the years to come. By design, arguably, the chief beneficiary of TRIPs has been the United States, which had already focused its energies on producing and selling intellectual property as Japan and other East Asian countries began to enjoy a competitive advantage in manufacturing. Intellectual property formed no more than 10 per cent of American exports in 1947, but this grew to 37 per cent by 1986 and over half by 1994.[6]

Seen in this light, TRIPs might be interpreted as the aftershock of the explosion of intellectual property rights within the United States itself, whose internal copyright, trademark, and patent protections had expanded rapidly since 1973. Yet the bigger, stronger intellectual property protections secured at home and globalised in TRIPs would be useless, from the American perspective, without industries capable of producing such property for export. Hand-in-hand with the expanded post-1973 enclosure of ideas, expressions, and symbols thus came the emergence of commercial biotechnology, much of whose market value lies in its patent

the United States Commercial Spaceship *Nostromo*: Concepts and Derivations' (Los Angeles: The Thinking Cap Company, 1980).
[4] On Scott's proclivities towards 'oriental style', see Jane Chi Hyun Park's discussion of *Blade Runner* and *Black Rain* in *Yellow Future: Oriental Style in Hollywood Cinema* (Minneapolis: Minnesota University Press, 2010), pp. 51–81, 114–22.
[5] Morley and Robins, p. 173.
[6] Vandana Shiva, *Protect or Plunder? Understanding Intellectual Property Rights* (London: Zed Books, 2001), p. 19.

portfolios. Biotechnology proper preceded the study of molecular genetics (fermentation is an early example), but the possibility of its industrialisation can be dated quite precisely to Stanley Cohen and Herbert Boyer's 1973 discovery of recombinant DNA techniques, the patent on which earned the inventors (and their universities) in the region of $200 million until its expiry in 1997. Major biotechnology companies such as Genentech ('genetic engineering technology') and Amgen ('applied molecular genetics'), dedicated to the exploitation of new developments in the field, cropped up in the latter half of the 1970s. It was not long before these and other companies and researchers set upon the human genome, parts of which, when isolated from their natural environment, became eligible for patent protection, the commodity-form cast on human life itself. American dominance in biotechnology has since prompted the European Union and Japan to invest heavily in their own biotechnology companies in the name of international competitiveness.[7]

My proposition in this chapter is that the post-1973 co-expansion of biotechnology and intellectual property rights, which reached their apotheosis in the drive to commodify the human genome, served as a focal point for the changing portrayal of race in three Hollywood science-fiction films released either side of the new millennium: Lana and Lilly Wachowski's *The Matrix* (1999), Michael Bay's *The Island* (2005), and Neill Blomkamp's *District 9* (2009).[8] The very innovations in biotechnology and intellectual property law intended to reassert American economic dominance became, in these narratives, means through which the dystopian imagination could reformulate its racial politics once 'Japan panic' had died down.[9] As we shall see, *The Matrix*

---

[7] Graham Dutfield, *Intellectual Property Rights and the Life Sciences Industry: Past, Present, and Future*, 2nd edn (Singapore: World Scientific, 2009), pp. 167–73.

[8] For a much longer and broader discussion of the shift from cyberpunk to 'biopunk', from the cyborg to the 'splice', see Lars Schmeink, *Biopunk Dystopias: Genetic Engineering, Society and Science Fiction* (Liverpool: Liverpool University Press, 2016). The films discussed in this chapter by no means exhaust Hollywood's engagement with biotechnology in the period covered by this monograph (*RoboCop*, *Jurassic Park* (1993) and its sequels, and *Gattaca* (1997) are other notable examples). I focus on *The Matrix*, *The Island*, and *District 9*, however, because they offer abundant evidence for the waning of the utopian imagination from the end of the twentieth century, as I shall show later.

[9] Japan's decline is not the only determinant of these shifting racial politics. Park attributes Hollywood's changing representation of East Asia to the rise of popular multicultural discourse in the 1980s and 1990s, as well as to the neoliberalism and renewed neoconservatism of the 1990s and 2000s (*Yellow Future*, pp. 165–66). LeiLani Nishime suggests that cyberpunk's geographic

uses biotechnology as a means of representing a universal, essentially colour-blind slavery. *The Island* goes further and imagines biotechnological enslavement as a phenomenon predominantly afflicting white bodies, the film's narrative resolution thus consisting in white people's return to the status of property owners, rather than property owned. *District 9* ostensibly stands against racist South African attitudes towards Black immigrants, but undermines this with its stereotypical portrayal of a Nigerian gang, whom it constructs as the mirror image of the multinational biotechnology behemoth.

What seems to interest these films about biotechnology, I would stress, is not so much the technology per se, but the threat of human ownership that accompanies the expansion of intellectual property rights into the domain of human life. That such developments seemed to threaten a new unfreedom, this superseding the Orientalist fear of Japanese authoritarianism, prompts *The Matrix*, *The Island*, and *District 9* to meditate on what it means to be free under capitalism, with varying results. Thus I shall argue that *The Matrix* depicts capitalism itself as a form of unfreedom, subjecting humans to a system massively outside of their control; that *The Island*, conversely, sees biotechnological slavery as capitalism gone wrong, at odds with the American dream; and that *District 9* initially articulates a perspicacious critique of capitalism's formal freedom—the freedom to be hungry, to be homeless, if one chooses not to sign a labour contract—before succumbing to its own (implicitly racist) moralism.

Enclosure and Disclosure

Expropriation rarely goes by its name. In Chapter 1, we considered the merits of framing certain specifically capitalist forms of expropriation as 'enclosures', and thus emphasising their continuity with the fencing off of English fields. In Chapter 2, we noted the Reagan administration's description of its own enclosures as 'privatisations', a term intended to situate such processes in a longer history and to legitimise them thereby. A chapter on the phenomenon we now rather unreflectively call 'intellectual property' must begin the same way, with a note on the

---

focus moved from Japan to Hong Kong as the latter grew as an economic power and returned to Chinese control ('*The Matrix* Trilogy, Keanu Reeves, and Multiraciality at the End of Time', in *Mixed Race Hollywood*, ed. by Mary Beltrán and Camilla Fojas (New York: New York University Press, 2008), pp. 290–312 (pp. 303–05)).

term's history and politics. In the eighteenth century, American lawyers and politicians tended to see patents and copyrights as monopolies rather than property, such framing being inherited from English patent law. According to William W. Fisher, this shifted over the course of the nineteenth century, such that, by the beginning of the twentieth, decisions in copyright and trademark law frequently and consciously invoked the language of property. The qualifier 'intellectual', which seemed to give its 'property' an air of refinement, entered into common usage only after the Second World War.[10] The now-widespread reduction of 'intellectual property' to its initialism depoliticises it: as 'IP', the social status of our creativity has come to sound like technical esoterica to be adjudicated in court, no longer a matter for public debate or political contestation.

Though this chapter will continue to refer to things like patents and copyrights as 'intellectual property', I would suggest they are best understood as forms of enclosure, separating us from the ideas, inventions, expressions, and techniques that we held in common. On the one hand, the notion of intellectual property as enclosure is already prevalent in much critical legal scholarship, which likewise conceives of the intangible things enclosed as commons (often 'information commons').[11] On the other hand, many of these scholars condemn only intellectual property law's most egregious incursions, not enclosure and commodification per se. They do so, Anthony McCann shows, on the basis that enclosure leads to poor 'resource management', and thereby regurgitate the very arguments formulated in favour of enclosure in the first place.[12] It follows that, while such accounts usefully document the expansion of intellectual property in the United States over the last 50 years, in them the relationship of such property to capitalism,

---

[10] William W. Fisher III, 'The Growth of Intellectual Property: A History of the Ownership of Ideas in the United States' (1999) <https://cyber.harvard.edu/property99/history.html> [accessed 17 May 2022] (paras 39–45 of 50).

[11] See, for just a few examples, Bollier, *Silent Theft*; James Boyle, *The Public Domain: Enclosing the Commons of the Mind* (New Haven: Yale University Press, 2008); and Christopher May, *The Global Political Economy of Intellectual Property Rights: The New Enclosures*, 2nd edn (London: Routledge, 2010).

[12] Anthony McCann, 'Enclosure Without and Within the "Information Commons"', *Information and Communications Technology Law*, 14.3 (2005), 217–40 (pp. 223–27). However, McCann's own redefinition of commodification (and thus of intellectual property rights) along Foucauldian lines, as something both 'dispositional' and 'discursive', downplays the fundamentally economic force driving such processes.

particularly to the pressures of profitability and overaccumulation, remains largely unexplored.[13]

What we call 'intellectual property' is a cluster of several distinct legal doctrines. Broadly defined (and not dwelling, here, on the myriad problems with such definitions), patents claim ownership of ideas and copyrights the expression of ideas; trademarks cover the symbols distinguishing one company's commodities from another's; trade secrets conceal economically valuable business information; geographical indicators prohibit generic use of the name of region-specific goods (say, champagne); and the right of publicity prohibits the misappropriation of one's identity for another's commercial benefit. The purpose of these doctrines (and the above is not an exhaustive list), Christopher May suggests, is to make such intangibles, which can normally be shared among different people to no one's detriment, scarce, the property of a single person or company.[14] At the same time, intellectual property rights are also intended to have a public function: after the period of protection, a patented design or copyrighted work is released into the public domain. Thus the scholarly literature typically conceives of intellectual property rights as a quid pro quo or, in the language of this study, an enclosure and a disclosure: you obtain exclusive property rights for a time, but you must later share what you have discovered or produced. The eventual disclosure is a distinguishing feature of intellectual property, since material goods are theoretically ownable in perpetuity. Trade secrets—'the ultimate form of private knowledge property', according to May—are the exception, as they need never be revealed.[15]

In the United States, Fisher argues, the history of each kind of intellectual property 'is involuted and idiosyncratic, but one overall trend is common to all: expansion'.[16] Fisher describes a steady growth

---

[13] Symptomatically, we find in May's text (whose second edition, published in 2010, acknowledges McCann's 2005 essay) a brief suggestion that 'what is driving attempts to expand the scope of intellectual property is a desire by capitalists to find new products and/or services that will allow their continued profitable market activity' (*Global Political Economy*, p. 52). Yet the framework May actually employs in his analysis tends to foreground the determining role of technological innovation, ideologies, and political actors, rather than capitalism's basic compulsions (the need to grow, produce surplus-value, resolve crises, and so on). Like Bollier and Boyle, May advocates reform of the intellectual property system (*Global Political Economy*, pp. 125–26), a position that assumes enclosure is incidental, not integral, to capital accumulation.

[14] May, pp. 32–35.

[15] May, p. 9.

[16] Fisher, 'Growth of Intellectual Property', para. 5.

from the eighteenth century, but since about 1970 the expansion seems particularly rapid (James Boyle goes as far as to describe this wave as the 'second enclosure movement').[17] For instance, the last 30 years of the twentieth century witnessed at least three major events in American copyright law: first, in 1976, the creation of a new Copyright Act (extending protection to 50 years after the author's death); in 1989, the United States' accession to the Berne Convention; and in 1998, the passing of the Digital Millennium Copyright Act (or DMCA, on which more in my reading of *The Matrix*). This period also saw the 'propertisation' of trademarks, as the latter expanded dramatically to include, not only text and image, but colours, sounds, scents, and slogans, while certain features of a product itself or its packaging also became eligible for protection. Finally, the post-1990 proliferation in patents is traceable in part to the 1982 establishment of the Court of Appeals for the Federal Circuit, which began to take a rather loose interpretation of what qualifies as a 'nonobvious' invention (one of the conditions for granting a patent). The rapid growth of patents has recently generated some counter-pressure, including efforts by the Supreme Court to tighten restrictions.[18]

We will turn to biotechnology, particularly the latter's claims to ownership of the human genome, shortly, but first I want to stress the fundamentally capitalist character of the abovementioned trends, whose effects exceed, by far, the impoverishment of the American public sphere. The expansion of intellectual property in the United States has in fact been a worldwide—that is to say, an imperialist—incursion. As Vandana Shiva argues, if the earliest American patent laws were designed to attract technological knowledge from elsewhere, to help the United States catch up with European states, modern international intellectual property law serves the opposite purpose: to prevent technology transfer from core to periphery. The challenge posed to American manufacturing by the likes of Japan in the 1980s was decisive in this respect, since it prompted the United States to rely more heavily on intellectual property exports, and hence to enforce global compliance with its own intellectual property laws.[19] The 1995 TRIPs agreement thus foisted Euro-American conceptions of property on its signatories and established a flow of

---

[17] Boyle, p. 45.
[18] For a detailed account of this history, see Oren Bracha, 'The Emergence and Development of United States Intellectual Property Law', *The Oxford Handbook of Intellectual Property Law*, ed. by Rochelle C. Dreyfuss and Justine Pila (Oxford: Oxford University Press, 2018), pp. 235–64.
[19] Shiva, pp. 14–20.

income from poorer nations to richer ones, the biggest winner of course being the United States.[20] The United States Trade Representative (USTR) has subsequently put pressure on those countries who continue to resist full integration into its intellectual property regime.[21] As even this brief overview suggests, the late twentieth-century expansion of intellectual property rights across the world cannot be separated from the problem of squeezed profitability in the United States.

In the domain of American gene patents in particular, the year 1980 formed a crucial turning point. The discipline of molecular biology and the patenting thereof underwent a revolution in the course of just six months.[22] First, in June, came the United States Supreme Court's decision, in *Diamond* v. *Chakrabarty*, that Ananda Chakrabarty's genetic engineering of a micro-organism—specifically, altering a bacterium's genes such that it could break down oil—counted as 'manufacture' and was thus eligible to be patented. In their decision, the Supreme Court affirmed that 'anything under the sun that is made by man' constitutes patentable matter.[23] Second, in October, Genentech put a million shares on the stock market. Venture capitalists bought voraciously, and Genentech's share price climbed from $35 to $88 during the first day. This success prompted a wave of investment in biotechnology firms, the value of such companies residing in their patent portfolios (so long does it take for biotechnological innovations to turn into products). Third, at the beginning of December, the abovementioned patent on Cohen and Boyer's recombinant DNA technology was awarded. Crucially, this new technology enabled other researchers to isolate and purify genes, and thus—if they wished—to patent them. Fourth, on 12 December 1980, Congress passed the Bayh–Dole Act, which allowed universities to claim

---

[20] May, pp. 95–96.

[21] May, p. 103. In fact, pressure from the USTR played a significant role in prompting net intellectual property importers to sign up to TRIPs in the first place. The USTR continues to challenge even those countries whose intellectual property law complies with TRIPs if their protections fall short of those of the United States (Dutfield, pp. 246, 255–56).

[22] Jacob S. Sherkow and Henry T. Greely, 'The History of Patenting Genetic Material', *Annual Review of Genetics*, 49 (2015), 161–82 (pp. 165–66).

[23] US Supreme Court, *Diamond* v. *Chakrabarty*, 447 US 303 (1980). The decision is here quoting from the Committee Reports accompanying the 1952 Patent Act. As Dutfield emphasises, the success of the case rested on the combined economic power of the many pro-patent organisations (such as Genentech, the Pharmaceutical Manufacturer's Association, and the American Patent Law Association) who offered favourable amicus briefs (*Intellectual Property*, pp. 197–98).

ownership of research produced by their faculties even where such work had received funding from federal government.

The first gene patent entered this brave new world in 1981; the first human gene patent joined it in 1982; and then the heavens opened. The final 15 years of the twentieth century saw a deluge of property claims on human genes—an 'exponential growth in all categories of nucleotide-related patenting from the mid-1980s up through 1998 or 1999', as one study puts it.[24] In 2005, Kyle Jensen and Fiona Murray concluded that American gene patents awarded thitherto amounted to ownership of 20 per cent of human genes in total. Certain genes, they noted, had been claimed by more than one patent, and some patents claimed more than one gene, with genes pertinent to healthcare attracting the most interest.[25] Some have argued that the true figure is lower than Jensen and Murray's calculation; others point out that between 41 per cent and 100 per cent of all human genes are theoretically patentable.[26] The rate of gene patenting levelled off in the early 2000s, a shift likely attributable to several factors: a decrease in ready venture capital; higher standards demanded of patent applications; and a possible lack of follow-on opportunities, such had been the frenzy of the previous decades.[27] Also significant in this context was the Supreme Court's 2013 ruling that the patents licensed to Myriad Genetics, a Utah-based molecular diagnostic company, on *BRCA1* and *BRCA2* genes (crucial in identifying early onset breast and ovarian cancer risk) were invalid, since the act of isolating the genes from their environment does not constitute 'novelty' or 'invention', the genes remaining a product of nature.[28]

Even at its height, however, the race to patent the human genome did not go unopposed. In closing our discussion of such patents, I want to draw attention to the fate of one particular protest against the creeping commodification of human DNA, namely cell biologist Stuart Newman's 1997 application to patent chimeras (specifically, beings containing both human and non-human cells), made with the intention of alerting the public to impending developments in biotechnology. Rejecting Newman's application two years later, the United States Patent and Trademark Office

---

[24] Gregory D. Graff and others, 'Not Quite a Myriad of Gene Patents', *Nature Biotechnology*, 31.5 (2013), 404–10 (p. 407)

[25] Kyle Jensen and Fiona Murray, 'Intellectual Property Landscape of the Human Genome', *Science*, 310 (2005), 239–40.

[26] See the discussion by Johnathon Liddicoat, Tess Whitton, and Dianne Nicol in 'Are the Gene-Patent Storm Clouds Dissipating? A Global Snapshot', *Nature Biotechnology*, 33.4 (2015), 347–52 (p. 347).

[27] Graff and others, pp. 407–08.

[28] Sherkow and Greely, pp. 172–75.

(USPTO) justified its decision with reference to the Constitution, which, it suggested, forbids the 'grant of a limited, but exclusive property right in a human being'.[29] Though the USPTO did not cite a particular clause, it seemed to be appealing to the 13th Amendment, the Constitutional prohibition of slavery (except as punishment for a crime). In 2002, a USPTO representative informed the *New York Times* that the office was no longer making the 13th-Amendment argument;[30] yet that the spectre of slavery stood, at the turn of the century, as a significant practical bulwark against the commodification of human life is worthy of our attention as we proceed to *The Matrix*'s portrayal of a specifically biotechnological enslavement.

Mysticism and Millennium

Blissfully unaware that their bodies are being harvested in great fields, billions of humans now live out their lives in the Matrix, the green-tinged simulation that gives film and trilogy their titles. Humanity has found itself here—enslaved to the machines, reduced to so many breathing batteries—because it lost its war with artificial intelligence. In the year 2199 (or thereabouts), when *The Matrix*'s action takes place, all that remains for the machines is to expunge the remaining human enclave, a subterranean city named Zion. The odds are stacked against humanity, yet one of Zion's military captains, Morpheus (Laurence Fishburne), learns from the Oracle (Gloria Foster)—a Matrix program whose true function becomes clear only in the sequels—that he will one day find 'The One', humanity's saviour, and begins his search.

The saviour turns out to be Neo (Keanu Reeves) or, as he is known in the Matrix, Thomas Anderson, a computer programmer who is often late for work. Having alerted Neo to the reality of the Matrix and prised his atrophied body from the machines, Morpheus takes him to speak to the Oracle. During the operation, a member of Morpheus's rebel crew betrays Morpheus, whom Agent Smith (Hugo Weaving), a program tasked to maintain the Matrix system, then captures and interrogates, seeking the codes for entry into Zion. Neo and his

---

[29] The language here derives from a 1987 note by Donald J. Quigg: 'Animals—Patentability', *Consolidated Listing of Official Gazette Notices Re Patent and Trademark Office Practices and Procedures*, 7 April 1987 <https://www.uspto.gov/web/offices/com/sol/og/2013/week53/TOCCN/item-137.htm> [accessed 17 May 2022] (4 paras). See Sherkow and Greely, p. 169.

[30] Andrew Pollack, 'Debate on Human Cloning Turns to Patents', *New York Times*, 17 May 2002, p. 14.

crewmate (and soon-to-be lover) Trinity (Carrie-Anne Moss) re-enter the Matrix to save Morpheus, and it is during that visit, where Neo must fight Agent Smith personally, hand-to-hand, that he comprehends its nature: it is just a simulation, and its laws can in many cases be bent or suspended. Neo holds Smith off but cannot stop the assault on Zion chronicled in *The Matrix Reloaded* and *The Matrix Revolutions* (both released in 2003), at the end of which Neo gives up his life to save Zion—at least for the time being.

That the code governing the Matrix manifests the world of private property, rather than some other form of social organisation, is no accident. As Morpheus learns while Agent Smith interrogates him, the Matrix he knows is only the latest version. The first one 'was designed to be a perfect human world, where none suffered, where everyone would be happy', Smith says, but this proved inimical to the machines' goals, since humans did not accept such utopianism. 'Entire crops'—that is, so many harvested humans—'were lost', failing to yield energy. The reasons for the human incredulity towards the first simulation remain unknown, Smith continues, before offering his own view: 'I believe that, as a species, human beings define their reality through misery and suffering. The perfect world was a dream that your primitive cerebrum kept trying to wake up from.' As such, the Matrix was redesigned to this, 'the peak of your civilisation', the year 1999.[31] Smith is not himself a neoliberal triumphalist, yet what he does suggest is that humans are constitutionally unable to believe in utopia; the best they think they can do is the world as rendered in the Matrix. What stimulates humans, what drives them to work, is only the circumscribed, nominal, essentially formal freedom of capitalism, where their access to means of subsistence is contingent on the wage. Humans belong, Smith suggests, in an anti-utopian utopia, enchained but propertied.

Yet because *The Matrix* does not necessarily endorse Agent Smith's suggestion that humans are innately anti-utopian, the significance of the year 1999 in the film remains ambiguous, and contrasts with its meaning in *Strange Days*. It matters that Smith frames his explanation as one among many and couches his view in the language of 'belief' (this being a recurring motif in the trilogy). Whether humans are really constituted so as to see the end of the twentieth century as their pinnacle, or whether Smith is in fact mistaken, and the alternative accounts— for instance, that the machines 'lacked the programming language to

---

[31] For a reading of *The Matrix* through its depiction of office work, the 'tech boom', and huge corporate mergers at turn of the millennium, see Joshua Clover, *The Matrix* (London: BFI, 2004), pp. 71–83.

describe [humans'] perfect world'—are correct, the original film does not itself judge. In *Strange Days*, on the other hand (and as we saw in Chapter 3), the millennium is cause for celebration: it marks the moment that Commissioner Strickland arrests the offending police officers and solves, through policing, the problem of white supremacist policing. 1999 here represents a state of affairs that, shorn of its excesses, extends happily into the year 2000, *Strange Days* having swallowed the blue pill whole.

Despite its ambiguity on the question of human belief in, and acceptance of, utopianism, *The Matrix* remains critical of the formal freedom represented in the sixth Matrix simulation. The film depicts in particular the dilemma of the 'free' worker, who is indeed free, in that sense, to leave their job, to forego the wage, as long as they are prepared to risk homelessness and starvation. In *The Matrix*, this worker is embodied by Neo himself in his life as Thomas Anderson, who, being late again, must face his boss's ultimatum: 'Either you choose to be at your desk on time from this day forth, or you choose to find another job.' The truth of such freedom, such 'choice', is then made explicit in the next scene. Having been captured by Agent Smith and taken for interrogation, Neo demands to have his phone call. 'You can't scare me with this Gestapo crap,' he says. 'I know my rights.' Neo may well know his rights, but it turns out that, like gravity, rights can be suspended in the Matrix. Agent Smith glues Neo's mouth shut and bugs him. Formal freedom slides quickly into real unfreedom, 'Gestapo crap', the film suggests.[32]

What the relationship posited here between the formal freedom of the labour contract and the unfreedom of Smith's interrogation is meant to imply, I think, is the continuity of capitalism and slavery. The intubation, harvesting, objectification of human life, the unhappy fate of humanity in the real world, signifies the truth, the reality hidden behind the formal freedoms of capitalism, the Matrix's mirage. Revealing the truth to Neo, Morpheus expresses the connection literally: 'You are a slave, Neo. Like everyone else, you were born into bondage, born into a prison that you cannot smell or taste or touch.'[33] It is only the imperceptibility

---

[32] In fact, just before the workplace scene, *The Matrix* shows Neo in his free time, when he codes and hacks. So it is that the opening scenes of the film dramatise his descent from free time to the time of formal freedom (work), and from there to really unfree time (police interrogation).

[33] The humans' oppression, undetectable by the senses, is precisely the opposite of Agent Smith's: foreshadowing his own rebellion against the Matrix in *Reloaded* and *Revolutions*, Smith tells Morpheus that he cannot stand being in the Matrix any longer because of humans' smell. (We shall consider the figure of slavery in *The Matrix* in more depth in the next section.)

of the bonds that conceals our real unfreedom in the workplace. The fields where all but a few humans are hooked up to the machines make manifest what capitalist 'equality' and 'freedom' mystify. The unhappy state of affairs obtaining in 2199 being merely the ironic culmination of humanity's own technological advancement, *The Matrix* implies that the transformation of human life itself into a form of property is the essence, the *telos* of capitalism as such.

Yet the machines do not simply capture and contain the humans: the latter must also do work, produce energy, sustain the machines. To be precise, then, what *The Matrix* imagines is not so much humans as property as humans as specifically biotechnological property. In doing so, the film penetrates to the heart of what biotechnology is, what it means, since the first use of the term—by Hungarian agricultural engineer Karl Ereky in 1917—pertains precisely to the exploitation of organic life as an energy source, as food. Ereky used *'Biotechnologie'* to describe an intensive, industrial, scientific approach to farming, at odds with the traditional methods of Hungary's peasantry, and put it into practice by setting up one of Europe's largest pig-fattening farms and slaughterhouses. In line with these principles, Ereky conceptualised his pigs as machines 'converting carefully calculated amounts of input into meat output'.[34] *The Matrix* seems to propose an extension of Ereky's notions: if animals are to be thought of thus, as so many machines converting energy from one form to another, why not also humans? Morpheus informs the newly awoken Neo that the 'human body generates more bioelectricity than a 120-volt battery and over 25,000 BTUs of body heat'; at the same time, we see an image of a human foetus, growing in its artificial sac, plugged into the machines. It is biotechnology in this full but speculative sense—humans become machines, machines supplanting humans—that *The Matrix* dramatises, and that it takes, metonymically, as emblematic of capitalism as a whole.

Yet if developments in biotechnology accompanied the expansion of intellectual property rights in the late twentieth century, so did the growth of networked computing, and *The Matrix* reminds us of this too. Neo's two lives (as Agent Smith puts it), one as a hacker, the other as a respectable software engineer, recall the late 1990s enclosure of the digital commons, whose spirit is perhaps best encapsulated by the DMCA, passed one year prior to *The Matrix*'s release. Suffice it to note here that the DMCA seeks not so much to expand the scope of copyrightable subject matter as to criminalise users' efforts to circumvent digital

---

[34] Robert Bud, *The Uses of Life: A History of Biotechnology* (Cambridge: Cambridge University Press, 1993), p. 34.

protections or encryptions of that matter, even if such circumvention is intended for 'fair use'. The result is that many examples of fair use—say, a lecturer excerpting part of a film to show in class—are now criminal.[35] In this context, Neo's job and his pastime seem to stand for opposed positions vis-à-vis digital property. In his life as a hacker, Agent Smith says, Neo is 'guilty of virtually every computer crime we have a law for', while Neo's employer, Metacortex, is a 'respectable software company', and would thus, in a reproduction of the real 1999, rely on precisely the sort of protections enshrined in the DMCA. In one life, Neo violates the laws of intellectual property; in the other, he produces that property.

The discussion of the film presented hitherto has emphasised its symbolic character: what *The Matrix* undertakes, I have suggested, is a process of unmasking (or, if you prefer, red-pill swallowing), as it shows the formal freedoms basic to capitalism to be, at root, unfreedoms, so many subjections of human beings to an apparatus that exceeds and dominates them. Capitalism *is* biotechnology. Yet what we must now add is that, in its second and third instalments, the *Matrix* trilogy begins to dilute the first's critical, socially symbolic content through its increasing reliance on abstract, mystical, anti-critical conceptions of balance and order. As we learn in *Reloaded*, the Oracle is the Architect's (Helmut Bakaitis) foil: in designing the Matrix, the Architect seeks to 'balance' the equations, while the Oracle 'unbalances' them. Neo personifies this unbalance; his life, the Architect says, 'is the sum of a remainder of an unbalanced equation inherent to the programming of the Matrix'. Agent Smith is likewise only Neo's negative, his opposite, 'the result of the equation trying to balance itself out', again. In the encounter between Neo and the Architect in *Reloaded*, and between Neo and the Oracle in *Revolutions* (the Oracle played in this film by Mary Alice), balance and unbalance become a metaphysical opposition structuring the diegetic universe.

Crucially, the centrality the sequels accord to 'balance' retroactively undermines *The Matrix*'s neutral presentation of Agent Smith's explanation: it prompts us to accept his anti-utopianism, which, we can now see, itself rests on the balance/unbalance dichotomy. Still speaking

---

[35] The debate over digital rights management, May notes, was particularly visible and public in the United States, compared with in Europe (*Global Political Economy*, p. 130). On the DMCA as a form of enclosure, see Bollier, pp. 124–25, and Boyle, pp. 85–121. On the commodification of software in general, see Boyle, pp. 160–71. My discussion here is in essence an elaboration of Nakamura's suggestion that '*The Matrix* can (and should) be read as a narrative about the Internet and its possibilities and dangers' (*Cybertypes*, p. 73).

to a barely conscious Morpheus, Smith explains what he sees as the *differentia specifica* of humans: 'Every mammal on this planet instinctively develops a natural equilibrium with the surrounding environment, but you humans do not. You move to an area and you multiply and multiply until every natural resource is consumed. The only way you can survive is to spread to another area.' Smith thus outs himself as a garden-variety Malthusian, for whom human reproduction exceeds nature's capacity to sustain human life. Humans begin in 'equilibrium'—a term that anticipates the Architect's and Oracle's 'balance'—but throw things out of joint by their drive to procreate. Humans can restore the balance only by 'spread[ing] to another area', by colonisation, in short. Humanity and nature are two terms of an equation that must ceaselessly rebalance itself. Smith's theory being validated by the framework governing the second and third films, the ambiguity attending his explanation evaporates. Smith speaks for both the Matrix and *The Matrix*: his anti-utopianism becomes the film's itself.

Copyright and Cloning

Perhaps the clearest way in which the *Matrix* trilogy's recourse to notions of balance can be seen to undermine its incipient criticisms is in its depiction of race. To observe this, however, it will first be helpful to take a look at Bay's *The Island*, whose overt white supremacy contrasts *The Matrix*'s subtler racism. *The Island* opens into a renovated American military facility, set just offshore, known as the 'Merrick Institute', after its director, Dr Bernard Merrick (Sean Bean). What the institute produces and sells to wealthy Americans are clones—'agnates' grown in translucent sacs—whose organs can later be harvested for their buyer (or 'sponsor'), or who can be used for surrogate births. The institute tells its customers that the clones are humanoid vegetables; in flagrant contravention of the 'eugenics laws of 2015', however, Merrick produces copies with consciousness, human beings in their own right able to learn, socialise, play, compete, and—at least in the more recent models—to question.

It is precisely this curiosity that prompts one of the clones, Lincoln Six Echo (Ewan MacGregor)—so named to reflect his owner, a luxury yacht designer named Tom Lincoln; the state in which the sponsor lives (six is code for Los Angeles); and his version (he is the fifth iteration of clone, version 'E' or 'Echo')—to ponder his and his fellow clones' existence, which is at present confined to the institute itself. Merrick has brainwashed the clones to believe that they are the survivors of a great contamination event that has left only one island pathogen-free.

The clones participate in a lottery promising its winner passage to the island, yet what really awaits the lucky agnate is the operating table. Having learnt the truth, Lincoln escapes the institute with his friend Jordan Two Delta (Scarlett Johansson), mimics his sponsor's identity—bringing about the latter's death at the hands of Albert Laurent (Djimon Hounsou), a security contractor hired by Merrick—and frees his fellow clones. In the film's closing shot, we see Lincoln and Jordon enjoying each other's company aboard Tom's yacht, the *Renovatio*, which property the designer seems to have unwittingly bequeathed to his double.

As this synopsis perhaps already indicates, the relations between *The Island* and the phenomenon of intellectual property are several. First, intellectual property is implicit in the very existence of the Merrick Institute, a cutting-edge biotechnology firm that claims ownership of human life. Second, believing he has killed the clone rather than its sponsor, Laurent reminds Lincoln that he has witnessed certain of Merrick's 'trade secrets', these too being a form of the institute's intellectual property. Third, *The Island* is rife with product placement (MSN, Xbox, Puma, and Calvin Klein, to name just a few), which process might in many cases more accurately be called 'trademark placement', for what is included in films is obviously not the commodity itself but its *sign*, its mark or branding. In a real sense, a film awash in product placement and branding such as *The Island* is not only about intellectual property, the ethics of the ownership of human life: it incorporates signs that are themselves others' property.[36]

On a fourth and still more basic level, *The Island* is the intellectual property of DreamWorks and Warner Bros (the former having won Caspian Tredwell-Owen's spec script at auction in 2004) and enjoys the protection of copyright law. But then so do many other films, as the two Hollywood giants were reminded when, shortly before *The Island*'s theatrical release, the producers of a little-known 1979 science-fiction film called *Parts: The Clonus Horror* accused them of copyright infringement. Like *The Island*, *Clonus* opens in its eponymous clone

---

[36] Notably, it was a science-fiction film, Steven Spielberg's *E.T.* (1982), whose astonishingly successful placement of Reese's Pieces heralded the beginning of a new era in Hollywood's product placement, when producers began actively to solicit placements. Other Hollywood science-fiction films with a significant amount of product placement include (somewhat ironically, given the film's satire of commodification) *Total Recall* and (another loose Philip K. Dick adaptation, initially written as a *Total Recall* sequel) *Minority Report* (2002). For an account of the post-*E.T.* growth in Hollywood's product placement, see Kerry Segrave, *Product Placement in Hollywood Films: A History* (Jefferson: McFarland, 2004), pp. 164–208.

colony in the United States, where wealthy citizens can pay to have their duplicates born and prepared for harvesting (in *Clonus*, the clones are not kept alive until they are needed, but rather frozen when they are sufficiently physically fit). As in *The Island*, too, the clones live in hope of freedom (though here it is not some unnamed 'island' they are promised, but 'America'). One clone, Richard (Tim Donnelly), questions his existence, flees the colony, and meets the man from whose DNA he was grown. The cloning company, Walker Industries, fails to cover its tracks, and the film concludes with its trade secrets being leaked at a press conference with a presidential candidate invested in the enterprise. Whether *The Island*'s narrative, shot construction, characters, dialogue, and so on are sufficiently similar to *Clonus* to suggest copying in the legal sense we will unfortunately never know, because DreamWorks and Warner Bros settled with Clonus Associates out of court, according to Bob Sullivan, one of *Clonus*'s screenwriters.[37]

In fact, *The Island* appears to have taken inspiration from a whole host of Hollywood science-fiction films, some of them already discussed in this book. From *The Matrix*, for instance, *The Island* borrows the notion that the harvested humans must be conscious in order for their bodies to yield adequate product (in this case, organs and babies, and in *The Matrix*, energy). The Merrick Institute grows its agnates in translucent, fluid-filled sacs, as the humans are grown in the *Matrix* trilogy, and the little mechanical bugs entering Lincoln's eye, whence they will gather data on his cognition, recall the mechanical bug that Agent Smith implants in Neo for much the same purpose. All this action, meanwhile, is set in the year 2019, the year that *Blade Runner* imagines. The two 2019s are quite different, but one notable commonality is the existence of memory imprinting, which give the agnates, like *Blade Runner*'s Replicants, the impression of having lived a real childhood. In particular, Jordan remembers her mother, and it is memories of her mother that Rachael has too, though in both cases such memories are retold to them by those already in the know, James McCord (Steve Buscemi) and Deckard. It does not seem too much of a stretch to read Laurent as a fully privatised blade runner, his task being to 'retire' the escaped agnates. We could go on: *The Island* also bears the influence of several 1970s Hollywood science-fiction films—particularly *THX 1138*

---

[37] Sullivan discusses the settlement in a 2007 interview with Albert Walker ('An Interview with Bob Sullivan, *Clonus* Screenwriter', *The Agony Booth*, 17 May 2007 <https://web.archive.org/web/20191013075446/https://www.agonybooth.com/interview-with-clonus-screenwriter-4507> [accessed 17 May 2022]).

Figure 6: White wish-fulfilment (*The Island*, dir. by Michael Bay (DreamWorks Pictures, 2005))

(1971), *Logan's Run* (1976), and *Coma* (1978)—whose tropes perhaps found their way into it via *Clonus*.

Yet despite these similarities with *The Matrix* (and the other films just noted), *The Island*'s conceptualisation of biotechnology is different, and articulates a racial politics distinct from *The Matrix*'s. *The Island* represents Merrick's biotechnological experiments as capitalism gone wrong, a violation of capitalist freedoms. That Merrick's work contravenes the official ethics of American capitalism, enshrined in the (fictional) 'eugenics laws of 2015', is one way the film indicates this; but the key detail, it need scarcely be noted, is that Bay names the clone primarily responsible for freeing his fellow slaves 'Lincoln', and thus drives a wedge between Merrick's slavery and the post-abolition United States.[38] What matters here is that, since only wealthy Americans can afford to be cloned, the slaves reproduce the racial composition of the American upper class, with the result that those enslaved are predominantly white.[39] Biotechnology being conceptualised as a divergence from American

---

[38] I am grateful to Tomos Hughes for pointing out the correlative significance of the name 'Jordan', which might be a reference to the crossing of the river Jordan narrated in the Bible. This became in turn a key metaphor for slave emancipation in the United States.

[39] The Black agnate accorded the greatest narrative significance is Starkweather Two Delta (Michael Clarke Duncan), a lottery winner sponsored by a famous American football player now in need of a new liver.

capitalism, even its antithesis, it becomes the perfect site on which to play out the fantasy of white enslavement, white victimisation, and fulfils the white person's wish to return to the apex of the racial hierarchy, whence they may reclaim their privileged relationship to property. This, I think, is what the closing shot of Lincoln and Jordan on the yacht is rather unabashedly meant to signify.

In *The Matrix*, on the other hand (and as we have already seen), biotechnological slavery is portrayed as the essence of capitalism. Consequently, the film transposes capitalism's purely formal equality onto that slavery, such that people of all races suffer the same oppression to the same degree. Slavery becomes universal, almost egalitarian, and loses its historical relationship to Blackness.[40] It might be objected that *The Matrix* projects racial oppression instead onto its antagonism between the freed humans and machines: note, for instance, the whiteness of Agent Smith, who beats down Morpheus (a scene that seems to recall the videotaped beating of Rodney King); the invocation of 'Zion', a significant term in African American Christian theology; and the multiracial Council, many of whose major figures are Black. As Jason Haslam shows, however, such an allegory breaks down, since, first, on the model of the 'buddy flick', the Black characters function as the assistants of the white protagonist, Neo, and, second, Neo's sacrifice in *Revolutions* keeps the Matrix, and thus the allegorically white power structure, in place.[41] Similarly, if Smith embodies the whiteness of American law enforcement in the first film, in the second he goes rogue, his whiteness disarticulated from the Matrix. The Matrix's ultimate representative in the sequels is as much the Oracle, who is Black, as the Architect, who is white, and as such (picking up, here, on my argument in the previous section) the trilogy finally conceives of race itself as a kind of equilibrium, Black balanced against white. *The Matrix*'s erasure of the racialised character of slavery foreshadows the failure, even reversal, of its antiracist allegory.

What further complicates the picture is that the concept of balance, discussed above, seems to derive from *The Matrix*'s fascination with

---

[40] For further discussion of the problems with *The Matrix*'s depiction of slavery in particular and race in general, see Kim D. Hester-Williams, 'NeoSlaves: Slavery, Freedom, and African American Apotheosis in *Candyman*, *The Matrix*, and *The Green Mile*', *Genders*, 40 (2004) <http://web.archive.org/web/20131112025835/http://www.genders.org/g40/g40_williams.html> [accessed 17 May 2022] (paras 10–23 of 43).

[41] Jason Haslam, *Gender, Race, and American Science Fiction: Reflections on Fantastic Identities* (New York: Routledge, 2015), pp. 134–60. Haslam thus reads Neo as white, but for an argument that *The Matrix* codes him as multiracial, see Park, pp. 179–88, and Nishime.

Figure 7: Yin and yang? (*The Matrix*, dir. by Lana Wachowski and Lilly Wachowski (Warner Bros., 1999))

East Asia, and is thus itself implicitly racialised. We can see this in the film's dojo scene, which Jane Chi Hyun Park reads as exemplary of the Wachowskis' 'oriental style'. The fight between Neo and Morpheus recalls Japanese videogames such as *Virtua Fighter* and *Tekken*, Park argues, while the scene's shot construction evokes noh theatre. Sonically, the film introduces the battle with a gong and accompanies it with a kind of New Age Asian music. Reeves is himself of mixed Asian ancestry, but it is only here, in the dojo, that his character—coded white, until this point in the film—learns kung fu, becomes racialised as Asian, and performs 'yellowface'.[42] I want to add to Park's incisive reading of the scene by drawing attention to one shot in particular: as Neo and Morpheus resume fighting, Morpheus having praised his opponent's adaptation and improvisation, we see them, suddenly, from above. From this perspective, with Neo's kicking leg caught in Morpheus's hand and Morpheus's likewise in Neo's, the two form the yin and yang symbol, Neo's light gown and black hair juxtaposed with Morpheus's black gown and light head. Neo and Morpheus are balanced against each other both physically (each stands on one leg) and metaphysically (*qua* yin and yang). If *The Matrix* conceives the relationship between Black and white—between Morpheus and Neo, between the Oracle and the Architect—as one of balance, the category of balance is itself, here in

---

[42] Park, pp. 188–91.

the dojo (and prior to its full thematisation in *Reloaded* and *Revolutions*), revealed to be East Asian in origin.

Though, by contrast with *The Matrix*, *The Island*'s cast is overwhelmingly white, it is Laurent, the Black security contractor, who holds the key to the film's racial politics. Laurent's ideological function, I would argue, is to reinforce *The Island*'s characterisation of biotechnological slavery as white, but also to suggest that Merrick's oppressive business model is, in essence, Black. Formerly an employee of GIGN (the specialist branch of the French police), Laurent now works for 'Blackhawk Security' and comes recommended to Merrick by the Defense Department—a perfunctory nod, we might note in passing, to the interpenetration of private and public sectors in Bay's 2019. His father having been killed in the 'Burkinabé rebellion' (whether this refers to a real historical event in Burkina Faso and, if so, what event, the film does not seem to indicate), Laurent and his brothers were branded (we are not told by whom) 'so others would know we were less than human', as he says to Merrick, a pointed analogy with the situation of the agnates, whom Laurent now believes Merrick to be killing needlessly, and thus to be treating as sub-human. Yet if Merrick stands for these undefined counter-forces, he is also, at the same time, Laurent himself: 'At some point,' the latter continues, reflecting on his own career, 'you realise that war is a business.' He turns around to face Merrick: 'So when did killing become a business for you?' In *The Island*'s allegorical structure, Laurent is both oppressed and oppressor: he is branded as other but also hired as a killer involved in the oppression of others. The effect on the film's depiction of race is double. First, by drawing a parallel between his own alterity and the agnates', Laurent sanctions the film's reimagining the historical oppression of Black people as one with mostly white victims. Second, by characterising the 'business of war' as something he learnt in his childhood in Burkina Faso, he defines such immoral business as Black.

This second point here functions as implicit praise for the United States and sheds light on *The Island*'s divergence from both *Clonus* and—another film that dramatises an 'escape from dystopia'—*The Truman Show*. If Burkina Faso is the place of business done wrong, business subordinated to the purpose of war, tainted by some end outside itself, the United States must be its opposite: capitalism in its pure form, where capital serves no function but the accumulation of more capital, the valorisation of yet more value. It is significant that when Lincoln and Jordan leave to find their sponsors, McCord, who is one of Merrick's employees, gives them his credit card and not simply cash. For the user, the credit card offers access to money outside the wage-relation, money unsullied by the labour process, while for the bank, the card represents interest-bearing capital, thus the possibility of earning more money without the nuisance of having workers make material things. In the credit card, the production process—which from the perspective of valorisation is 'an unavoidable middle term, a necessary evil for the purpose of money-making'[43]—disappears, and capital seems to take its simplest form. Capitalist America represents capital in motion, frictionless circulation—this symbolised in the hovering Amtrak train, one of the few speculative 'innovations' included in *The Island*—as opposed to the Merrick Institute, where production appears directly in the agnates' slave labour and is thereby dissociated from capitalism in its pure, American incarnation.[44]

The Island's America is no longer the America of *Clonus*, then: the clones' promised land that turns out to be a lie and in fact signifies their freezing. Bay's substitution of some unspecified island for *Clonus*'s 'America' is as clear a mark as any of the distinct political ambitions of the two films—though we ought to add that *Clonus* somewhat redeems the United States, since the journalist's brandishing of the stolen tape, which reveals the Clonus operation, is alone supposed to assure us that such a practice will come to an end, and thus reveals undue faith in the immediate political efficacy of such journalism. It appears that Truman's escape from his eponymous set into Los Angeles is likewise an emergence into the United States *qua* utopia, but crucially (as I emphasised in Chapters 3 and 4) the outside world is no truer, no more authentic than life in Seahaven. The film's conclusion, where two security guards celebrate Truman's exit from the world of images and then immediately set about deciding what to watch next, is not a punchline extrinsic to the message of the film but rather the latter's essence. America is the society of the spectacle; Seahaven literalises it.

We might formalise this difference between *The Island* and *The Matrix*, on the one hand, and films like *Clonus* and *The Truman Show*, on the other, in the distinction (also developed in Chapter 4) between the critical, utopian dystopias produced mostly before the mid-1990s and the increasingly anti-utopian ones made after. As we have seen, what characterises the utopian dystopia is the contrast between some utopian fragment or principle, placed in the foreground, and the overwhelmingly dystopian background that, being incompatible with the former, throws it

---

[43] Marx, *Capital*, II, 137.
[44] Revealing the truth of their existence to Lincoln and Jordan, McCord describes clone technology, with its promise of longer lives, as a 'new American dream'. In condemning Merrick, the film subsequently implies that the old one was enough.

into relief. By 'utopia' here, I do not mean simply 'desire for a better way of being' (as per Levitas), but rather the representation of a form of life incompatible with, and implicitly critical of, enclosure. It is on this basis that the utopian dystopia must be distinguished from its anti-utopian variant, which maintains the background while excising the utopian element and, with it, consequently, the critique of the new enclosures.

Superficially, of course, *The Island* and *The Matrix* do generate contrasts between a worse and a better state of affairs. *The Island* distinguishes Merrick's dystopian facility from the American dream, while *The Matrix* juxtaposes the machines' enslavement of humans with Zion. As such, a formal definition of utopia, one indifferent to matters of content, is obliged to conclude that these two texts are no more or less utopian than the likes of *RoboCop*, *Blade Runner*, *Total Recall*, and *The Truman Show*. All the films named here evince desire for some better way of being or living, but the political insignificance of such a criterion becomes clear when we see that it corrals into the same generic space both a work as reactionary as *The Island* and a genuinely critical text like *RoboCop*. Beneath the similarity of these films' form lie deep differences in content, *The Island* rendering white supremacist apologia for capitalism, while *RoboCop* takes Reaganite privatisation as the object of its critique.

Ethics and Experiment

One of the ways that we might begin to distinguish *District 9* from *The Matrix* and *The Island* is in the role it accords biotechnology, which is no longer inflated into a metonym for capitalism or dismissed as capitalism gone awry. On one level, the film can be read as a rather straightforward denunciation of biopiracy, the process by which imperialists patent indigenous knowledge and claim it as their own. *District 9* centres on the efforts of its corporate giant, Multinational United (MNU), which, drawing on all the sophistication of twenty-first-century science, tries to harvest hybrid human–alien genetic material from Wikus van de Merwe (Sharlto Copley), a newly promoted bureaucrat working for MNU in Johannesburg. This lucrative opportunity has arisen because Wikus accidentally inhaled a black fuel while inspecting an alien dwelling, which he entered as part of his work clearing the aliens from District 9, where almost two million of them have mysteriously settled, and moving them, ostensibly with their consent, to a concentration camp named District 10. Having exposed himself to the fuel, Wikus begins to transform into an alien, and MNU detains him in its testing facility. The company soon finds out that Wikus's modified genome allows him to operate alien weaponry (something that no ordinary humans can do, since the firearms react to alien touch alone). MNU—and this is the place of biopiracy in *District 9*—thus decides to harvest Wikus's hybrid DNA, which represents 'hundreds of millions, maybe billions of dollars of biotechnology' for the company. The second half of the film proceeds to chart Wikus's efforts to evade capture and, by securing the help of the aliens, to turn himself back into a human.

As in the above discussions of *The Matrix* and *The Island*, my reading of *District 9* will eventually seek to disclose the relationship between the film's depiction of biotechnology and its racial politics. I propose that we begin, however, where Blomkamp himself did: with *Alive in Joburg*, a short film he directed in 2006, which stages interviews with Black South Africans about aliens who have recently settled in Johannesburg. A clear precursor to *District 9*, *Alive in Joburg* tests what would become many of the feature film's signal devices: found footage, including interviews both with the public and with experts; shots of aliens living in squalor; and spectacular militarised combat between aliens and security forces. According to Blomkamp, the interviews in *Alive in Joburg*, which generally reveal a fearful and prejudicial view of the aliens, are in fact real, Blomkamp having simply asked his interviewees about Black Nigerians and Zimbabweans.[45] Blomkamp's approach renders the ideological function of *Alive in Joburg* more or less transparent: the film takes such dehumanising remarks literally and turns the Black Nigerians and Zimbabweans who are their object into actual aliens. We, the film's viewers, are supposed to conclude that the interviewees' comments, identical as they are to real criticisms of marginalised groups, do not capture the qualities of those groups. Such is Blomkamp's sympathetic portrayal of the aliens that the interviewees' remarks do not seem fair even to these latter.

In turning *Alive in Joburg* into *District 9*, however, Blomkamp decided to transform the object of the documentary, though the prejudicial interviews—and the ideological 'message' intended of their inclusion—remain. It seems that *District 9* begins as a mere elaboration of *Alive in Joburg*: this is a documentary about aliens, about the South Africans' attempts to expropriate them. Wikus appears to be the film's presenter, the one who will guide us through the alien settlement, introduce us to alien custom and culture. Yet when, during that fateful inspection, he inhales the fuel and demands that the handheld camera, still trained

---

[45] Meredith Woerner, '5 Things You Didn't Know about *District 9*', *Gizmodo*, 19 October 2009 <https://io9.gizmodo.com/5-things-you-didnt-know-about-district-9-5341120> [accessed 17 May 2022] (paras 10–11 of 11).

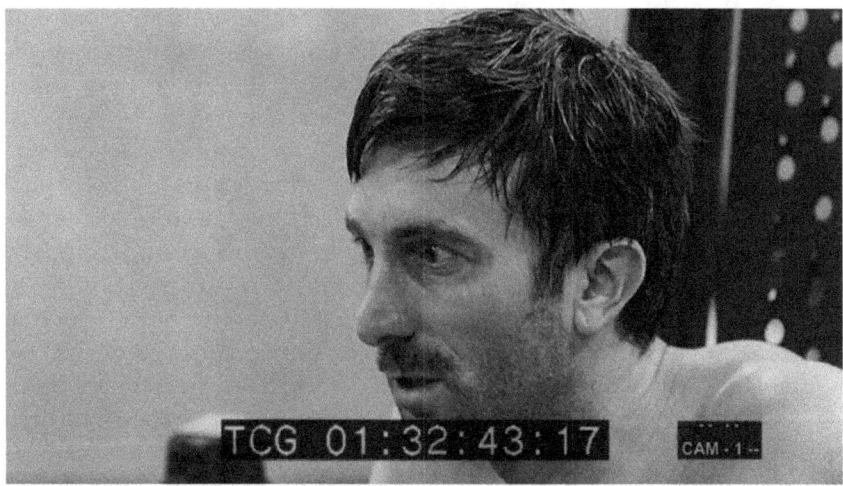

Figure 8: Wikus as filmic object (*District 9*, dir. by Neill Blomkamp (TriStar Pictures, 2009))

on him, be turned off, we realise that Wikus is not, in fact, in control of this documentary. Several other times Wikus tells the cameraperson to stop filming, or not to show what has been filmed (especially when his masculinity is at stake, as when an alien injures him), and yet such moments are included in the film anyway. These episodes, where authorial control eludes Wikus, hint at what will shortly become obvious: that it is he who forms the film's object.

Wikus's shift from subject, with agency over the image, to object, the focal point of the image itself, mirrors his changed relationship to human rights, which his transformation into an alien seems to forfeit entirely. The doctor having revealed his alien claw, Wikus is rushed down to MNU's testing laboratory, hooked up to alien weaponry, and forced (with an electric prod) to shoot various things, including finally an alien. The experiment having been a success, MNU decides to harvest Wikus's genetic material, a process over which he of course has no say. (At least Murphy had technically signed away the rights to his body prior to his resurrection as RoboCop.) These events are captured on handheld cameras; indeed, stressing Wikus's shift from presenter to documentary object, Blomkamp conspicuously places in the frame an MNU photographer taking photos of Wikus prior to his operation. In just one of the film's many ironies, when a server refuses to sell the part-transformed Wikus food (he is a fugitive, and his picture has just flashed up on the shop's television screen), Wikus recalls his old bureaucratic lexicon and states, 'You are legally obliged to serve me.' Yet it seems that the server is not, in fact, obliged: another employee returns with a shotgun, by which time Wikus appears to have learnt that his human rights no longer apply in this context.

That the corporation so brusquely divests Wikus of his rights—that Wikus finds himself lifted straight from the public spaces of the hospital to the laboratories of the MNU building, from the place of healthcare to the cauldron of biotechnology—is not, by this point, especially surprising. The film spends its first half an hour showing us not so much that the aliens do not have rights as that those rights are merely formal. The MNC sends its staff, along with private military contractors, to serve the aliens their eviction notices (a process observed by human rights groups), which require the resident alien's signature.[46] Whether this is actually legal in the first place is questionable: the alien Christopher Johnson (played, like the other aliens, by Jason Cope) tells Wikus that it is not, and generally refuses to cooperate. 'You don't have a choice in the matter; you just have to sign this document,' Thomas (Kenneth Nkosi), the armed guard accompanying Wikus, responds. The direct appeals failing to work, Wikus threatens to take Christopher's son on contrived grounds, namely that the litter outside their house constitutes 'dangerous conditions' for the child. What matters is not the legality of the process but the outcome: in another incident, an alien bats away the paperwork but, because his claw touched the paper, the imprint left counts as valid scrawl, and therefore as consent. The film devotes much energy to showing that, in transactions between humans and aliens, and hence between the human groups for whom those two allegorically stand (on which more shortly), 'force decides'.[47]

The humans feel that they have to trick the aliens, in part, because

---

[46] Incidentally, *District 9* was shot in Tshiawelo, where people who had lived in the shacks we see in the film were themselves being moved out, into state-subsidised housing. The production thus 'bought up the shacks that remained, fenced off the area and created a controlled environment in which to shoot' (Andrew Worsdale, 'Joburg Inspired Blomkamp', *Screen Africa*, October 2009, p. 35). I am grateful to Sarah Smyth for alerting me to this detail.

[47] The phrase is Marx's, in a different but not entirely unrelated context; see *Capital*, I, 344. At the end of *District 9*, we learn that Fundiswa Mhlanga (Mandla Gaduka), an MNU employee who shadowed Wikus on the latter's first trip around the alien settlement, 'is currently awaiting trial for exposing MNU's illegal genetic research programme'. The contradiction here is that the very whistleblowing practices that would enable the proper functioning of the law are themselves criminal. Again, the film seems to point to the law's latent class content.

the latter do not understand 'the concept of ownership of property' (though Christopher's claim that MNU's evictions are illegal suggests that the more astute ones might in fact have got their heads around it). 'We have to say, "Listen, this is our land; please will you go?"' Wikus states before the handheld camera. In a sense, then, MNU's attempt to expropriate Wikus's hybrid genome, which would confer private property rights on a 'product of nature', is only a grimly ironic repetition of Wikus's expropriation of alien settlements, which likewise intends to impose the property-form on things not already so organised. This irony is threaded through the early stages of Wikus's transformation, when he finds his fingernails and teeth falling out (this evoking, of course, David Cronenberg's *The Fly* (1986)), one of his hands turned into a claw, and then, shortly after, the growth and yellowing of his left eye. What is significant about such mutations is that they occur in parts of the human body that typically express one's individuality: the fingers and hand for signatures, the teeth for DNA identification, the eye for retinal scans. The first casualty in Wikus's transformation is his own status as a juridical subject, an individual capable of giving consent.[48]

The aliens being tricked into leaving their land, and Wikus forced to render his hybrid DNA, *District 9* shows us that expropriation is only superficially at odds with bourgeois conceptions of freedom: the latter, under the guise of 'consent', is a legal fiction invoked to legitimise the former. Yet the film's politics are not quite as straightforward as this: I now want to suggest that they contradict themselves, and bear the mark of that anti-utopianism characteristic of Hollywood's twenty-first-century science fictions.[49] Such anti-utopianism manifests itself in *District 9*'s efforts to represent Black immigrants, who were absent in *Alive in Joburg* but appear in the feature film as a stereotypical Nigerian gang. Within the *District 9* narrative, the gang is constructed as the opposite of MNU, since it seeks to achieve the same goal—operating the alien firearms—with an inverse *modus operandi*. Thus, where the MNU building abounds

[48] This irony is also refracted through space: as Landi Raubenheimer notes, near the end of the film, Wikus finds himself injured amidst the rubble of the alien township, 'a place where his apartheid-era white identity is fundamentally one of non-belonging' ('Nostalgic Dystopia: Johannesburg as Landscape after *White Writing*', *Journal of Literary Studies*, 36.4 (2020), 123–42 (p. 129)).

[49] I treat *District 9* as a Hollywood film on the basis that TriStar Pictures was involved in its production and distribution, but it must also be added that much of the film's funding came from QED International, an independent American production company, and that *District 9* has links to New Zealand (through Peter Jackson, one of its producers) and, of course, South Africa.

in cutting-edge technology, the Nigerians operate out of shacks and seem to have a proclivity for magic. The gang also organises a number of subsidiary businesses, including a prostitution ring and cat food retail, the latter a more or less blatant attempt to defraud the aliens. These, Teju Cole argues, are stereotypes of Nigerians that one finds in Nollywood, but there they at least benefit from Nollywood's 'humanising, narrative context'.[50] Blomkamp's film perpetuates the same dehumanisation of Black Nigerians that *Alive in Joburg* sought to criticise.

I want to argue that the very possibility of this relapse, where *District 9* revives the prejudices it began to challenge, is already implicit in the form of its judgement on biotechnology. Near the end of the film, Wikus and Christopher escape from MNU, where they have retrieved the alien biofuel—Christopher because the fuel will allow him to return to the mothership, and Wikus because Christopher has told him that technology upon that ship can reverse his transformation. In a break in the fighting, Christopher reveals to Wikus that this reversal will in fact take three years, much longer than he had earlier suggested. (The implication here is that Christopher already knew this and has simply manipulated Wikus, another instance of the film's irony, and a hint that the aliens are much cannier than the humans assume.) Wikus reminds him that they had a 'deal' but, enraged by the alien corpses he just witnessed in the MNU building, Christopher retorts, 'I will not let my people be medical experiments!' This is the ideological crux of the film: the aliens, and hence whomever they allegorise, deserve to be treated as humans, accorded the protections of human rights.

Yet the potency of Christopher's remark is at odds with *District 9*'s earlier critique of bourgeois rights. According to this first critique, as we have seen, such rights are formal, and serve simply as a means of legitimising expropriation. What Christopher suggests, however, is that it is not rights themselves that are the problem as much as their incomplete coverage. Christopher implies that it is wrong that his kind

---

[50] Teju Cole, 'Comment: *District 9* and the Nigerians', *Africa Is a Country*, 11 September 2009 <https://africasacountry.wordpress.com/2009/09/11/comment-district-9-and-the-nigerians> [accessed 17 May 2022] (para. 3 of 9). Carina Ray likewise criticises the stereotypical portrayal in 'Humanising Aliens or Alienating Africans?', *New African*, December 2009, pp. 32–33. It is worth noting that, though the Nigerians attempt to defraud the aliens by selling the latter cat food for their weapons, this ruse actually backfires: it seems the only way humans can use the weapons is by ingesting the black fuel, such that the Nigerians are actually giving the aliens food in exchange for something useless to them. This is another suggestion that the aliens are much more intelligent, more cunning than the humans suppose.

are experimented on, that they lack the legal shield from which humans benefit. Christopher's is a moral appeal according to which the dignity of his particular group, the aliens, makes them unacceptable objects of medical experiments. What such an appeal leaves intact, or even directly implies, is that *other* people or organisms, ones lower than aliens in the natural hierarchy, might still reasonably be experimented on. *District 9* does not leave us to guess who remains an acceptable object in this sense: it fills the place of this 'other', this alterity, with the Nigerian gang, which, desperate to use their own stock of alien weaponry, constantly experiment on themselves (the leader, notably, tries drinking some of Wikus's blood) in order to attain hybridity. The fundamental contradiction of *District 9* is that the film dehumanises the very group represented by the aliens—the immigrant Nigerians and Zimbabweans—and that is thus to be accorded the same human rights for which Christopher appeals.[51]

The question of how a film with some antiracist commitments can also regurgitate the oldest racist stereotypes has troubled *District 9*'s critics.[52] Trying to explain the contradiction, Cole offers two options: the portrayal of the Nigerian gang is either a blind spot or an effort to objectify the racism itself, to literalise the racist prejudice symbolised by the humans' attitude towards the aliens.[53] Yet if we see the film's racism as a corollary of its moralism, the dark underside of its moralistic critique, as I have just argued, then the contradiction no longer appears as such. It seems to me that *District 9* conceives of Christopher's moralism as a supplement, a boost to the earlier, more thoroughgoing critique of bourgeois rights. It does so for the simple reason that, in the enclosed

[51] This explains Joshua Clover's observation, echoed by Rebecca Duncan, that it is impossible to establish who the aliens 'really are', for whom they really stand (Clover, 'Allegory Bomb', *Film Quarterly*, 63.2 (2009), 8–9 (p. 8); Duncan, 'From Cheap Labour to Surplus Humanity: World-Ecology and the Postapartheid Speculative in Neill Blomkamp's *District 9*', *Science Fiction Film and Television*, 11.1 (2018), 45–72 (p. 64)). The only group that can possibly occupy this place is the same one that, on another level, the film suggests does not merit the sympathy we eventually give the aliens. Thus the allegory's referent appears empty.

[52] 'I am not convinced that Blomkamp really had a progressive agenda at heart in making *D9*,' Ray writes. 'If he did something terrible happened along the way' ('Humanising Aliens', p. 32). Similarly, Duncan suggests that Blomkamp's depiction of the Nigerians as primitive 'avatars of evil' reinforces anti-immigrant sentiment, and that, contrasted with the film's critique of capitalism, this xenophobia is 'inexplicabl[e]' ('Cheap Labour', p. 69).

[53] Cole, para. 9 of 9.

social world of the twenty-first century, it fears that the first critique no longer suffices, that it no longer convinces its audience, such that a bonus moralism might increase the force of its objections.

This, I think, finally accounts for the prominence of arms manufacturing in *District 9*. It is significant that what the expropriation of alien DNA promises is not simply billions of dollars' worth of biotechnology (the riches no doubt flowing from an imminent patent claim on the expropriated materials), but the use of appreciably more powerful weapons. That is, what the film seems to suggest is reprehensible about the (attempted) expropriation is not merely that a multinational will profit from it, but that MNU is indifferent to the ends to which its products will be put. It matters that MNU is not any old seller of commodities but an arms dealer, the 'second largest manufacturer of weapons in the world', as one of the interviewees emphasises. Again, a kind of supplementation is at work: the critique of commodification (specifically, of the formal freedom requisite to it) not being enough, *District 9* adds to it the bonus that the commodities themselves, the weapons, are immoral, or will likely be used immorally. Except that these weapons feature spectacularly in the action sequences, they have no narrative necessity. We do not see them produced, sold, and mobilised en masse against either humans or aliens. They serve simply to give an edge to the critique, and to emphasise, in case we prove unsusceptible to that critique, that MNU is evil.

So it is that *District 9* must finally be counted with *The Matrix* and *The Island* as cinematic manifestations of the anti-utopian dystopia. What is notable about these films in particular (and I hope justifies the lengthy treatment given them in this chapter) is that each offers some sort of critique of enclosure that goes astray. *The Matrix* enlarges the biotechnological commodification of human life to the point where it becomes slavery, yet in doing so it elides the racial constitution of that concept. *The Island* likewise imagines biotechnology as human enslavement but puts that to reactionary ends, to fantasise the return of the white American to their private property. *District 9*'s allegorical biopiracy and critique of formal freedom give way to a moralism from which the film's stereotypical representation of the Nigerian gang springs. That this structure is not a peculiarity of the three films studied here, but rather a tendency of the Hollywood science-fiction film in the twenty-first century, the next chapter will seek to demonstrate through readings of two post-crisis films: *Repo Men* and *The Purge*.

Chapter 6

Speculation
Credit, Crisis, and Foreclosure in *Repo Men* and *The Purge*

When, exactly, did the late noughties global financial crisis begin? Did it start, as many accounts proclaim, in 2008, on 15 September, when Lehman Brothers filed for bankruptcy and global credit markets froze? Or had it already begun the previous year, in July 2007, when Bear Stearns revealed that two of its hedge funds, heavily invested in subprime mortgage debt, had lost all their value? Yet perhaps even summer 2007 is too late. The investment banks collapsed into the rubble of a growing foreclosure crisis, where millions of American homeowners, unable to keep up with mortgage payments, had defaulted on their loans and suffered eviction. The wave of foreclosures began in late 2006, but did not draw comment from the American press until it struck wealthier, white homeowners in Florida, California, Nevada, and Arizona in mid-2007.[1] To write (or, as we shall see, film) an account of the financial crisis is thus to confront a problem of narrativisation, in particular of what one deems the 'equilibrium' that, as Tzvetan Todorov observes, narratives unsettle and eventually restore.[2] Retellings of the crisis that begin in July 2007 or September 2008 treat bank solvency as their equilibrial state, while those departing from the foreclosures of mid-2007 take white homeownership as theirs.

To these two equilibria and the periodisations they imply also correspond the disparate temporalities and iconographies of the financial and the foreclosure crises. If the events of 2007–08 can be described as a 'crash', 'crunch', or 'collapse'—the punctum of failure—the post-2006 period of rising foreclosure rates is better thought of as a 'wave'— something durative—cresting around 2010. Contrasting but ultimately

---

[1] David Harvey, *The Enigma of Capital: And the Crises of Capitalism* (London: Profile, 2011), pp. 1–2.
[2] Tzvetan Todorov, 'Structural Analysis of Narrative', trans. by Arnold Weinstein, *Novel*, 3.1 (1969), 70–76 (p. 75).

related to the ubiquitous images of falling share prices, scrolling red digits whose precise meaning is inaccessible to most of us, is the picture of the boarded-up home, the import of which needs no explanation. I would submit that this dual presentation of the crisis—its appearance as, on the one hand, a banking collapse, product of Wall Street's mortgage-backed bacchanalia, and, on the other, a foreclosure crisis, with its roots in the homeowner's inability to keep up with mortgage payments when their property values fall[3]—creates a major representational challenge for the filmmaker who wishes to tell its story. The cinema depicting such a crisis must be mediatory and connective, linking its diverse forms and sites of expression.

As we shall see, however, the majority of American fiction and documentary films seeking to narrate the crisis have baulked at the challenge and contented themselves with focalising events narrowly, through the traders and bankers dealing in mortgage-backed securities. It typically falls to the film's designated conscientious banker to express, in moral outrage, the effects of their dealings on the American working class. In this context, the novelty of the two Hollywood science fictions I discuss in this chapter—Miguel Sapochnik's *Repo Men* (2010) and James DeMonaco's *The Purge* (2013)—is that they do indeed manage to mediate finance and foreclosure, albeit in different ways. *Repo Men* imagines a dystopia in which a company loans artificial organs at predatory interest rates and employs its own 'repo men' to retrieve those organs when the debtor is sufficiently overdue. Telling the story from the perspective of one such agent, who later becomes a borrower himself and then delinquent, *Repo Men* renders the relation between credit and debt, between loaning and repayment, in concrete, visceral terms. *The Purge* connects the two expressions of crisis through allegory. On the one hand, its characters symbolise the gendered and racialised aspects of foreclosure. On the other, the Sandin household, on which the film's action centres, serves as a critique of the 'household analogy'

---

[3] This duality, I am keen to stress, is not unique to the post-2006 foreclosure/2007–08 banking crisis. Rather, all capitalist crises are at one and the same time crises of capital's reproduction—its inability to change form from money capital to commodity capital to productive capital and so on—*and* of social reproduction—the reproduction of social groups, their ability to sustain themselves—since capitalism functions precisely by making the latter dependent on the former, by making human subsistence dependent on the wage, thus on the health of the economic system that pays out wages. Notably for us, it is enclosure that, in severing our direct access to subsistence, ties social reproduction to the reproduction of capital, such that shocks in the latter course through the former.

of government spending elaborated by austerians in the wake of the crisis, as concerns about public debt displaced those about private debt.

Yet this is not to say that *Repo Men* and *The Purge* are without their limitations, politically. Like the other late-1990s and post-2000 films discussed in this book, their criticisms founder on a more thoroughgoing anti-utopianism, as each film comes to naturalise, and thereby to support, the institution of private property. While *Repo Men*'s representations of organ excision are so many efforts to render foreclosure horrifying, such repossessions belong mainly in the film's downtown spaces. The metropolitan centre extrapolates the processes of capitalist urbanism and renders a cityscape much like (indeed, derivative of) *Blade Runner*'s nightmarish Los Angeles, but *Repo Men*'s suburb remains pristine, its inhabitants protected from financial expropriation. The film's suburb projects a fantasy of the permanence of the private home, which has warded off the threat of foreclosure. In *The Purge*, meanwhile, the suspension of American law seems to mean only the decriminalisation of murder, as the purgers are rather more interested in killing their compatriots than in stealing property. Isolated counterexamples crop up in the prequel and sequel films, yet it remains murder, the sanction of killing, that drives their plots.[4] The effect, again, is that property rights are naturalised, elevated to the status of natural law, thus unable to be abrogated.

Finance and Foreclosure

That the crises of banking and foreclosure came into being together, entailed one another, should have been no surprise. Looking back at the twentieth century, David Harvey notes that the 1973 global crisis (often attributed to that same year's oil shock), the late 1980s American savings and loan crisis, the Japanese crisis of the 1990s, the 1992 nationalisation of Swedish banks, and the economic collapse of East and Southeast Asia in 1997–98 were all linked to crashes in property markets. There is even evidence to suggest that the Great Depression stemmed from a property boom. In a country such as the United States, where mortgage debt constitutes about 40 per cent of GDP, housing crisis and national recession cannot be but intimately bound.[5]

---

[4] I write this chapter prior to the July 2021 theatrical release of the final *Purge* film (directed by Everardo Gout), which nonetheless falls outside this book's temporal scope.

[5] David Harvey, *Rebel Cities: From the Right to the City to the Urban Revolution*, 2nd edn (London: Verso, 2019), pp. 30–34.

But why is housing so often the epicentre of crisis? Harvey's explanation returns us to the theory of overaccumulation, according to which the surpluses of capital arising from capitalist production must find profitable reinvestment. While this imperative is what drives the new enclosures, enclosure is equally only one such 'fix' in the capitalist's toolbox. Credit is another, its flow into the economy allowing capitalists who cannot sell their surplus product to invest in future production, which generates, in turn, additional demand elsewhere in the economy.[6] In the case of housing, credit fuels both demand *and* supply (in fact, sometimes the same bank finances a building's construction and its mortgages), and therein lies the issue. Because the time taken to build and sell a property (its 'turnover time') is very long, the credit lent out to buyers whips up demand quicker than supply. (Typically it is difficult to increase a country's housing stock by more than 2 or 3 per cent per year, Harvey observes.) The result, as lenders rush towards buyers rather than builders—as more money chases roughly the same number of homes—is a housing bubble.[7]

The theory of overaccumulation offers a broad and general explanation for the importance of urban development to capitalism. What then were the specific pressures inflating the American housing bubble of the early 2000s? Behind the growth in property values, paradoxically, was the long-term decline in real wages in the United States, which had decreased as a proportion of GDP since the late 1960s. Such decline would have translated into extremely weak effective demand, exacerbating the problem of overaccumulation, were it not for several countervailing factors: an increase in two-earner households, longer working hours, workers taking on more jobs, and, perhaps most importantly, the expansion of household debt (which reached 100 per cent of GDP in 2007).[8] It was precisely the massive inflow of cheap credit to workers with stagnant or falling real wages that fuelled the demand for housing and produced the post-2000 housing bubble. Rising house prices then stimulated further borrowing, as workers began to secure additional loans against their homes. Thus, despite booming house prices, the ratio of homeowners' equity to the value of their household real estate fell from 68 per cent in the 1980s, to 59 per cent in the 1990s, to 57

---

[6] Harvey, *Enigma*, pp. 110–12. In the city especially, enclosure and finance seem to come together, twin scissor blades cutting up the urban fabric, since the sheer scale and duration of privatised urban construction requires that its projects be debt-financed.

[7] Harvey, *Rebel Cities*, pp. 45–47.

[8] John Bellamy Foster and Fred Magdoff, *The Great Financial Crisis: Causes and Consequences* (New York: Monthly Review, 2009), pp. 129–31.

per cent between 2000 and 2005.⁹ During the housing bubble, Annie McClanahan remarks, 'the home no longer gave refuge from the volatility of the market but instead came to symbolise the spectacular magic of speculative investment'.¹⁰

The growing reliance of the American economy on household debt created a situation that banks sought to exploit. Since at least the 1980s, commercial banks had begun to shift their operations towards investment banking, and increasingly drew their profits from fees associated with loan origination and securitisation rather than from interest. As part of this process, banks began to bundle up securities in now-infamous 'collateralised debt obligations' (CDOs): portfolios of prime and subprime mortgage debt, consumer debts, corporate debts, and regular bonds, *inter alia*, which are then sorted into 'tranches' according to their risk (and thus, also, to the investor's reward). CDOs proved immensely profitable and popular, so the banks began to set up their own hedge funds and 'structured investment vehicles' (SIVs) to buy them, while lenders simultaneously generated more such securities by granting mortgages more widely and freely. This expanded lending centred on wealthier, white Americans between 2001 and 2003, but once that market had been exhausted, lenders sought the poorer, Black and Hispanic populations that, deemed 'high risk', had been denied mortgages throughout the twentieth century.¹¹ Far from remedying the injustice, lenders sold many of these poorer homeowners predatory 'adjustable-rate' mortgages, which usually began with a low interest rate for two years and then jumped to unaffordable levels. The crisis began in 2006 when homeowners started to default on their subprime mortgages; then it spread to the prime sector, where rising interest rates and falling house prices caused a wave of additional defaults. The hedge funds and SIVs invested in CDOs lost their money, and, unable to borrow from the money market, sought help from the banks that had set them up. So it was that the banks themselves, who thought they

---

⁹ Foster and Magdoff, pp. 32–33.
¹⁰ Annie McClanahan, *Dead Pledges: Debt, Crisis, and Twenty-First-Century Culture* (Stanford: Stanford University Press, 2017), p. 99.
¹¹ The practice of subprime lending goes back to the 1990s, when the Clinton administration's National Partners in Homeownership initiative prompted financial institutions to start offering mortgages to poorer, marginalised populations. In that decade, the percentage of subprime mortgages granted to those in minority neighbourhoods grew from 2 per cent to 18 per cent (Matthew Hall, Kyle Crowder, and Amy Spring, 'Variations in Housing Foreclosures by Race and Place, 2005–2012', *The Annals of the American Academy of Political and Social Science*, 660 (2015), 217–37 (p. 221)).

had so cleverly contrived to reap profits from CDOs without increasing their liabilities, started to suffer losses, and ceased to trade with each other in the money market. Insolvent and lacking liquidity, many banks themselves collapsed.[12]

Yet it was the working-class American household that paid the highest price. Between 2007 and 2010, annual home foreclosures across the United States increased from around 650,000 to 2.9 million, but they were not evenly distributed, either by location or by the homeowner's race. The Mountain states felt the foreclosure crisis earliest and most acutely: foreclosures began to rise at the end of 2006 from a rate of about 0.2 per 100 homes to more than 0.8 per 100 during 2009 and 2010. By the end of 2012, nearly one in six homes in the Mountain region had been foreclosed on, while approximately one in eight homes in the Pacific region and one in 11 in the South Atlantic region had suffered the same fate. Black and Hispanic homeowners were more likely to be victims of predatory lending practices, more likely to be laid off when the recession hit, and thus, unsurprisingly, more likely than white Americans to lose their homes. The common picture of the crisis as one predominantly afflicting white suburban homeowners or urban minority neighbourhoods is thus not borne out by the data, which suggest that white neighbourhoods had lower foreclosure rates, generally, than Black, racially mixed, and especially Hispanic communities. Black and Hispanic homeowners were already more likely than white ones to enter foreclosure, but at the height of the crisis, the disparities stretched still wider, as Black households became more than twice, and Hispanic households more than three times, as likely to have their properties foreclosed. 'By 2013,' one study concludes, 'about one in thirteen whites had experienced a foreclosure start, more than one in six black homeowners did, and nearly one in four Hispanic homeowners had gone through a foreclosure.'[13]

The home dispossessions consequent on this crisis are conceptually distinct from enclosures, since the houses in question are not thereby constituted, for the first time, as specifically capitalist private property. That being said, foreclosures do enable other, indirect forms of profit-making, in at least two ways. First, because evictions generally devalue

---

[12] I draw here from two complementary accounts published shortly after the irruption of the banking crisis: Costas Lapavitsas, 'Financialised Capitalism: Crisis and Financial Expropriation', *Historical Materialism*, 17.2 (2009), 114–48, and Gary A. Dymski, 'Racial Exclusion and the Political Economy of the Subprime Crisis', *Historical Materialism*, 17.2 (2009), 149–79.

[13] Hall, Crowder, and Spring, p. 233. All the data presented in this paragraph derive from Hall, Crowder, and Spring's study.

the property, they offer those buying foreclosed homes a positive return on their investment. Compounding this, the foreclosure of one property tends to devalue neighbouring ones, pushing other homeowners towards default and opening up further investment opportunities.[14] Second, mortgage lenders make money by charging fees on 'delinquent' loans (those in which the debtor's payments are overdue). They do so, principally, through their own subsidiary companies, which might bill the lender for insurance, appraisals, title searches, or legal services. The lender then passes the cost on to the buyer of the foreclosed property. It follows that a longer period of delinquency, running up ever greater fees, is good for the lender (not to mention that the late fees charged by lenders already typically amount to 6 per cent of monthly payments). It was precisely the profitability of delinquent loans that confounded the Obama administration's 2009 foreclosure-prevention programme, which believed good-hearted lenders simply lacked enough staff to process applications for relief.[15]

Representing Crisis

So much for my own account of the banking and foreclosure crises. How has American cinema presented the relationship between them? Let us consider three documentaries released after 2008. Michael Moore's *Capitalism: A Love Story* (2009) uses 'capitalism' as a heuristic for connecting banking to foreclosure, excess to poverty, though what Moore calls 'capitalism'—what he really abhors—is in fact simply financial deregulation. Thus, despite its emotive images of eviction and worker resistance, Moore's film portrays the crisis as one of American politics, which it takes to be insufficiently democratic, undermined by the alliance of Washington and Wall Street. Moore's 'revolving door' theory of crisis also forms the working hypothesis of Charles Ferguson's *Inside Job* (2010), which focuses on the practices of bankers and traders themselves and their close, too-friendly relationships with economics departments and government. Foreclosure is one regrettable effect of the

---

[14] 'With home prices down more than a third from their peak and the market swamped with foreclosures,' the *New York Times* reported in 2012, 'large investors are salivating at the opportunity to buy perhaps thousands of homes at deep discounts and fill them with tenants' (Motoko Rich, 'Buying Homes by the Thousands: Investors Aim to Stockpile Fixer-Uppers to Fill With Tenants', *New York Times*, 3 April 2012, p. B1).

[15] Peter S. Goodman, 'Late-Fee Profits May Trump Plans to Modify Loans', *New York Times*, 30 July 2009, pp. A1, A3.

crisis, according to *Inside Job*, but it is not the *story* of the crisis, which instead centres on deregulation and greed. *Money for Nothing* (2013), directed by Jim Bruce, takes aim at the Federal Reserve, in particular the low interest rates it set in the 2000s, to which the film attributes the housing bubble and subsequent banking crisis. Bankers, Federal Reserve officials, and economists are the privileged narrators of such a crisis—Bruce interviews no one else—which derives, if *Money for Nothing* is to be believed, from Alan Greenspan's and Ben Bernanke's misjudged monetary policy.

These documentaries' tendency to emphasise the bankers' and politicians' role in the crisis persists in *Too Big to Fail* (2011), Curtis Hanson's television film, which recreates the 2008 negotiations between Henry Paulson (William Hurt), the US Treasury Secretary from 2006 to 2009, and major American investment banks. The narrative unfolds in sumptuous panelled halls and boardrooms, and foreclosure appears only at its conclusion, in the closing titles, which note the insufficiency of the Treasury's cash injection into the banks. Adam McKay's *The Big Short* (2015) tries to bridge the gap between mortgage securitisation and foreclosure by explaining the complexities of the former to those who might have been vulnerable to the latter. That is, while the film looks at the world of banking—albeit askance, from the perspective of those 'outsiders' who foresaw, and profited from, the failure of the market for mortgage-backed securities—it interpellates its viewer as an ordinary American homeowner, whose financial activity is the object of the bankers' dealings, but who equally finds themselves alienated from such dealings by financial jargon. Foreclosure itself appears in *The Big Short* briefly: first, when the employees of the FrontPoint Partners hedge fund visit Florida to meet those at risk of being foreclosed on, and, second, during the photo montages between scenes, which include pictures of foreclosed properties.

Hanson's and McKay's films purport to portray things more or less truthfully (and *The Big Short* takes some pleasure in it: 'Mark Baum really did that,' Jared Vennett (Ryan Gosling) says, turning to camera, after Baum (Steve Carrell) challenges a speaker at a business forum), but the years following the crisis also saw the release of several fiction films, centred on Wall Street, in which the correspondence between characters and investors is no longer straightforward, one-to-one. Oliver Stone's *Wall Street: Money Never Sleeps* (2010)—a sequel to Stone's 1987 *Wall Street*—takes place around the financial crisis, and like many of the films and documentaries surveyed above, depicts it as primarily a banking failure, some of its fictional financiers, most notably Louis Zabel (Frank Langella), having invested in subprime loans. Filial relations connect the banking crisis to foreclosure: the film's protagonist, stock trader Jake Moore (Shia LeBoeuf), glimpses this second dimension of the crisis through his mother, who has invested in several properties but cannot keep up with payments, and who periodically comes to him looking for money. *Margin Call* (2011), an independent film directed by J. C. Chandor, takes place almost entirely in the offices of its unnamed investment bank (likely an allegory for Goldman Sachs and Lehman Brothers), whose risk managers are only just beginning to appreciate the scale of their toxic-asset problem. While, in many of the abovementioned films, it falls upon the conscientious banker or trader to articulate the stakes of their financial failure for the ordinary person (Paulson does this in *Too Big to Fail*, Baum and Ben Rickert (Brad Pitt) in *The Big Short*), here we have the opposite: a trader, Will Emerson (Paul Bettany), who, arguing that the availability of credit, thus of cars and homes, to American consumers depends on investment banking, denies those consumers his sympathy. 'They only reason that they all get to continue living like kings is because we've got our fingers on the scales in their favour,' Emerson says, before concluding: 'Fuck normal people.'

The fraudulent or unwise banker thus garners much attention in post-2008 American cinema, but at least two films buck the trend and offer the dispossessed representation.[16] Sam Raimi's 2009 horror film *Drag Me to Hell* dramatises the conflict between Christine Brown (Alison Lohman), a loan officer working at Wilshire Pacific Financial Centre, and Sylvia Ganush (Lorna Raver), an elderly client whose entreaties for an extension to her mortgage Brown rejects, thinking this will curry favour with her boss. Ganush curses Brown, who is then pursued, and eventually claimed, by an evil spirit called the Lamia, the debtor's answer to the sorceries of speculation and securitisation, which appear to summon profits *ex nihilo*.[17] Ramin Bahrani's *99 Homes* (2014) lingers still longer on the foreclosed home and evicted family. *99 Homes* tells

---

[16] To be clear, I am not criticising the above-discussed films, on an individual basis, for focusing on finance rather than foreclosure. Neither the post-2006 wave of foreclosures nor the 2007–08 banking collapse is the true locus of the crisis, which (as we saw in Chapter 1) lies instead in the contradiction between the imperative to produce surplus-value and the limits of the market—that is, in the problematic of overaccumulation. My claim here is simply that the discrepant temporalities and iconographies of the two dimensions of the crisis generate a representational challenge for filmmakers who wish to give an account of it. For ease of narrative continuity, then, many of them choose to focus on one side rather than the other.

[17] For a reading of *Drag Me to Hell* as a critique of mortgage securitisation, see McClanahan, pp. 163–69.

the story of Dennis Nash (Andrew Garfield), a construction worker whose last job fell through mid-build, when the lender funding the project cut their finance. Unable to keep up with his own mortgage, Nash, his mother, and his son are evicted from his home by real-estate broker Rick Carver (Michael Shannon), who then employs Nash to fix up the foreclosed homes that he is hoping to sell on. The function of *99 Homes* is documentary, even didactic: by following Nash's descent into the underworld of real-estate brokerage, we learn how the latter generates its profits. The business of foreclosure is as fraudulent here as that of mortgage securitisation is, emphatically, for most of the other films about the crisis.

Vanishing Mediators

Repo Men counts, along with *99 Homes*, as one of the few post-2008 American films to focus on the work of dispossession itself. On the most basic level, *Repo Men* might be read as a response to an actual expansion of the American debt-collection business, which, tracking rising household debt in the 1990s and 2000s, grew from around 12 firms in 1996 to more than 500 by 2005.[18] The film begins with one such firm, The Union, loaning its desperate customers exorbitant new artificial organs ('artiforgs') at soaring interest rates. 'You owe it to your family. You owe it to yourself,' Frank Mercer (Liev Schreiber), the Union's manager, tells customers concerned about the 19.6 per cent APR. Mimicking the economics of mortgage lending, which (as we have already seen) generates profits precisely in and through delinquent loans, Frank tells Remy (Jude Law), one his 'repo men', that customers who pay in full are unprofitable. By repossessing organs, Remy and his fellow debt collector Jake (Forest Whitaker) reclaim, at low cost, expensive artiforgs that the company can sell again at full price, profiting doubly.

Convinced by Frank (who is anything but), the unhappy buyer signs. The first half of *Repo Men* thus shows us, in contrast with Frank's platitudes and reassurances, the bloody process of repossession, as Remy travels across the city to reclaim overdue body parts from the Union's debtors. Yet Remy is not without his own problems: Carol (Carice van Houten), his wife, has been pushing him to move from repossession to sales, where he will work shorter hours. Remy eventually accedes to Carol's demands, but not before completing one last job: the repossession of Jimmy T-Bone's (RZA) heart. Jake is determined to stop his childhood

---

[18] Foster and Magdoff, pp. 34–35.

friend from transferring out of repo, so he rigs the defibrillator Remy will use on T-Bone, and the machine backfires, knocking Remy out. When Remy wakes, he finds Frank and Jake smiling by his bedside, the two of them having taken the liberty to loan him a new heart.

Unable to pay his organ debt through a mere sales job, and unwilling to continue repossessing others' artiforgs, Remy soon falls overdue and takes flight. He befriends Beth (Alice Braga), a singer whose body mostly comprises overdue organs, and concocts an elaborate plan to wipe not only her debt but indeed all organ debt. Remy and Beth succeed, and their story ends happily on a white beach, where Jake appears to have joined them. But if this denouement seems a little too clean for a film that spends much of its time conjuring the goriness of organ removal, that is because it is. In reality, Jake bludgeons the delinquent Remy into a vegetative state, and *Repo Men* concludes with Jake paying up front for Remy's heart and the M.5 Neural Net, a Union product that allows the brain-damaged Remy to dream a computer-generated dream. His and Beth's overthrow of the Union, we learn, was one such dream.

Repo Men's premise, it need scarcely be noted, is that the human body has quite literally become commodified, with organs available on credit.[19] 'My job is simple,' Remy explains in his voiceover at the start of the film. 'Can't pay for your car? The bank takes it back. Can't pay for your house? The bank takes it back.' Just as reasonably, it follows, the bank reserves the right to take back your artiforgs. When the tables have turned and Remy finds himself pursued, he calls the repo man coming for him a 'landlord' and affirms the continuity, in *Repo Men*'s diegetic world, between the body and real estate (though in this particular framing Remy has become a tenant rather than a homeowner). At other moments, the repossession of organ and home seem to go together. When Remy compliments T-Bone's mansion, the musician responds that it 'ain't really mine no more'. The implication, of course, is that T-Bone is mired in other debts too, a substantial portion of which he has secured against his house.

In fact, the relation drawn in the film between organ repossession and home foreclosure is already implicit in the term 'mortgage' itself, a French word that literally means 'dead pledge'. 'As collateral for a loan,' McClanahan notes, unpacking the term, and prompting us to think about the uncanniness of the mortgaged home,

---

[19] *Repo Men* thus both nods to, and goes beyond, the 1984 film *Repo Man* (directed by Alex Cox), whose debt-collecting protagonist, Otto Maddox (Emilio Estevez), works for a car repossession firm.

property could be either 'dead' to the lender, if the loan was paid, or 'dead' to the borrower, if he defaulted. What this etymology suggests is that the house has a kind of liminal status while the loan is still owed; neither living nor dead, the mortgaged home has a strange ontology. The dead pledge of the mortgage defamiliarizes domestic space, which instead of being a place of comfort and security becomes a space of unease and alienation.[20]

What at first seems an analogy—Remy's equation of car and home repossession with organ extraction—is rather a simple transferral of epithet, as the death of the home to the delinquent borrower becomes, with the tweak of the taser and the application of the scalpel, the death of the borrower in their home (which is then, *ispo facto*, suddenly no longer their home). Remy's voiceover began with an account of Schrödinger's cat, and the latter finds its allegorical purpose in this context: the dead-and-alive cat mimics the status of the mortgaged house, which too is 'neither living nor dead', but somehow both at the same time.

Repo Men plays with, and thereby thematises, the above-discussed question of perspective: from whose point of view can (and should) the crisis of foreclosure be narrated? When we first hear Remy's voiceover, we think him to be speaking as a Union employee who identifies on some level with his company's ethos, such that his car–house–body comparison seems an attempt to justify repossessions of the last. Only later, when we learn that Remy is in hiding, and spends his time novelising his experiences, do we realise that his voiceover, and the story it tells (the film's first embedded narrative), comes from the position of one of the Union's debtors, someone threatened by the foreclosure of their organs. Remy's voiceover is not a promotion or justification but rather a grim, sardonic description of the 'repossession mambo'—the victim's vain resistance, prior to the extraction of their organs, that forms the title of his novel (and is in fact the title of Eric Garcia's 2009 novel, from which the film derives). The employee is always already the dispossessed, *Repo Men* thus seems to suggest: the former's identification with their job is contingent, and means nothing to capital, which cares more for the interest payments and the profits to be made from repossession than it does for the individual. Remy and Jake perform such indifference themselves: 'A job's a job,' they repeat during their shifts, a mantra that registers the contingent relation between the proletarian and the line of work into which they happen, temporarily, to have fallen.

---

[20] McClanahan, pp. 126–27.

Yet Remy and Jake's job is not a typical job. It occupies, rather, a symbolically significant position within the circuits of capital accumulation. From the perspective of valorisation (and as we saw in the previous chapter), the production process appears as 'a necessary evil for the purpose of money-making'. Capitalists cannot simply buy cheap and sell dear, but must rather employ workers who generate, through their labour-time, more value than they receive in wages. Yet the figure of interest perpetuates the fantasy of pure, production-less accumulation: the bank lends out money, and a year later, as if by magic, a slightly larger sum returns. It is in this context that the repo-man character-type must be read, as their very existence attests to the material difficulties, the impasses attendant on making profit—which must, after all, come from somewhere—without employing proletarians. What the film calls the 'repossession mambo'—the dance of two bodies as the repo man tries to subdue the writhing, resisting debtor—is simply an aestheticised corporeal expression of such difficulties. *Repo Men*'s body horror also becomes comprehensible in this light: the sheer violence of each extraction puts blockages in accumulation (here, a debtor's non-payment) in visceral terms. The straightforward removal of the organ, which is not replaced, and which leaves a hole in the victim, punishes the debtor's body by allegorising precisely those holes or breaks in circulation that their unpaid debt creates.

The repo man always wins the struggle, and capital claims what it is due. The confirmation of this, *Repo Men*'s ultimately pessimistic message, is the purpose of the film's second embedded narrative, which begins at the climax of Remy's 'mambo' with Jake. In reality, Jake defeats Remy by striking him over the head with an industrial metal hook, but, after a volley of out-of-sequence flashbacks (which we take to signify Remy's brief unconsciousness), we see Beth picking Remy up, the latter apparently having resisted his repo man. The film convinces us that Remy's is a happy ending, where he, Beth, and Jake escape the forces of capital and wind up on the beautiful beach. The shattering of the illusion, which occurs when the neural net glitches and Jake vanishes from his deckchair, is then equally the viewer's realisation that capital has again been victorious. *Repo Men* tests, even mocks our credulity. Did we really think that love and friendship (and some nifty combat skills) would overcome the compulsions of capital accumulation?[21] As if to stress the

---

[21] In her review of *Repo Men*, Sherryl Vint reads the second embedded narrative as a critique of Hollywood itself, and particularly of the latter's tendency to represent the hero's victory over an oppressive system ('*Repo Men*', *Science Fiction Film and Television*, 4.2 (2011), 306–9 (pp. 307–8)). We

point, the film then shows Jake using his commission to pay for Remy's neural net and new heart so as to sustain him in his vegetative state, Remy having acquired the same dead-and-alive status as Schrödinger's cat (and the mortgaged property). In the process, Remy's debts shift onto Jake's shoulders. The neural net will keep Remy happy, the technician reassures Jake, 'as long as someone's paying for the system'.

Capital typically justifies such repossessions with the fiction that the worker's purchase, thus their entry into debt, is free and willed, such that they might then justly be punished if they buy more than they can afford. Much like *The Matrix* and *District 9*, however, *Repo Men* thematises the purely formal character of such freedom. Two moments stand out on this point. First, during *Repo Men*'s exposition, we watch Frank persuade a potential customer, who needs a new pancreas but seems concerned about the interest rate, to agree to the Union's predatory terms. Remy is looking on, and his voiceover puts it bluntly: 'He'll sign it. Everybody signs it.' Frank's appeals to familial duty are too powerful to resist, the market here no longer that 'Eden of the innate rights of man' where people meet and decide, freely and equally, on the terms of their exchange.[22] 'We want them buying, not thinking!' Frank reminds Remy shortly afterwards. Second, when, having gone 96 days delinquent on their loan, the debtor finds themselves confronted by a repo man, the latter must (by law) remind them of their right to have an ambulance on standby during the extraction. Because debtors tend to resist such repossession, the repo man often stuns them and reads out their rights while they are incapacitated. The debtor is not really free to decide, and no ambulance is called. The exception is Remy's repossession of T-Bone's artificial heart, when, accepting his fate, T-Bone yields willingly to Remy, such that he is in fact awake to hear his rights read. As Remy informs him, however, T-Bone's credit history means that the hospital would not give him a new heart anyway. He can ask for an ambulance, but his decision makes no difference: it is an empty, merely formal gesture.

find the same idea in *Total Recall*, which teases us with the possibility that Schwarzenegger's heroics, saving the oppressed human populace on Mars, might likewise be part of a dream.

[22] Jake's own stated opinion contradicts this: he confers responsibility on the debtor and, moreover, a parallel responsibility on those paid to chase the debt. 'What do you think keeps a world like this's shit together?' he asks Remy. 'It's not magic. It's not. It's rules. It's people abiding by the terms of the deals that they've signed themselves. It's rules. You know what's more important than rules, though? It's the enforcement of those rules. We've got a responsibility, you and me.'

Geographically, the metropolitan centre serves as the arena for most of Remy's and Jake's repossessions. Cruising through the streets in Remy's black SUV, the pair point their artiforg scanner at the city's passers-by and threaten those who have fallen behind on their payments. Yet if downtown is the repo man's playground, repossession in the white, middle-class suburb is a different affair. When, during a work barbeque hosted at Remy's house, Jake extracts a debtor's organs out the front, Carol catches him and, disgusted, takes their son, Peter (Chandler Canterbury), from the house. 'I went as fast as I could, man,' Jake says to Remy: organ repossession, which repo men threaten freely and publicly in the city, becomes illicit in white suburbia. What is notable here is that Carol objects not to the organ extraction (and its attendant grotesquerie) but rather to the intrusion of Remy's work into the domestic sphere. Carol has already voiced her annoyance with Remy's long, irregular hours and urged him to transfer to sales, where he will earn less but work 9 to 5. So it is that the problems of dispossession represented in *Repo Men*'s metropolitan spaces yield, in the suburb, to a set of different but not unrelated economic questions, principally regarding 'work–life balance'.

Carol's indifference to the bloodshed itself, the gore and violence constitutive of her husband's labour, might be understood simply as the film's means of emphasising the degree to which organ repossession has become naturalised, accepted as an ordinary event, in its speculative United States. But the response can also be read another way, as a means of reassuring us that foreclosure belongs downtown, in the metropolitan centre, and not white suburbia. That Carol's indifference signifies both things at the same time derives, I think, from a split within the film itself, visible particularly in how it constructs and contrasts city and suburb. The city, we note, is portrayed at night, and recapitulates *Blade Runner*'s urban aesthetic (noted in the previous chapter): crowded, dark, steamy, vertical, Orientalised. Such worldbuilding is highly derivative, but it at least serves to stress, by extrapolation, and as it does in *Blade Runner*, capital's ever deeper penetration into the urban fabric, and thus the centrality of urbanism to capital accumulation. The American suburb, on the other hand, has undergone no such transformation: it looks more or less the same in the film's 2025 as it does in the viewer's 2010. The marks of technological change wrought across the metropolitan centre, where all that is holy has well and truly been profaned, vanish in the suburb, which appears to have enjoyed shelter from such processes. In this context, it is quite plausible that Carol's indifference to the violence of organ repossession suggests less the naturalisation of that violence, more its irrelevance to the white suburb, whose fences keep the vicissitudes of capital accumulation at bay.[23]

The suburb thus marks *Repo Men*'s ideological limits, the place where its criticisms of dispossession disappear, leaving behind only an affirmation of the longevity of white, middle-class suburbia. Though it mocks us for believing that that Remy's beach holiday is real, that he really did manage to destroy the system, the film's construction of the suburb suggests that the family home is the true holiday, the 'life' outside of labour that ought to be balanced, correctly, with work. Falling deeper into debt and resolving to take the sales job, Remy returns home to explain the situation to Carol. Unlike Remy's previous visit, where Sapochnik's camera alternated between a shot from Remy's perspective outside the door and a counter-shot from Carol's just inside, now we see things from Remy's exterior point of view alone.[24] Silent, Carol hands Remy a letter marked 'Past Due'. That 'something changed', as Remy puts it, does not matter: Carol's cold look blames him for his delinquency. Refinancing the house to pay off the debt—a trick employed by many of the film's American viewers in the years leading up to its release—does not seem to be an option. In fact, the opposite occurs: burdened with debt, Remy is banished from the house and seems to lose his property right therein. When Carol holds the letter through the doorway, she rejects the debt-relation as such, wards off the threat of dispossession and repossession. No longer some 'dead pledge' haunted by the prospect of foreclosure, the suburban house reassumes its prior status as a shelter from the market's volatility, ground zero of the American dream.[25]

---

[23] In her review, Vint argues that *Repo Men* 'is on the right topic for effective satire but too often succumbs to the pleasures of spectacle, losing track of their context' ('*Repo Men*', p. 306). *Pace* Vint, I would suggest that it is precisely where that spectacle, and the science-fictional processes of extrapolation driving it, end—in the suburb—that its satire falters.

[24] Between these two visits, Remy attempts a repossession in the suburbs, but fails, the suburb offering a kind of resistance to such action. Another failed repossession, Remy's attempt to reclaim T-Bone's artificial heart, also seems to take place outside the city centre (though geographical markers in the vicinity of T-Bone's mansion are scarce).

[25] As George W. Bush put it, 'Right here in America if you own your own home, you're realizing the American Dream' ('President Calls for Expanding Opportunities to Home Ownership', 17 June 2002 <https://georgewbush-whitehouse.archives.gov/news/releases/2002/06/20020617-2.html> [accessed 17 May 2022] (para. 21 of 47)).

A Model Household

> America was collapsing. A quadruple-dip recession followed by a full market crash. A skyrocketing debt, multiple wars, and a significant dollar devaluation, all precipitating the worst economic disaster in the history of the United States. Crime and poverty rose exponentially, and the New Founding Fathers, just months after being elected, came up with this audacious notion: the decriminalisation of murder for one night—a lawful outlet for American rage.

So the newsreader tells us at the commencement of the Purge of 2022, recounted in the first film of the series, titled simply *The Purge*. In fact, murder is only one of the freedoms that the Purge permits, since, for the 12 hours in which it takes place, *anything* goes. Police, fire, and medical services stand down, and the American people act as they wish, unconstrained by American laws. *The Purge*, the first narration of the event (though *The First Purge* (2018), a later film, recounts an earlier Purge), centres on the Sandin family, who, ensconced in an apparently neighbourly gated community, expect an uneventful and safe Purge night. The patriarch, James Sandin (Ethan Hawke), returns home from work an hour or so before the Purge commences, and he brings some good news: his division has sold the most upgraded security systems. The Sandins' home being protected by one of these systems, James and his wife Mary (Lena Headey) reassure their children, Zoey (Adelaide Kane) and Charlie (Max Burkholder), as the Purge begins, that they have nothing to fear. Of course, when expressed in Hollywood horror films, such reassurances are false *a priori*: during the original *Purge* film, no fewer than four different individuals or groups enter the Sandin mansion. Zoey's boyfriend, Henry (Tony Oller), sneaks in to murder her father, who disapproves of their relationship, and ends up killing Henry. The Bloody Stranger (Edwin Hodge), a homeless Black man fleeing a group of white hunters, gains entry after Charlie disables the security system for him. The hunting party demands the Stranger's release, and when the Sandins (eventually) refuse, force their own entry. Finally, the Sandins' neighbours, who had wished them a safe night only a few hours before, kill off the hunters in order to claim the Sandins as their own. James dies at the hands of the lead hunter, but the Stranger repays the Sandins by saving Mary and her children from the neighbours.

As the above-quoted newsreader suggests, the Purge is a policy response to economic crisis, a 'quadruple-dip recession followed by a full market crash'. That this recession, like 2007–08, also included a subprime mortgage crisis we do not learn until *The First Purge*, yet the context of foreclosure remains relevant to the original *Purge* film. Crucially, when the hunters confront James at his door, and their leader makes a point of mentioning that the stranger to whom they have given sanctuary is homeless, the Stranger begins to occupy, symbolically, the place of the evicted Black homeowner, who was, as we have seen, more likely to have experienced foreclosure than white Americans. In sheltering in their house and thereby passing the risk of his death on to the Sandins, moreover, the Stranger stands for precisely those 'subprime' borrowers whose foreclosures set off the nationwide run of property devaluations that caused, in turn, the dispossession of many 'prime' borrowers too. It is significant that the home security systems on which James has built his wealth—and which have paid for the Sandins' recent home extension, as we find out at the beginning of *The Purge*—seem to be largely psychological in their effects: James reveals that their defence systems are mainly deterrents, and a sufficiently determined purger seeking entry to their home can breach them. James, as well as the many neighbours to whom he has sold his system, quite literally enjoys a false sense of security on Purge night. 'Things like this are not supposed to happen in our neighbourhood,' James—instantiating the 'prime' homeowner who thought themselves safe from 'financial expropriation'—curses when things start to go wrong.[26]

Yet the Stranger is not the first intruder in the Sandin home. His escape from the street into the house is intercut with events unfolding simultaneously in Zoey's bedroom, back into which Henry had snuck before James activated the security system. At this moment the gendered dynamics of subprime lending come into view. Henry reassures Zoey that he simply wishes to talk to her father, who disapproves of their age difference; but really he is out for blood, so he heads to the top of the spiral staircase, whence he intends to shoot James. However, James has just unholstered his own gun to defend his family from the Stranger, whom Charlie allowed through the front door. James spins around and, shooting and killing Henry, reasserts his paternal authority against the boyfriend who sought to challenge it. If Henry's function in the film is therefore to emphasise, by his defeat, James's paternal guardianship, the Stranger's simultaneous entry represents a feminisation, as his ingress prompts that very guardianship, and he then benefits from it. Repeating this gendering, James later tells the Stranger that he can 'die like a man' if, rather than endangering the Sandins by remaining inside, he leaves

---

[26] On the foreclosure crisis as a form of 'financial expropriation', see Lapavitsas, pp. 130–31.

voluntarily to confront the hunters himself. The moment he occupies a home he could never afford and begins to benefit from its protection, then, the Stranger is feminised, and fits even closer the profile of the typical 'subprime' homeowner.[27]

The Stranger's gendering as male but feminised carries over into the film's dual construction of his Blackness as defencelessness and danger. On the one hand, as we have just seen, the Stranger is a fugitive in the Sandins' home and seeks cover in its darkness (the power having been cut by his pursuers). On the other, without warning, his vulnerability flips into terror, as he suddenly emerges from that darkness with a gun to Zoey's head, demands that the Sandins protect him, and thus makes her survival contingent on his own. Initially James refuses and, with some help from Mary, manages to free Zoey from the Stranger's grip. Yet it is Zoey who then prompts her parents' change of heart: 'Look at what you're doing,' she utters as James and Mary bind the Stranger in preparation for returning him to his hunters. It is crucial that Zoey urges her parents to 'look': the house's darkness at this point is meant to symbolise the lapsing of their judgement, their moral blindness, while the subsequent lighting of it (diegetically, by the purgers' bright spotlights from outside) signifies a renewed clarity, as the Sandins accept the Stranger as one of their own and fight off the white supremacists (from whom they have now been safely distinguished). The film exploits the Stranger's skin pigmentation for its continuity with the darkness, and transfers the vulnerability and danger associated with the Stranger onto the darkness itself—which then becomes, as it were, an extension of his skin—while the Sandins are not only white but all wear white (James, Zoey, and Charlie have white shirts, while Mary changes into white trousers). *The Purge* thus constructs blackness, both as skin colour and as absence of light, as ambivalence—danger and vulnerability, in the face of which white morality loses its bearings—while light and whiteness guarantee clarity, resolve, and unity.

If the Sandin home functions as a site on which the gendered and racialised character of the foreclosure crisis can be played out, it also seems to allegorise the economy itself. In the wake of the crisis, as the United States (and many other Western nations besides)

---

[27] 'Despite higher credit scores,' Amy Castro Baker observes, 'single female homeowners are overrepresented among subprime mortgage holders by 29.1 percent, and African American women in particular are 256 percent more likely to have a subprime mortgage than a white man with the same financial profile' ('Eroding the Wealth of Women: Gender and the Subprime Foreclosure Crisis', *Social Service Review*, 88.1 (2014), 59–91 (pp. 61–62)).

embraced austerity—economic policy geared towards reducing budget deficits, often by cutting public spending—American politicians began to speak of the economy as though it were a household, its income and expenditure independent of one another.[28] 'Families across the country are tightening their belts and making tough decisions,' Obama said in 2010. 'The federal government should do the same [...] Like any cash-strapped family, we will work within a budget to invest in what we need and sacrifice what we don't.'[29] The 'household fallacy' (as it has subsequently been called) came under fire from Keynesians in particular, who argue that expenditure (on, say, infrastructure projects) can in fact boost government income (through higher tax receipts) and create a 'multiplier effect', raising the economy from the doldrums.[30] 'Why is austerity in a depressed economy a bad idea?' Paul Krugman, one of America's foremost Keynesians, recently asked. He answered: 'Because an economy is not like a household, whose income and spending are separate things. In the economy as a whole, my spending is your income and your spending is my income.'[31]

It is in this context that the second assault on the Sandin household, the neighbours' efforts to kill the Sandins, gains its significance. What has annoyed the neighbours, apparently, is their discovery that expenditure in one place is income in another, as the money they spent buying James's security systems has turned into the Sandins' new extension. 'Some people are saying that this neighbourhood paid for that new addition on your home,' Grace Ferrin (Arija Bareikis) tells Mary at the start of the film. Later on, when the neighbours capture the Sandins, Grace reiterates the point and reveals that she is one such envious neighbour: 'You made so much money off of us and then you just stuck it in our faces.' Like good Keynesians, stimulating economic activity, the Sandins are not tightening their belts but looking to expand their conspicuous consumption. At the beginning of the Purge, Mary and James find peace in the pages of the catalogue, as Mary leafs

---

[28] On the history of austerity as concept and practice in the United States, see Richard McGahey, 'The Political Economy of Austerity in the United States', *Social Research*, 80.3 (2013), 717–48.

[29] Barack Obama, 'Remarks by the President in State of the Union Address', 27 January 2010 <https://obamawhitehouse.archives.gov/the-press-office/remarks-president-state-union-address> [accessed 17 May 2022] (para. 68 of 110).

[30] Roger E. A. Farmer and Pawel Zabczyk coined the term in 'The Household Fallacy', *Economics Letters*, 169 (2018), 83–86.

[31] Paul Krugman, 'The Legacy of Destructive Austerity', *New York Times*, 30 December 2019, p. A18.

through a homeware brochure while James looks at yachts on his tablet. '10 years ago, we could barely afford rent,' James reflects. 'Now we're thinking about buying a boat. Crazy.' The Sandin household is less the austerian 'household' model of the economy than it is the Keynesian one, and allegorises, in the transformation of others' expenditure into their income, the flow of value through the economy as a whole.

Extending the Keynesian inclinations of the original *Purge* film, the later instalments in the series increasingly define the Purge itself as a form of austerity: a means of cutting back on public expenditure by eliminating those citizens most dependent on it. In *Anarchy* (2014), watching a video posted online by an anti-Purge protest group, in which Carmelo Johns (Michael Kenneth Williams) asserts that it is the poor who die on Purge night, Cali Sanchez (Zoë Soul) explains to her grandfather that this is the intended outcome, engineered for fiscally conservative reasons: 'They're keeping the population down by getting rid of people like us to save money.' Dante Bishop—who we met as the Bloody Stranger in *The Purge*—makes the same point in *Election Year* (2016): 'For the past 20 years, the NFFA [New Founding Fathers of America] has taken to legalised murder to decrease the poor population, which, in turn, keeps the government spending down— less welfare, less healthcare, less housing.' These critiques of the New Founding Fathers are, of course, correct, verified in *The First Purge* by Arlo Sabian (Patch Darragh), the NFFA Chief of Staff. 'This country is overpopulated, Doctor,' he says to the behavioural scientist shocked at the NFFA's manipulation of her Purge experiment. 'There's too much crime, too much unemployment, and a bankrupt government that can't afford to care for its own citizenry. People don't want us to raise taxes? Our debt has tripled. We can't pay for anything.'

As the series proceeds, the *Purge* films bind this austerian economic ideology ever more tightly into various threads of contemporary Republicanism. In *Election Year*—released in 2016, an actual election year, in which American voters chose between Hillary Clinton and Donald Trump—the New Founding Fathers become associated with evangelical Christianity (their candidate for the election, Edwidge Owens (Kyle Secor), being a minister reportedly based on Ted Cruz, the Republican Senator for Texas),[32] while the Purge generates profit (so its detractors claim) for the National Rifle Association and insurance companies. The

---

[32] Alex Godfrey, 'Making America Gory Again: How the *Purge* Films Troll Trumpism', *The Guardian*, 4 July 2018 <https://www.theguardian.com/film/2018/jul/04/how-the-purge-trolls-trumps-america-jason-blum-first-purge> [accessed 17 May 2022] (para. 7 of 16).

mercenaries the NFFA hires to kill their rival candidate, Charlie Roan (Elizabeth Mitchell)—an independent whose states are nonetheless coloured blue on the electoral map, and who seems to stand fairly straightforwardly for Clinton—are white supremacists bearing the words 'white power' and Confederate and Nazi insignias on their uniforms.[33] These allegorical elements become more or less explicit in the promotion for the next film, 2018's *The First Purge*, one of whose posters portrayed, against a white backdrop, a simple red cap emblazoned with the words 'The First Purge', a reference to the red 'Make America Great Again' hats associated with Trump and his supporters. Unbeknown, presumably, to Trump's campaign team, their 2020 slogan—'Keep America Great'—also happened to be the tagline of *The First Purge*.

Crucially, at least as regards any evaluation of the *Purge* films' utopianism, *Election Year* represents the ballot box as the proper place of social change. From its very beginning, the film's Black characters articulate their scepticism of American politicians. While discussing the forthcoming election, for instance, Joe Dixon (Mykelti Williamson) warns his employee Marcos Dali (Joseph Julian Soria) that 'hope can lead to a lot of let-down', a thinly veiled criticism of Obama, who ran under the slogan 'Hope' in 2008. Later on, Laney Rucker (Betty Gabriel) derides politicians as 'goddamned conniving, duplicitous, crooked, cocksucking'. Senator Roan, who sits next to Rucker, takes the point, but adds that not all politicians are 'that bad'. Laney replies, 'My experience, Senator? My people are on their own, no matter what y'all say or promise.' Yet *Election Year* gives voice to this discontent in order to disprove it—to raise the white woman's assertion above Black experience. The film suggests that the direct action planned by Bishop (namely, killing members of the NFFA on Purge night) will delegitimise their valid political cause. 'I need to win this thing fair and fucking square,' Roan asserts when she learns that Bishop's forces plan to kill Owens. 'If they assassinate him,' she adds later, 'he becomes a martyr. We lose.' When Bishop and Roan meet at the church, Bishop initially disregards her warning—'If you do this, you will be no different than them'—but when Owens implores Bishop to kill him and Bishop realises that he is simply carrying out NFFA

---

[33] *Election Year*'s depiction of Confederacy supporters brings us back, full circle, to the original *Purge* film. As Craig A. Warren points out, *The Purge* belongs to a cycle of films released around the sesquicentennial of the American Civil War (from 2011 to 2015). *The Purge* counts among such films, Warren argues, because it recalls the Fugitive Slave Act of 1850, which mandates that fugitive slaves (for which the Stranger stands, symbolically) be returned to their owners. See Warren, 'Patriotism as Institutional Racism: *The Purge* and the Fugitive Slave Act', *Film and History*, 50.1 (2020), 29–40.

policy, he backs down, allowing Owens to contest the election. Roan's subsequent victory vindicates her electoralism and prompts a change in the previously sceptical Black characters' attitudes. The morning after the election, Laney walks into Joe's shop (now owned by Marcos) and smiles when she learns that Roan has won, her critique of professional politics having apparently been answered. Hope, the film suggests, need *not* lead to 'a lot of let-down'.

Yet this hope is ultimately anti-utopian in character—a phenomenon that should warn us against treating utopianism as merely an expression of hope—not least because the victory of the good politician, Roan (that is, Clinton), constitutes its happy ending, and thus offers a qualified defence of the American political system. In the domain of economics, correlatively, *The Purge* and its prequel and sequels are anti-austerity—the Purge being represented as the austerian policy par excellence—but do not elaborate this into a more thoroughgoing anticapitalism. While the Purge permits all crime, 'including murder' (as the broadcast stresses), the purgers behave as though murder were previously the only prohibition, and thus that private property has an extra-legal, transcendental status in this diegetic world, much as it seems to in the *Repo Men* suburb. Larceny is completely absent from the first *Purge* film and appears only sporadically in later instalments, in which murder, or the threat thereof, drives the plot.[34] For the *Purge* films—to invoke the oft-quoted characterisation of capitalist realism that will be our subject in the Conclusion—it is easier to imagine an apocalyptic war of all on all than even a temporary abrogation of private property rights.

---

[34] References to and representations of theft are occasional and ornamental. In *Anarchy*, the business district is empty, the banks having moved out their money. Passing through the district, the group encounter, strung up from the front of a bank, a murdered stockbroker who had stolen pension money. In *Election Year*, two young women try to pilfer some candy from Joe's store (though this happens before the Purge begins). And in *The First Purge*, a man attempts to break open an ATM, but is then promptly murdered.

Conclusion

Negation
Capitalism at the End of the World

November 2009 saw the publication by the newly established imprint Zer0 Books of a slim volume titled, provocatively, *Capitalist Realism: Is There No Alternative?* The book's author, Mark Fisher, was one of Zer0's founders; the other, his friend and colleague Tariq Goddard, had asked him to write something for Zer0, whose mission statement took aim at 'the informal censorship propagated by the cultural workers of late capitalism', this having generated 'a banal conformity that the propaganda chiefs of Stalinism could only have dreamt of imposing'.[1] Fisher's book was accordingly to break through the climate of intellectual stagnation. Preparing his manuscript in the evening or at weekends, Fisher collated much of the material for *Capitalist Realism* from his blog, *k-punk*, which he wrote while he worked as a philosophy lecturer at a Further Education college in Kent, in the United Kingdom.[2] As such, *Capitalist Realism* carries over the blog's eclecticism, and jumps from Marxist and psychoanalytic theory to pop culture and parliamentary politics and back again. What the book adds to the blogs is an organising concept, 'capitalist realism', and an overarching argument: that it is no longer possible even to imagine an alternative to capitalism.

I first encountered *Capitalist Realism* in 2016, on the recommendation of a colleague, shortly after I had started research on this project.

---

[1] 'Zer0 Books Statement', in *k-punk: The Collected and Unpublished Writings of Mark Fisher (2004–2016)*, ed. by Darren Ambrose (London: Repeater, 2018), p. 103.

[2] '[P]art of what Zer0 was about was harvesting the work that has been developed on the blog networks. Zer0 is about establishing a para-space, between theory and popular culture, between cyberspace and the university' (Mark Fisher, 'They Can Be Different in the Future Too: Interviewed by Rowan Wilson for *Ready Steady Book*', in *k-punk*, ed. by Ambrose, pp. 627–36 (p. 630)). Fisher and Goddard would later leave Zer0 to set up Repeater Books.

Fisher's thesis about the rise of capitalist realism, the stultification of the anti- or post-capitalist imagination, had become quite well known in British academia by then, and soon it begin to guide my own thinking. My suggestion here that Hollywood's science-fiction films turned away from utopia in the 1990s owes much to Fisher's periodisation, according to which the collapse of really existing socialism, the exhaustion of modernism, and the universalisation of capitalism sapped even the increasingly limited critical energies of much popular culture produced in the Reagan–Thatcher period.[3] The post-2000 dystopias I have discussed in Chapters 5 and 6, in which the utopian critique of private property seems to have more or less disappeared, would seem to corroborate such a thesis.

Returning to Fisher's book now, however, I cannot help but wonder whether there is something at stake in his describing this phenomenon as 'realism' rather than, as I have preferred in the preceding chapters, 'anti-utopianism'. What does Fisher mean by 'realism', and to what end does 'capitalist' modify it? What are the merits of invoking 'realism' to characterise an imaginative impasse? What practical implications do our terminological choices have for the interpretation of post-1990 American popular culture? By way of answering these questions, I hope not only to underscore the influence of Fisher's book on this one, but also to show how the language of 'utopianism', at least in the sense in which I have argued for its use, prompts appreciably different judgements of dystopian texts to those Fisher offers in *Capitalist Realism*.

Let us take a closer look at what Fisher means by 'capitalist realism'. In his book, Fisher begins by quoting the observation attributed to Jameson (and, mistakenly, Slavoj Žižek), and now often given as the definition of capitalist realism itself, that 'it is easier to imagine the end of the world than it is to imagine the end of capitalism'.[4] Fisher's actual definition is

---

[3] Mark Fisher, *Capitalist Realism: Is There No Alternative?* (Winchester: Zer0 Books, 2009), pp. 7–9.

[4] This saying has somewhat elusive origins. Fisher does not ascribe it to Jameson and Žižek, but rather writes in the passive voice that it is 'attributed', by unspecified others, to them (*Capitalist Realism*, p. 2). As Matthew Beaumont shows, however, the sentiment is really Jameson's, its first written use being in the preface to *The Seeds of Time* (p. xii) before Jameson returns to it in his essay 'Future City' (*New Left Review*, 21 (2003), 65–79 (p. 76)), where he suggests that he had himself read it elsewhere first. Tracking down the source, Beaumont points out that Jameson is 'probably misremembering some comments made by H. Bruce Franklin about J. G. Ballard' ('Imagining the End Times: Ideology, the Contemporary Disaster Movie, *Contagion*', in *Žižek and Media Studies: A Reader*, ed. by

in fact an explication of that slogan: capitalist realism, he writes, is 'the widespread sense that not only is capitalism the only viable political and economic system, but also that it is now impossible even to *imagine* a coherent alternative to it'. The italics are Fisher's: the distinctiveness of his concept lies in its recognition that the drawing-in of our political horizons is also a cultural, even an aesthetic phenomenon. Though Fisher associates capitalist realism with neoliberalism (on which more below), what is at stake is not merely the dominance of a particular political and economic logic (marketisation, privatisation, precarisation), but a cultural one. Thus Fisher suggests that his notion of capitalist realism 'can be subsumed under the rubric of postmodernism as theorized by Jameson', with the qualification that the 'cultural logic' Jameson diagnosed in the 1980s (the waning of affect, the loss of historicity, a new depthlessness, and so on) has become still deeper, more pervasive.[5]

Unsurprisingly, then, the early pages of *Capitalist Realism* are as much a threnody for a dead culture as they are bracing socio-political analysis. It is for this reason that Fisher turns to a Hollywood dystopia, Alfonso Cuarón's 2006 film *Children of Men*, one of whose scenes imagines various historic works of art, such as Michelangelo's *David* and Picasso's *Guernica*, preserved in a renovated Battersea Power Station, itself a monument to the past. Fisher reads this moment in *Children of Men* as an acknowledgement of the cultural sterility of capitalist realism. '[H]ow long can a culture persist without the new?' Fisher asks, such being, in his view, the film's central concern. Fisher then pivots to T. S. Eliot's essay 'Tradition and the Individual Talent' (1919) and draws from it the implication that 'the exhaustion of the future does not even leave us with a past', and that a 'culture that is merely preserved is no culture at all'.[6] The later pages of *Capitalist Realism* circle back to this theme, cultural stagnation, and propose a new 'paternalism' (albeit 'without the Father'), which would 'treat audiences as adults, assuming that they can cope with cultural products that are complex and intellectually demanding'.[7]

Despite his characterisation of capitalist realism as a cultural, not merely a political and economic, paralysis, Fisher does not mean the word 'realism' in its sense as literary or cinematic realism, or indeed as philosophical or political realism. Capitalist realism is 'more like realism

---

Matthew Filsfeder and Louis-Paul Willis (New York: Palgrave, 2014)), pp. 79–89 (p. 79)). For Franklin's discussion of Ballard, see 'What Are We to Make of J. G. Ballard's Apocalypse?' <http://www.jgballard.ca/criticism/ballard_apocalypse_1979.html> [accessed 17 May 2022] (53 paras).

[5] Fisher, *Capitalist Realism*, p. 7.
[6] Fisher, *Capitalist Realism*, p. 3.
[7] Fisher, *Capitalist Realism*, p. 75.

in itself', realism independent of its disciplinary articulations, Fisher suggests, somewhat enigmatically.[8] Later he reiterates that capitalist realism 'cannot be confined to art or the quasi-propagandistic way in which advertising functions'.[9] Yet the centrality Fisher accords to cultural forms in *Capitalist Realism* suggests that the distinction between his 'realism' and realism as genre is not so clear-cut. In an interview given three years after the publication of *Capitalist Realism*, Fisher notes that *The Wire* (2002–08)—which he had not seen when he wrote the book—'exemplifies so much of what I wanted to say in *Capitalist Realism*. In fact, if you want to know what capitalist realism is, go watch *The Wire*!'[10] We should take Fisher seriously here, since his comment reflects his working method in *Capitalist Realism*, which summons cultural texts because they represent capitalist realism realistically, mimetically. It is on this basis, for example, that Fisher contrasts Michael Mann's *Heat* (1995) with *The Godfather* (1972) and *Goodfellas* (1990): Mann's portrayal of 'branded Sprawl' reflects the real post-Fordist Los Angeles, Fisher claims, while Coppola's and Scorsese's films depend on 'the local colour, the cuisine aromas, the cultural idiolects' of a bygone era.[11] It would seem that 'realism in itself' cannot be so easily separated from realism as genre—that a certain literary, cinematic, and televisual realism allows us to glimpse the inner mechanism of capitalist realism.

Even when Fisher turns to a science-fiction film such as *Children of Men*, it is still its realism that matters. We might get a clearer sense of how *Children of Men* fits into Fisher's argument, and in what sense Fisher takes it to be realist, if we turn to the blog post that he later edited into the book. Posted on 26 January 2007, shortly after Fisher watched *Children of Men* on DVD, the blog registers his immediate enthusiasm for Cuarón's film. 'British cinema, for the last thirty years as chronically

---

[8] Fisher, *Capitalist Realism*, p. 4. In his writings and interviews, Fisher sometimes refers to capitalist realism as a kind of 'belief' or 'attitude', but as he notes in a discussion with Jodi Dean, neither of these terms is quite accurate: capitalist realism is 'more like a transpersonal psychic infrastructure'. 'It's ideological,' Fisher continues, 'not in the sense that it directly persuades people of the truth of its propositions, but more because it convinces people that it is an irresistible force' (Mark Fisher and Jodi Dean, 'We Can't Afford to be Realists: A Conversation with Mark Fisher and Jodi Dean', in *Reading Capitalist Realism*, ed. by Alison Shonkwiler and Leigh Claire La Berge (Iowa City: University of Iowa Press, 2014), pp. 26–38 (pp. 26–27)).

[9] Fisher, *Capitalist Realism*, p. 16.

[10] Mark Fisher, 'Preoccupying: Interviewed by the *Occupied Times*', in *k-punk*, pp. 663–69 (p. 665).

[11] Fisher, *Capitalist Realism*, pp. 31–32.

sterile as the issueless population of *Children of Men*, has not produced a version of the apocalypse that is even remotely as well realised as this,' Fisher begins. What stands out about *Children of Men* for Fisher is its contemporaneity, which he imputes to three things: first, that the catastrophe is present already, is simply 'being lived through'; second, that the dystopia is 'specific to late capitalism', especially in its portrayal of the compatibility of 'ultra-authoritarianism and Capital'; and, third, that the film represents the very cultural sterility to which Fisher sees it as the exception. In all three cases, what Fisher is extolling is the film's realism, its clear-eyed diagnosis of the peculiarity of its time. 'At a certain point,' Fisher adds, 'realism flips over into delirium', but the delirium too is realistic, as the film's refugee camp at Bexhill admits of comparison with 'Yugoslavia in the Nineties, Baghdad in the Noughties, Palestine any time'. Cuarón's 'formal realism', combined with 'despondent lyricism', Fisher marks out for particular praise.[12]

What seems to occur to Fisher when he reworks the post into the opening of his book, however, is that *Children of Men* is not realist but capitalist realist. Having quoted Jameson's dictum about imagining the end of capitalism and then supplied his own definition of capitalist realism, Fisher adds, in the next sentence, a comment on dystopian culture that did not appear in the blog: 'Once, dystopian films and novels were exercises in such acts of imagination, the disasters they depicted acting as narrative pretext for the emergence of different ways of living.'[13] Fisher here produces a new criterion for evaluating dystopias, which demands that he reappraise *Children of Men*. What now matters is not so much the accuracy of the extrapolation but the dystopia's function: does it act 'as a narrative pretext for the emergence of different ways of living'? In Fisher's view, *Children of Men* does not. Its diegetic world 'seems more like an extrapolation or exacerbation of ours than an alternative to it'. Fisher's position has flipped completely: now the extrapolation, generating the film's realism, and which Fisher praised in the blog, forestalls utopian imaginings, bears the mark of capitalist realism.[14]

---

[12] Mark Fisher, 'Coffee Bars and Internment Camps', in *k-punk*, ed. by Ambrose, pp. 179–182. Fisher describes *Children of Men* as a British film, but it was made by an American production company and distributed by Universal. As such, it is equally a Hollywood film.

[13] Fisher, *Capitalist Realism*, p. 2.

[14] We might also detect an inconsistency between Fisher's new criterion and his re-evaluation of *Children of Men*. If Fisher asks dystopias to function as pretexts for the emergence of the new, it is not incumbent on a dystopia to present its fictional world as an 'alternative': by Fisher's own logic, it

The shift between blog post and book speaks less to a refinement of Fisher's argument than it does to an equivocation in his thought about the political efficacy of realism, this uncertainty being latent in his writings but, again, coming to the surface in interview. According to an interviewer for the *Occupied Times*, who spoke to Fisher in 2012—this is the same piece from which I earlier quoted Fisher's comments on *The Wire*—*Capitalist Realism* shows how 'commercial pop and hip-hop music and films like *Children of Men* and *Wall-E* [2008], even when purporting to critique authority and the system, in fact leave only a message of its inevitable perpetuation'. Responding, Fisher denies that the popular culture he discusses in the book has no 'political potentials'; rather, his claim is that 'anti-capitalism at the level of a film's message does nothing *in itself* to disrupt the super-hegemony of capital', such anti-capitalism being more or less routine in Hollywood, in Fisher's view. 'The issue,' Fisher continues,

> is how culture connects up with struggles, and you can't second guess that. It's possible that any of the films I talked about could contribute to the development of class consciousness or inspire people to engage in struggles. Conversely, it's possible that even those films or television programs which inventory the features of capitalist realism end up reinforcing it. Take something like *The Wire*: yes, it exemplifies practically everything I say about capitalist realism, but, for that very reason, you could say it supports, rather than subverts, capitalist realism. You could very easily take away the message that struggling to change things is pointless; the system wins in the end.[15]

Fisher's remarks seem to amount to a denial that one can determine, from close reading alone, the relationship between a realist text and capitalist realism. Perhaps those films that 'inventory the features of capitalist realism'—that are, in some sense, realistic—'end up reinforcing it', but perhaps they will instead cultivate 'class consciousness'. Realism might be capitalist realist or it might not.

I want to suggest that Fisher's uncertainty here derives, not immediately from some imprecise conception of realism itself, but from his underlying notion of utopianism, which he never spells out in the book. It is, once more, only in interview that Fisher confronts the relation between the

---

need act only as a *pretext* for the imagination of alternatives, which is a different thing from showing those alternatives directly.

[15] Fisher, 'Preoccupying', p. 669.

two concepts, here in response to a question from Jodi Dean regarding the possibility that neoliberalism has a 'utopian core'. Fisher replies that 'on the face of it capitalist realism can be characterized by its repudiation of any utopianism. That repudiation is what the "realism" consists of'. He proceeds to observe that, 'if there is an ineradicable utopian core to neoliberalism', this is what distinguishes the latter from capitalist realism.[16] Fisher's notion of utopianism is then not quite as definitionally neutral or 'analytic' as Levitas's—according to which (as we saw in Chapter 4) one cannot discern utopian from anti-utopian material at the level of form, content, or function—since he does observe limits to what can be considered utopian: capitalist realism marks them precisely. Nonetheless, Fisher does use the term here in a *politically* neutral manner: he is happy to describe pro-capitalist visions (specifically, neoliberal ones) as utopian, and dismisses thereby the relevance of the distinction between degree and kind, reform and revolution, to definitions of utopia.

If Fisher's concept of utopianism is politically neutral, what does this imply about his notion of anti-utopianism, of which capitalist realism is apparently one expression? It must suggest that anti-utopias, too, can be either pro- or anti-capitalist: they can 'repudiate' either the pro-capitalist triumphalism of neoliberalism or, say, the communist vision of a world unbound by private property. Crucially, as Fisher notes in his conversation with Dean, it is anti-utopianism that becomes the category 'realism' in his blog posts and book: Fisher's 'realism' *is* anti-utopianism in this apolitical sense. The consequence is that the political neutrality of the latter must also pass into Fisher's analysis of realist texts. One cannot say whether realist texts support or reject the status quo, cannot 'second guess' their politics, since such 'realism' is really code for 'anti-utopianism', and anti-utopianism is defined neutrally. This is also why Fisher qualifies with the word 'capitalist' those specific realisms he wishes to criticise: because his 'realism' is not by definition pro-capitalist, an adjective must separate those realisms that are from those that are not.

Herein lies the core difference between what I have tried to propose in the present book and what Fisher posits in his. Though I am suggesting, along the same lines as Fisher, that American popular culture—or at least one specific form of it, the Hollywood science-fiction film—became increasingly anti-utopian in the late 1990s, I have taken 'anti-utopia' to define not simply a bundle of formal properties, but a specific political orientation towards capitalism, or more precisely, towards private property. As I argued in Chapter 4, utopia is the critique of private property by representations of its negation: it is the unity of More's Book

---

[16] Fisher and Dean, pp. 34–35.

I and Book II, the critique of enclosure and the imagination of a world unenclosed. The consequence is that we must characterise anti-utopianism as the rejection of that critique and the corollary imaginings, and therefore as necessarily pro-capitalist.

If we look at *Children of Men*'s utopianism from this perspective, using a political rather than a neutral concept of utopia, how might we characterise its politics? Crucially for us, *Children of Men* has little to say about property in its nightmarish future: its 'utopian' moment, juxtaposed with the grim sterility of the dystopia, is the birth of a baby. The newborn suspends the fighting between refugees and government, each side looking upon her with awe. Human life, *Children of Men* suggests, is intrinsically meaningful, hence the film's pejorative representation of the rebels, who want to use the baby as a means to their revolutionary ends. Miriam (Pam Ferris) explains the rebels' killing of Theo's (Clive Owen) friend in the same way: 'It's all part of a bigger thing,' she says, in a manner that suggests she does not quite believe the justification herself. It might be objected that, as Cuarón himself notes, the baby's mother, a Black woman named Kee (Clare Hope-Ashitey), is an illegal immigrant, such that *Children of Men* shows the 'future of humanity' resting on 'the dispossessed'.[17] Yet the film's use of a miraculous childbirth as a potential solution frames dispossession as an original sin, attributable to no material cause, rather than a historical condition. It is not rebel politics, politics oriented towards some 'bigger thing', but a miracle that will undo humanity's primordial dispossession, *Children of Men* implies.

Must a dystopia reserve its sharpest critique for dispossession? Is it not enough that *Children of Men* presents the authoritarian state, anti-immigrant sentiment, and militarisation, *inter alia*, negatively, as dystopian? Such questions assume that dispossession is one among many injustices of the modern world, that it can be heaped atop those others just mentioned. Yet what is intrinsic to utopias, I have suggested, is their perception that expropriation prepares the ground on which modern forms of domination play out.[18] We have seen Hythloday make a similar point about theft, which problem, he argues, cannot be solved

---

[17] Annie Wagner, 'Politics, Bible Stories, and Hope: An Interview with *Children of Men* Director Alfonso Cuarón', *The Stranger*, 28 December 2006 <https://www.thestranger.com/seattle/Content?oid=128363> [accessed 17 May 2022].

[18] Dispossession, as Nichols theorises it (here drawing from and extending Marx), 'comes to name a distinct logic of capitalist development grounded in the appropriation and monopolization of the productive powers of the natural world in a manner that orders (but does not directly determine) social pathologies related to colonization, dislocation, and class stratification

in isolation, by harsher punishments, but must rather be understood as a consequence of the enclosure of English fields, the separation of people from their means of subsistence. Expropriation is not one of many lamentable 'negative externalities' of capital accumulation, but rather the foundation, constantly renewed, on which such accumulation and its distinctive inequalities and oppressions rest. It follows that the absence of a critique of private property—rather than the film's failure to offer an 'alternative', as Fisher argues—is what marks *Children of Men*'s limits, politically. This lack of any sense of the determinate historical origins of such problems is precisely what accounts for the film's evocation of unremitting, ahistorical evil, solvable only by miracle.

By way of conclusion, I would like to draw attention to three remakes or sequels of dystopias that I have already discussed, which, precisely because they *are* remakes or sequels, demonstrate with particular lucidity the turn away from the problematic of property, thus away from utopia, that *Children of Men* exemplifies and that I have sought to document more broadly in the second half of this book. Take Len Wiseman's 2012 remake of *Total Recall*, which keeps much of Verhoeven's plot but transposes the colonial relation between Earth and Mars onto the 'United Federation of Britain' and the 'Colony' (located in Australia), these having become the sole habitable regions of Earth when chemical war broke out at the end of the twenty-first century. The geographical shift serves to downplay the original film's concern with commodification: Wiseman excises the sale of air on Mars and, with it, as a resolution to that problem, the utopian image of atmospheric renewal. Douglas Quaid (Colin Farrell) manages to prevent Britain's imminent invasion of the Colony; we feel relieved for the oppressed, but that is all. The narrative's motivating conflict becomes overpopulation instead of enclosure, since it is because Britain is overcrowded that its Chancellor (Bryan Cranston) determines to engineer a takeover of the Colony, during which, giving the Britons extra room, he intends to kill everyone living there. The Marxist problematic vanishes and, with it, *Total Recall*'s critique of enclosure.

In a similar way, José Padilha remakes *RoboCop* without the concept of privatisation. As we saw in Chapter 2, Verhoeven's *RoboCop* thematises the growing intimacy between public and private sectors (recall Jones's claim that OCP 'practically are the military'); his film sees the privatisation of public services as something worthy of note, vulnerable to satire, such that it forms an essential part of the dystopian Detroit through which RoboCop moves. While policing is indeed private in Padilha's 2014

and/or exploitation, while simultaneously converting the planet into a homogeneous and universal means of production' (*Theft is Property!*, p. 84).

version, the dramatic tension attendant on the relation between public and private in the original, on the contested *process* of privatisation, has more or less dissipated. Padilha also engineers another shift: it is now not OCP but the police department that maintains ties with crime, as RoboCop (Joel Kinnamen) busts two officers and the police chief for working with Antoine Vallen (Patrick Garrow), the remake's Boddicker. Padilha is less keen than Verhoeven was to equate 'free enterprise' with theft: OmniCorp is guilty in the remake primarily for its callous maltreatment of Alex Murphy's wife and son.

Released in 2017, Denis Villeneuve's *Blade Runner 2049* completes this book's historical trajectory. As in Cuarón's film, the apparently utopian moment here is childbirth: K (Ryan Gosling) learns at the beginning of the narrative that a Replicant mother, who turns out to be Rachael, gave birth to Replicant offspring, a 'miracle' that the film's other Replicants interpret as the harbinger of their liberation. 'This breaks the world,' K's boss, Lieutenant Joshi (Robin Wright), says, urging K to kill the offspring, while the Replicant rebel leader Freysa (Hiam Abbass) reads the baby's existence as proof they are 'more than just slaves'. Allegorically, the labour of gestation signifies a release from the slave labour for which the Replicants are built; as Joi (Ana de Armas) puts it, the miraculous Replicant offspring (she thinks it is K himself) is 'born, not made', the product of a different kind of work. Yet what is utopian about the figure of the child here? If Replicant labour is highly instrumentalised and disaggregated, each Replicant having been produced as a specific 'model' for a specific task, the baby signifies, by contrast, wholeness. It is thus Deckard's (Harrison Ford) fear that his child would be not only found, but 'taken apart, dissected'. Despite *Blade Runner 2049*'s opening images of highly industrialised agriculture, its 'protein farms' appearing as so many enclosed fields from the bird's-eye establishing shot, the questions about property and labour that it raises yield, ultimately, to a valorisation of unity in the abstract.

It is not my view that these later science-fiction films are meritless, the earlier ones beyond reproach. The present work has sought only to document, in Hollywood's speculative cinema since the mid-1990s, the fading of a specific kind of critique, one aimed at enclosure in particular and private property in general. These films evince our inability, not just to imagine the end of capitalism, or to plan what would come after, but also to criticise its fundaments, the regime of property rights on which the whole exploitative edifice stands. Capitalist realism is thus an analytic deficit quite as much as it is an imaginative or aesthetic one. It is a pervasive anti-utopianism, a negation of the utopian negation, which cannot but deaden what is radical and speculative in works of science fiction.

Bibliography

Adorno, Theodor, *Introduction to Dialectics*, ed. by Christoph Ziermann, trans. by Nicholas Walker (Cambridge: Polity, 2017)
——, *Minima Moralia: Reflections on a Damaged Life*, trans. by E. F. N. Jephcott (London: Verso, 2005)
'An Interview with Bob Sullivan, *Clonus* Screenwriter', *The Agony Booth*, 17 May 2007 <https://web.archive.org/web/20191013075446/https://www.agonybooth.com/interview-with-clonus-screenwriter-4507> [accessed 17 May 2022]
Arrighi, Giovanni, *The Long Twentieth Century: Money, Power, and the Origins of Our Times* (London: Verso, 2010)
Baker, Amy Castro, 'Eroding the Wealth of Women: Gender and the Subprime Foreclosure Crisis', *Social Service Review*, 88.1 (2014), 59–91
Balasopoulos, Antonis, 'Unworldly Worldliness: America and the Trajectories of Utopian Expansionism', *Utopian Studies*, 15.2 (2004), 3–35
Barkan, Joanne, 'Death by a Thousand Cuts: The Story of Privatising Public Education in the USA', *Soundings*, 70 (2018), 97–116
Beaumont, Matthew, 'Imagining the End Times: Ideology, the Contemporary Disaster Movie, *Contagion*', in *Žižek and Media Studies: A Reader*, ed. by Matthew Filsfeder and Louis-Paul Willis (New York: Palgrave, 2014), pp. 79–89
Bel, Germà, 'The Coining of "Privatization" and Germany's National Socialist Party', *Journal of Economic Perspectives*, 20.3 (2006), 187–94
Bellamy, Edward, *Equality* (Frankfurt: Outlook, 2019)
——, *Looking Backward: 2000–1887* (Oxford: Oxford University Press, 2007)
Benjamin, Walter, *Charles Baudelaire: A Lyric Poet in the Era of High Capitalism*, trans. by Harry Zohn (London: Verso, 1983)
Benson-Allott, Caetlin, 'Dreadful Architecture: Zones of Horror in *Alien* and Lee Bontecou's Wall Sculptures', *Journal of Visual Culture*, 14 (2015), 267–78
Best, Steven, '*RoboCop*: In the Detritus of Hi-Technology', *Jump Cut*, 34 (1989) <http://www.ejumpcut.org/archive/onlinessays/JC34folder/RobocopBest.html> [accessed 17 May 2022] (49 paras)

Bhandar, Brenna, *The Colonial Lives of Property: Law, Land, and Racial Regimes of Ownership* (Durham, NC: Duke University Press, 2018)
Bhose, Indra, 'Paul Verhoeven Tackles Science Fiction', trans. by Alexandra Valentine Proulx, in *Paul Verhoeven: Interviews*, ed. by Margaret Barton-Fumo (Jackson: University Press of Mississippi, 2016), pp. 47–54
Bollier, David, *Silent Theft: The Private Plunder of Our Common Wealth* (London: Routledge, 2003)
Bonefeld, Werner, 'Primitive Accumulation and Capitalist Accumulation: Notes on Social Constitution and Expropriation', *Science and Society*, 75.3 (2011), 379–99
Boyle, James, *The Public Domain: Enclosing the Commons of the Mind* (New Haven: Yale University Press, 2008)
Bracha, Oren, 'The Emergence and Development of United States Intellectual Property Law', *The Oxford Handbook of Intellectual Property Law*, ed. by Rochelle C. Dreyfuss and Justine Pila (Oxford: Oxford University Press, 2018), pp. 235–64
Brenner, Robert, *The Boom and the Bubble: The US in the World Economy* (London: Verso, 2002)
——, 'What Is, and What Is Not, Imperialism?', *Historical Materialism*, 14.4 (2006), 79–105
Bud, Robert, *The Uses of Life: A History of Biotechnology* (Cambridge: Cambridge University Press, 1993)
Bush, George W., 'President Calls for Expanding Opportunities to Home Ownership', 17 June 2002 <https://georgewbush-whitehouse.archives.gov/news/releases/2002/06/20020617-2.html> [accessed 17 May 2022] (47 paras)
Butler, Stuart M., 'Privatizing Federal Services: A Primer', *Heritage Foundation Backgrounder*, 488 (1986), 1–13
Byars, Jackie, and others, 'Symposium on *Alien*', *Science Fiction Studies*, 7 (1980), 278–304
Chan, Edward K., 'Race in the *Blade Runner* Cycle and the Demographic Dystopia', *Science Fiction Film and Television*, 13.1 (2020), 59–76
Chang, David A., 'Enclosures of Land and Sovereignty: The Allotment of American Indian Lands', *Radical History Review*, 109 (2011), 108–19
Chu, Seo-Young, *Do Metaphors Dream of Literal Sleep? A Science-Fictional Theory of Representation* (Cambridge, MA: Harvard University Press, 2010)
Claeys, Gregory, *Dystopia: A Natural History* (Oxford: Oxford University Press, 2017)
——, *Utopia: The History of an Idea* (London: Thames & Hudson, 2020)
Clover, Joshua, 'Allegory Bomb', *Film Quarterly*, 63.2 (2009), 8–9
——, *The Matrix* (London: BFI, 2004)
Cobb, Ron, 'The Authorized Portfolio of Crew Insignias from the United States Commercial Spaceship *Nostromo*: Concepts and Derivations' (Los Angeles: The Thinking Cap Company, 1980)
Cockburn, Alexander, 'Al Gore's Teapot Dome', *The Nation*, 17 July 2000, p. 10

Cole, Teju, 'Comment: *District 9* and the Nigerians', *Africa Is a Country*, 11 September 2009 <https://africasacountry.wordpress.com/2009/09/11/comment-district-9-and-the-nigerians> [accessed 17 May 2022] (9 paras)

Congress for the New Urbanism, 'Charter of the New Urbanism' (1996) <https://www.cnu.org/who-we-are/charter-new-urbanism> [accessed 17 May 2022]

Cornea, Christine, *Science Fiction Cinema: Between Fantasy and Reality* (Edinburgh: Edinburgh University Press, 2007)

Creed, Barbara, *The Monstrous-Feminine: Film, Feminism, Psychoanalysis* (Oxon: Routledge, 1993)

Cunningham, Douglas A., 'A Theme Park Built for One: The New Urbanism vs. Disney Design in *The Truman Show*', *Critical Survey*, 17.1 (2005), 109–30

Davis, Mike, *City of Quartz: Excavating the Future in Los Angeles*, 2nd edn (London: Verso, 2006)

De Angelis, Massimo, *The Beginning of History: Value Struggles and Global Capital* (London: Pluto, 2007)

Debord, Guy, 'The Decline and Fall of the Spectacle–Commodity Economy', in *Situationist International Anthology*, ed. and trans. by Ken Knabb, revised edn (Berkeley: Bureau of Public Secrets, 2006), pp. 194–203

——, *The Society of the Spectacle*, trans. by Ken Knabb (London: Rebel Press, 2004)

Decherney, Peter, *Hollywood's Copyright Wars: From Edison to the Internet* (New York: Columbia University Press, 2012)

Dick, Philip K., 'We Can Remember It for You Wholesale', in *Selected Stories of Philip K. Dick* (Boston: Houghton Mifflin Harcourt, 2013), pp. 325–45

Duncan, Rebecca, 'From Cheap Labour to Surplus Humanity: World-Ecology and the Postapartheid Speculative in Neill Blomkamp's *District 9*', *Science Fiction Film and Television*, 11.1 (2018), 45–72

Dutfield, Graham, *Intellectual Property Rights and the Life Sciences Industry: Past, Present, and Future*, 2nd edn (Singapore: World Scientific, 2009)

Dymski, Gary A., 'Racial Exclusion and the Political Economy of the Subprime Crisis', *Historical Materialism*, 17.2 (2009), 149–79

Ecker, Martha, 'Efforts to Privatize the United States Postal Service', *Labor Studies Journal*, 43 (2018), 173–88

Eisen, Lauren-Brooke, *Inside Private Prisons: An American Dilemma in the Age of Mass Incarceration* (New York: Columbia University Press, 2018)

Ellin, Nan, *Postmodern Urbanism*, 2nd edn (New York: Princeton Architectural Press, 1999)

Elliott, Brian, 'Debord, Constant, and the Politics of Situationist Urbanism', *Radical Philosophy Review*, 12.1/2 (2009), 249–72

Farmer, Roger E. A., and Pawel Zabczyk, 'The Household Fallacy', *Economics Letters*, 169 (2018), 83–86

Federici, Silvia, *Caliban and the Witch: Women, the Body, and Primitive Accumulation* (Brooklyn: Autonomedia, 2004)

Felker-Kantor, Max, *Policing Los Angeles: Race, Resistance, and the Rise of the LAPD* (Chapel Hill: University of North Carolina Press, 2018)

Ferguson, Priscilla Parkhurst, *Paris as Revolution: Writing the Nineteenth-Century City* (Berkeley: University of California Press, 1994)

Fisher, Mark, *Capitalist Realism: Is There No Alternative?* (Winchester: Zer0 Books, 2009)

——, 'Coffee Bars and Internment Camps', in *k-punk: The Collected and Unpublished Writings of Mark Fisher (2004–2016)*, ed. by Darren Ambrose (London: Repeater, 2018), pp. 179–82

——, 'Preoccupying: Interviewed by the *Occupied Times*', in *k-punk*, ed. by Ambrose, pp. 663–69

——, 'They Can Be Different in the Future Too: Interviewed by Rowan Wilson for *Ready Steady Book*', in *k-punk*, ed. by Ambrose, pp. 627–36

Fisher, Mark, and Jodi Dean, 'We Can't Afford to be Realists: A Conversation with Mark Fisher and Jodi Dean', in *Reading Capitalist Realism*, ed. by Alison Shonkwiler and Leigh Claire La Berge (Iowa City: University of Iowa Press, 2014), pp. 26–38

Fisher III, William W., 'The Growth of Intellectual Property: A History of the Ownership of Ideas in the United States' (1999) <https://cyber.harvard.edu/property99/history.html> [accessed 17 May 2022] (50 paras)

Fitting, Peter, 'Unmasking the Real? Critique and Utopia in Recent SF Films', in *Dark Horizons: Fiction and the Dystopian Imagination*, ed. by Raffaella Baccolini and Tom Moylan (London: Routledge, 2003), pp. 155–66

Flusty, Steven, 'The Banality of Interdiction: Surveillance, Control, and the Displacement of Diversity', *International Journal of Urban and Regional Research*, 25.3 (2001), 658–64

Foster, John Bellamy, and Fred Magdoff, *The Great Financial Crisis: Causes and Consequences* (New York: Monthly Review, 2009)

Franklin, H. Bruce, 'What Are We to Make of J. G. Ballard's Apocalypse?' <http://www.jgballard.ca/criticism/ballard_apocalypse_1979.html> [accessed 17 May 2022] (53 paras)

Freedman, Carl, *Critical Theory and Science Fiction* (Middletown: Wesleyan University Press, 2000)

——, 'Kubrick's *2001* and the Possibility of a Science-Fiction Cinema', *Science Fiction Studies*, 25.2 (1998), 300–18

Geisler, Charles, 'Disowned by the Ownership Society: How Native Americans Lost Their Land', *Rural Sociology*, 79 (2014), 56–78

Gibbons, Andrea, *City of Segregation: 100 Years of Struggle for Housing in Los Angeles* (London: Verso, 2018)

Glenn, Brian J., 'Privatisation as a Strategy in the United Kingdom, the United States, and Beyond', in *Domestic Policy Discourse in the US and the UK in the 'New World Order'*, ed. by Lori Maguire (Newcastle: Cambridge Scholars Publishing, 2010), pp. 179–205

Godfrey, Alex, 'Making America Gory Again: How the *Purge* Films Troll Trumpism', *The Guardian*, 4 July 2018 <https://www.theguardian.com/film/2018/jul/04/how-the-purge-trolls-trumps-america-jason-blum-first-purge> [accessed 17 May 2022] (16 paras)

Goldberger, Paul, 'The Rise of the Private City', in *Breaking Away: The Future of Cities*, ed. by Julia Vitullo-Martin (New York: Twentieth Century Fund Press, 1996), pp. 135–47

Goodman, Peter S., 'Late-Fee Profits May Trump Plans to Modify Loans', *New York Times*, 30 July 2009, pp. A1, A3

Graff, Gregory D., and others, 'Not Quite a Myriad of Gene Patents', *Nature Biotechnology*, 31.5 (2013), 404–10

Grant, Jill, *Planning the Good Community: New Urbanism in Theory and Practice* (London: Routledge, 2006)

Greer, Allan, 'Commons and Enclosure in the Colonization of North America', *The American Historical Review*, 117.2 (2012), 365–86

Hackworth, Jason, 'Destroyed by HOPE: Public Housing, Neoliberalism and Progressive Housing Activism in the US', in *Where the Other Half Lives: Lower Income Housing in a Neoliberal World*, ed. by Sarah Glynn (London: Pluto Press, 2009), pp. 232–56

Hall, Matthew, Kyle Crowder, and Amy Spring, 'Variations in Housing Foreclosures by Race and Place, 2005–2012', *The Annals of the American Academy of Political and Social Science*, 660 (2015), 217–37

Harvey, David, *A Brief History of Neoliberalism* (Oxford: Oxford University Press, 2005)

——, *The Enigma of Capital: And the Crises of Capitalism* (London: Profile, 2011)

——, *The Limits to Capital*, 2nd edn (London: Verso, 2006)

——, *The New Imperialism* (Oxford: Oxford University Press, 2003)

——, *Rebel Cities: From the Right to the City to the Urban Revolution*, 2nd edn (London: Verso, 2019)

——, 'The Right to the City', *New Left Review*, 53 (2008), 23–40

——, *Spaces of Hope* (Berkeley: University of California Press, 2000)

Haslam, Jason, *Gender, Race, and American Science Fiction: Reflections on Fantastic Identities* (New York: Routledge, 2015)

Henig, Jeffrey R., 'Privatization in the United States: Theory and Practice', *Political Science Quarterly*, 10 (1989–90), 649–70

Henry, Nicholas, 'The Contracting Conundrum in the United States: Or, Do We Really Understand Privatization?', in *Privatization or Public Enterprise Reform? International Case Studies with Implications for Public Management*, ed. by Ali Farazmand (Westport, CT: Greenwood Press, 2001), pp. 95–126

Hester-Williams, Kim D., 'NeoSlaves: Slavery, Freedom, and African American Apotheosis in *Candyman*, *The Matrix*, and *The Green Mile*', *Genders*, 40 (2004) <http://web.archive.org/web/20131112025835/http://www.genders.org/g40/g40_williams.html> [accessed 17 May 2022] (43 paras)

Hickenlooper, George, 'The Vitality of Existence', in *Paul Verhoeven: Interviews*, ed. by Barton-Fumo, pp. 57–63

Hodkinson, Stuart, 'The New Urban Enclosures', *City*, 16.5 (2012), 500–18

Hughes, David, *Tales from Development Hell: Hollywood Film-Making the Hard Way* (London: Titan, 2003)

Hyde, Lewis, *The Gift: How the Creative Spirit Transforms the World* (Edinburgh: Canongate, 2012)

Ince, Onur Ulas, 'Between Equal Rights: Primitive Accumulation and Capital's Violence', *Political Theory*, 46.6 (2017), 885–914

Irwin, David T., 'Privatization in America', in *The Municipal Year Book, 1988* (Washington, DC: International City Management Association, 1988), pp. 43–55

Jameson, Fredric, *Archaeologies of the Future: The Desire Called Utopia and Other Science Fictions* (London: Verso, 2007)

——, 'Future City', *New Left Review*, 21 (2003), 65–79

——, 'Of Islands and Trenches: Neutralization and the Production of Utopian Discourse', in *The Ideologies of Theory* (London: Verso, 2008), pp. 387–414

——, *The Political Unconscious: Narrative as a Socially Symbolic Act* (Abingdon: Routledge, 2002)

——, *Postmodernism: Or, The Cultural Logic of Late Capitalism* (London: Verso, 1991)

——, 'Progress versus Utopia; Or, Can We Imagine the Future?', *Science Fiction Studies*, 9.2 (1982), 147–58

——, *Raymond Chandler: The Detections of Totality* (London: Verso, 2016)

——, 'Reification and Utopia in Mass Culture', in *Signatures of the Visible* (Abingdon: Routledge, 2007), pp. 11–46

——, *The Seeds of Time* (New York: Columbia University Press, 1994)

——, 'World-Reduction in Le Guin: The Emergence of Utopian Narrative', *Science Fiction Studies*, 2.3 (1975), 221–30

Jeffords, Susan, *Hard Bodies: Hollywood Masculinity in the Reagan Era* (New Brunswick: Rutgers University Press, 1994)

Jensen, Kyle, and Fiona Murray, 'Intellectual Property Landscape of the Human Genome', *Science*, 310 (2005), 239–40

Kautsky, Karl, *Thomas More and His Utopia*, trans. by H. J. Stenning (Whitefish: Kessinger, 2003)

King, Geoff, *New Hollywood Cinema: An Introduction* (London: I.B. Tauris, 2002)

King, Geoff, and Tanya Krzywinska, *Science Fiction Cinema: From Outerspace to Cyberspace* (London: Wallflower, 2000)

Kohn, Margaret, *Brave New Neighborhoods: The Privatization of Public Space* (New York: Routledge, 2004)

Krugman, Paul, 'The Legacy of Destructive Austerity', *New York Times*, 30 December 2019, p. A18

Lapavitsas, Costas, 'Financialised Capitalism: Crisis and Financial Expropriation', *Historical Materialism*, 17.2 (2009), 114–48

Lesjak, Carolyn, *The Afterlife of Enclosure: British Realism, Character, and the Commons* (Stanford: Stanford University Press, 2021)

Levitas, Ruth, *The Concept of Utopia* (Oxford: Peter Lang, 2011)

——, *Utopia as Method: The Imaginary Reconstitution of Society* (London: Macmillan, 2013)

Liddicoat, Johnathon, Tess Whitton, and Dianne Nicol, 'Are the Gene-Patent Storm Clouds Dissipating? A Global Snapshot', *Nature Biotechnology*, 33.4 (2015), 347–52

Linebaugh, Peter, 'Karl Marx, the Theft of Wood, and Working-Class Composition', in *Stop, Thief! The Commons, Enclosures, and Resistance* (Oakland: PM Press, 2014), pp. 43–64

Locke, John, 'Second Treatise of Government', in *Second Treatise of Government and A Letter Concerning Toleration* (Oxford: Oxford University Press, 2016), pp. 1–120

Loukaitou-Sideris, Anastasia, 'Privatisation of Public Open Space: The Los Angeles Experience', *The Town Planning Review*, 64.2 (1993), 139–67

Low, Setha M., 'Incorporation and Gated Communities in the Greater Metro-Los Angeles Region as a Model of Privatization of Residential Communities', *Home Cultures*, 5.1 (2008), 85–108

Lukács, Georg, *The Historical Novel*, trans. by Hannah and Stanley Mitchell (London: Penguin, 1981)

——, *History and Class Consciousness: Studies in Marxist Dialectics*, trans. by Rodney Livingstone (Cambridge, MA: MIT Press, 1971)

Maddison, Ben, 'Radical Commons Discourse and the Challenges of Colonialism', *Radical History Review*, 108 (2010), 29–48

Marquardt, Nadine, and Henning Füller, 'Spillover of the Private City: BIDs as a Pivot of Social Control in Downtown Los Angeles', *European Urban and Regional Studies*, 19.2 (2012), 153–66

Marx, Karl, *Capital: A Critique of Political Economy*, trans. by Ben Fowkes and David Fernbach, 3 vols (London: Penguin, 1976–81)

——, 'Chapitre XXVI: Le secret de l'accumulation primitive' (1872) <https://www.marxists.org/francais/marx/works/1867/Capital-I/kmcapI-26.htm> [accessed 17 May 2022] (14 paras)

——, *A Contribution to the Critique of Political Economy*, trans. by N. I. Stone (Chicago: Kerr & Company, 1904)

——, *Grundrisse: Foundations of the Critique of Political Economy*, trans. by Martin Nicolaus (London: Penguin, 1993)

——, Letter to Ferdinand Lassalle, 22 February 1858, in *Marx–Engels Collected Works*, 50 vols (London: Lawrence and Wishart, 1975–2004), XL (1983), 268–71

May, Christopher, *The Global Political Economy of Intellectual Property Rights: The New Enclosures*, 2nd edn (London: Routledge, 2010)

McCann, Anthony, 'Enclosure Without and Within the "Information Commons"', *Information and Communications Technology Law*, 14.3 (2005), 217–40

McClanahan, Annie, *Dead Pledges: Debt, Crisis, and Twenty-First-Century Culture* (Stanford: Stanford University Press, 2017)

McGahey, Richard, 'The Political Economy of Austerity in the United States', *Social Research*, 80.3 (2013), 717–48

Megginson, William L., *The Financial Economics of Privatization* (Oxford: Oxford University Press, 2005)

Midnight Notes Collective, 'Introduction to the New Enclosures', *Midnight Notes*, 10 (1990) <http://www.midnightnotes.org/pdfnewencl.pdf> [accessed 17 May 2022] (pp. 1–9)

Miéville, China, 'Cognition as Ideology: A Dialectic of SF Theory', in *Red Planets: Marxism and Science Fiction*, ed. by Mark Bould and China Miéville (Middletown: Wesleyan University Press, 2009), pp. 231–48

Miller, Wilbur R., *A History of Private Policing in the United States* (London: Bloomsbury, 2019)

Mizejewski, Linda, 'Total Recoil: The Schwarzenegger Body on Postmodern Mars', *Post Script*, 12.3 (1993), 25–34

More, Thomas, *Utopia*, trans. by Dominic Baker-Smith (London: Penguin, 2012)

Morley, David, and Kevin Robins, *Spaces of Identity: Global Media, Electronic Landscapes and Cultural Boundaries* (London: Routledge, 1995)

Morris, William, 'Foreword to Thomas More's *Utopia*' (1893) <https://www.marxists.org/archive/morris/works/1893/utopia.htm> [accessed 17 May 2022] (8 paras)

——, '*Looking Backward*' (1889) <https://www.marxists.org/archive/morris/works/1889/commonweal/06-bellamy.htm> [accessed 17 May 2022] (12 paras)

——, *News from Nowhere: Or, An Epoch of Rest* (Oxford: Oxford University Press, 2003)

Moylan, Tom, *Scraps of the Untainted Sky: Science Fiction, Utopia, Dystopia* (New York: Routledge, 2018)

Mulvey, Laura, 'Visual Pleasure and Narrative Cinema', *Screen*, 16.3 (1975), 6–18

Nakamura, Lisa, *Cybertypes: Race, Ethnicity, and Identity on the Internet* (London: Routledge, 2002)

Neeson, J. M., *Commoners: Common Right, Enclosure and Social Change in England, 1700–1820* (Cambridge: Cambridge University Press, 1993)

Nelson, Eric, 'Greek Nonsense in More's *Utopia*', *The Historical Journal*, 44.4 (2001), 889–917

Neocleous, Mark, *A Critical Theory of Police Power: The Fabrication of Social Order*, 2nd edn (London: Verso, 2021)

Nichols, Robert, *Theft is Property! Dispossession and Critical Theory* (Durham, NC: Duke University Press, 2020)

Nishime, LeiLani, '*The Matrix* Trilogy, Keanu Reeves, and Multiraciality at the End of Time', in *Mixed Race Hollywood*, ed. by Mary Beltrán and Camilla Fojas (New York: New York University Press, 2008), pp. 290–312

Nolan, Petra, *Hardboiled Heroes, Deadly Dames: Modernity and 1940s Film Noir* (Saarbrucken: VDM Verlag, 2008)

Obama, Barack, 'Remarks by the President in State of the Union Address', 27 January 2010 <https://obamawhitehouse.archives.gov/the-press-office/remarks-president-state-union-address> [accessed 17 May 2022] (110 paras)

Park, Jane Chi Hyun, *Yellow Future: Oriental Style in Hollywood Cinema* (Minneapolis: Minnesota University Press, 2010)

Parker, Jennifer, 'Seaside, About the Community and the Building of the Seaside Research Portal' [n.d.] <https://seaside.library.nd.edu/essays/the-community-and-building-the-portal> [accessed 17 May 2022]

Parrinder, Patrick, 'Revisiting Suvin's Poetics of Science Fiction', in *Learning from Other Worlds: Estrangement, Cognition, and the Politics of Science Fiction and Utopia*, ed. by Patrick Parrinder (Liverpool: Liverpool University Press, 2000), pp. 36–50

Perelman, Michael, *The Invention of Capitalism: Classical Political Economy and the Secret History of Primitive Accumulation* (Durham, NC: Duke University Press, 2000)

Peterson, Marina, 'Patrolling the Plaza: Privatized Public Space and the Neoliberal State in Downtown Los Angeles', *Urban Anthropology and Study of Cultural Systems and World Economic Development*, 35.4 (2006), 355–86

Pollack, Andrew, 'Debate on Human Cloning Turns to Patents', *New York Times*, 17 May 2002, p. 14

Postone, Moishe, *Time, Labor, and Social Domination: A Reinterpretation of Marx's Critical Theory* (Cambridge: Cambridge University Press, 1993)

Prawer, S. S., *Karl Marx and World Literature* (London: Verso, 2011)

President's Commission on Privatization, *Privatization: Toward More Effective Government* (Washington, DC: The Commission, 1988)

President's Private Sector Survey on Cost Control, *Report on Privatization* (Washington, DC: US Government Printing Office, 1983)

Quigg, Donald J., 'Animals—Patentability', *Consolidated Listing of Official Gazette Notices Re Patent and Trademark Office Practices and Procedures*, 7 April 1987 <https://www.uspto.gov/web/offices/com/sol/og/2013/week53/TOCCN/item-137.htm> [accessed 17 May 2022] (4 paras)

Rahall, Karena, 'The Siren is Calling: Economic and Ideological Trends toward Privatization of Public Police Forces', *University of Miami Law Review*, 68 (2018), 633–75

Raubenheimer, Landi, 'Nostalgic Dystopia: Johannesburg as Landscape after *White Writing*', *Journal of Literary Studies*, 36.4 (2020), 123–42

Ray, Carina, 'Humanising Aliens or Alienating Africans?', *New African*, December 2009, pp. 32–33

Reagan, Ronald, 'Statement on the President's Commission on Privatization', 3 September 1987 <https://www.reaganlibrary.gov/archives/speech/statement-presidents-commission-privatization> [accessed 17 May 2022] (6 paras)

Rhodes, John David, *Spectacle of Property: The House in American Film* (Minneapolis: University of Minnesota Press, 2017)

Rich, Motoko, 'Buying Homes by the Thousands: Investors Aim to Stockpile Fixer-Uppers to Fill With Tenants', *New York Times*, 3 April 2012, p. B1

Rieder, John, *Science Fiction and the Mass Cultural Genre System* (Middletown: Wesleyan University Press, 2017)

Roberts, William Clare, *Marx's Inferno: The Political Theory of Capital* (Princeton: Princeton University Press, 2017)

——, 'What Was Primitive Accumulation? Reconstructing the Origin of a Critical Concept', *European Journal of Political Theory*, 19.4 (2020), 532–52

Robertson, Michael, 'Property and Privatisation in *RoboCop*', *International Journal of Law in Context*, 4 (2008), 217–35

Rosenman, Ellen, 'On Enclosure Acts and the Commons', *BRANCH* [n.d.] <http://www.branchcollective.org/?ps_articles=ellen-rosenman-on-enclosure-acts-and-the-commons> [accessed 17 May 2022] (13 paras)

Sargent, Lyman Tower, 'The Three Faces of Utopianism Revisited', *Utopian Studies*, 5.1 (1994), 1–37

Schatz, Thomas, 'The New Hollywood', in *Film Theory Goes to the Movies*, ed. by Jim Collins, Hilary Radner, and Ava Preacher Collins (New York: Routledge, 1993), pp. 8–36

Schmeink, Lars, *Biopunk Dystopias: Genetic Engineering, Society and Science Fiction* (Liverpool: Liverpool University Press, 2016)

Seaside Institute, 'Our Mission' [n.d.] <https://www.seasideinstitute.org/mission> [accessed 17 May 2022]

Seeger, Sean, and Daniel Davison-Vecchione, 'Dystopian Literature and the Sociological Imagination', *Thesis Eleven*, 155 (2019), 45–63

Segrave, Kerry, *Product Placement in Hollywood Films: A History* (Jefferson: McFarland, 2004)

Sherkow, Jacob S., and Henry T. Greely, 'The History of Patenting Genetic Material', *Annual Review of Genetics*, 49 (2015), 161–82

Shiva, Vandana, *Protect or Plunder? Understanding Intellectual Property Rights* (London: Zed Books, 2001)

Shoemaker, Nancy, *A Strange Likeness: Becoming Red and White in Eighteenth-Century North America* (Oxford: Oxford University Press, 2004)

Situationist International, 'Editorial Notes: Unitary Urbanism at the End of the 1950s', trans. by Paul Hammond (1959) <https://www.cddc.vt.edu/sionline/si/unitary.html> [accessed 17 May 2022] (14 paras)

Skinner, Quentin, 'Sir Thomas More's *Utopia* and the Language of Renaissance Humanism', in *The Languages of Political Theory in Early Modern Europe*, ed. by Anthony Pagden (Cambridge: Cambridge University Press, 1987), pp. 123–58

Smith, Adam, *The Wealth of Nations: Books I–III* (London: Penguin, 1999)
Sobchack, Vivian, *Screening Space: The American Science Fiction Film*, 2nd edn (New Brunswick: Rutgers University Press, 1987)
Soiland, Tove, 'A Feminist Approach to Primitive Accumulation', in *Rosa Luxemburg: A Permanent Challenge for Political Economy*, ed. by Judith Dellheim and Frieder Otto Wolf (London: Palgrave Macmillan, 2016), pp. 185–217
Sontag, Susan, 'The Imagination of Disaster', in *Against Interpretation and Other Essays* (London: Penguin, 2009), pp. 209–25
Stengers, Isabelle, *In Catastrophic Times: Resisting the Coming Barbarism* (London: Open Humanities Press, 2015)
Stepovich, Romi, '*Strange Days*: A Case History of Production and Distribution Practices in Hollywood', in *The Cinema of Kathryn Bigelow: Hollywood Transgressor*, ed. by Deborah Jermyn and Sean Redmond (London: Wallflower, 2003), pp. 144–58
Suvin, Darko, *Metamorphoses of Science Fiction: On the Poetics and History of a Literary Genre*, 2nd edn (Oxford: Peter Lang, 2016)
Sweedler, Milo, 'Class Warfare in the *RoboCop* Films', *Jump Cut*, 56 (2014–15) <https://www.ejumpcut.org/archive/jc56.2014-2015/SweedlerRobocop/index.html> [accessed 17 May 2022] (pp. 1–2)
Telotte, J. P., *Science Fiction Film* (Cambridge: Cambridge University Press, 2001)
Thompson, E. P., *Customs in Common* (London: Penguin, 1993)
Todorov, Tzvetan, 'Structural Analysis of Narrative', trans. by Arnold Weinstein, *Novel*, 3.1 (1969), 70–76
US General Accounting Office, *Government Contractors: Are Service Contractors Performing Inherently Governmental Functions?* (Washington, DC: US General Accounting Office, 1991)
Vint, Sherryl, '*Repo Men*', *Science Fiction Film and Television*, 4.2 (2011), 306–09
Wagner, Annie, 'Politics, Bible Stories, and Hope: An Interview with *Children of Men* Director Alfonso Cuarón', *The Stranger*, 28 December 2006 <https://www.thestranger.com/seattle/Content?oid=128363> [accessed 17 May 2022]
Warren, Craig A., 'Patriotism as Institutional Racism: *The Purge* and the Fugitive Slave Act', *Film and History*, 50.1 (2020), 29–40
Wells, H. G., *A Modern Utopia* (London: Penguin, 2005)
Williams, Raymond, *The Country and the City* (London: Hogarth, 1993)
——, 'Utopia and Science Fiction', in *Tenses of Imagination: Raymond Williams on Science Fiction, Utopia and Dystopia*, ed. by Andrew Milner (Oxford: Peter Lang, 2010), pp. 93–112
Woerner, Meredith, '5 Things You Didn't Know about *District 9*', *Gizmodo*, 19 October 2009 <https://io9.gizmodo.com/5-things-you-didnt-know-about-district-9-5341120> [accessed 17 May 2022] (11 paras)

Wood, Neal, *John Locke and Agrarian Capitalism* (Berkeley: University of California Press, 1984)

Worsdale, Andrew, 'Joburg Inspired Blomkamp', *Screen Africa*, October 2009, p. 35

Wyatt, Justin, *High Concept: Movies and Marketing in Hollywood* (Austin: University of Texas Press, 1994)

Yelling, J. A., *Common Field and Enclosure in England 1450–1850* (London: Macmillan, 1977)

Yu, Timothy, 'Oriental Cities, Postmodern Futures: *Naked Lunch, Blade Runner*, and *Neuromancer*', *MELUS*, 33.4 (2008), 45–71

'Zer0 Books Statement', in *k-punk*, ed. by Darren Ambrose, p. 103

Filmography

2001: A Space Odyssey, dir. by Stanley Kubrick (Metro-Goldwyn-Mayer, 1968)
99 Homes, dir. by Ramin Bahrani (Broad Green, 2015)
Alien, dir. by Ridley Scott (20th Century Fox, 1979)
Alive in Joburg, dir. by Neill Blomkamp (Spy Films, 2005)
The Big Short, dir. by Adam McKay (Paramount Pictures, 2015)
Black Rain, dir. by Ridley Scott (Paramount Pictures, 1989)
Blade Runner, dir. by Ridley Scott (Warner Bros., 1982)
Blade Runner 2049, dir. by Denis Villeneuve (Warner Bros., 2017)
Bonnie and Clyde, dir. by Arthur Penn (Warner Bros.-Seven Arts, 1967)
Brazil, dir. by Terry Gilliam (20th Century Fox, 1985)
Buck Rogers, dir. by Ford Beebe and Saul A. Goodkind (Universal Pictures, 1939)
Capitalism: A Love Story, dir. by Michael Moore (Overture Films, 2009)
Children of Men, dir. by Alfonso Cuarón (Universal Pictures, 2006)
Close Encounters of the Third Kind, dir. by Steven Spielberg (Columbia Pictures, 1977)
Coma, dir. by Michael Crichton (Metro-Goldwyn-Mayer, 1978)
District 9, dir. by Neill Blomkamp (TriStar Pictures, 2009)
Double Indemnity, dir. by Billy Wilder (Paramount Pictures, 1944)
Drag Me to Hell, dir. by Sam Raimi (Universal Pictures, 2009)
E.T. the Extra-Terrestrial, dir. by Steven Spielberg (Universal Pictures, 1982)
The First Purge, dir. by Gerrard McMurray (Universal Pictures, 2018)
Flash Gordon, dir. by Frederick Stephani and Ray Taylor (Universal Pictures, 1936)
Flesh and Blood, dir. by Paul Verhoeven (Orion Pictures, 1985)
The Fly, dir. by David Cronenberg (20th Century Fox, 1986)
Forbidden Planet, dir. by Fred M. Wilcox (Metro-Goldwyn-Mayer, 1956)
Frankenstein, dir. by James Whale (Universal Pictures, 1931)
Gattaca, dir. by Andrew Niccol (Sony, 1997)
The Godfather, dir. by Francis Ford Coppola (Paramount Pictures, 1972)
Goodfellas, dir. by Martin Scorsese (Warner Bros., 1990)

The Graduate, dir. by Mike Nichols (Embassy Pictures, 1967)
Heat, dir. by Michael Mann (Warner Bros., 1995)
Imagining 'Total Recall', dir. by Jeffrey Schwarz (Artisan Entertainment, 2001)
Inside Job, dir. by Charles Ferguson (Sony, 2010)
Invasion of the Body Snatchers, dir. by Don Siegel (Allied Artists Pictures, 1956)
The Invisible Ray, dir. by Lambert Hillyer (Universal Pictures, 1936)
The Island, dir. by Michael Bay (DreamWorks Pictures, 2005)
Jaws, dir. by Steven Spielberg (Universal Pictures, 1975)
Jurassic Park, dir. by Steven Spielberg (Universal Pictures, 1993)
Logan's Run, dir. by Michael Anderson (Metro-Goldwyn-Mayer, 1976)
Margin Call, dir. by J. C. Chandor (Lionsgate, 2011)
The Matrix, dir. by Lana Wachowski and Lilly Wachowski (Warner Bros., 1999)
The Matrix Reloaded, dir. by Lana Wachowski and Lilly Wachowski (Warner Bros., 2003)
The Matrix Revolutions, dir. by Lana Wachowski and Lilly Wachowski (Warner Bros., 2003)
Metropolis, dir. by Fritz Lang (Universum Film, 1927)
Minority Report, dir. by Steven Spielberg (20th Century Fox, 2002)
Money for Nothing: Inside the Federal Reserve, dir. by Jim Bruce (Java Films, 2013)
Murder, My Sweet, dir. by Edward Dmytryk (RKO Pictures, 1944)
Parts: The Clonus Horror, dir. by Robert S. Fiveson (Group 1 Films, 1979)
The Purge, dir. by James DeMonaco (Universal Pictures, 2013)
The Purge: Anarchy, dir. by James DeMonaco (Universal Pictures, 2014)
The Purge: Election Year, dir. by James DeMonaco (Universal Pictures, 2016)
Repo Man, dir. by Alex Cox (Universal Pictures, 1984)
Repo Men, dir. by Miguel Sapochnik (Universal Pictures, 2010)
RoboCop, dir. by José Padilha (Columbia Pictures, 2014)
RoboCop, dir. by Paul Verhoeven (Orion Pictures, 1987)
RoboCop 2, dir. by Irvin Kirshner (Orion Pictures, 1990)
RoboCop 3, dir. by Fred Dekker (Orion Pictures, 1994)
The Running Man, dir. by Paul Michael Glaser (Tri-Star Pictures, 1987)
Soldier of Orange, dir. by Paul Verhoeven (Tuschinski Film Distribution, 1977)
Star Wars: Episode IV—A New Hope, dir. by George Lucas (20th Century Fox, 1977)
Strange Days, dir. by Kathryn Bigelow (20th Century Fox, 1995)
The Terminator, dir. by James Cameron (Orion Pictures, 1984)
The Thing from Another World, dir. by Christian Nyby (RKO Pictures, 1951)
THX 1138, dir. by George Lucas (Warner Bros., 1971)
Too Big to Fail, dir. by Curtis Hanson (HBO, 2011)
Total Recall, dir. by Len Wiseman (Columbia Pictures, 2012)
Total Recall, dir. by Paul Verhoeven (TriStar Pictures, 1990)

The Truman Show, dir. by Peter Weir (Paramount Pictures, 1998)
Wall Street, dir. by Oliver Stone (20th Century Fox, 1987)
Wall Street: Money Never Sleeps, dir. by Oliver Stone (20th Century Fox, 2010)

Index

Arrighi, Giovanni 24–25
autonomism 22–23

Bahrani, Ramin
   99 Homes (2014) 155–56
Bay, Michael
   Island, The (2005) 2, 6–7,
      119–20, 131–40, 146
Bear Stearns 147
Bellamy, Edward
   Looking Backward (1888) 6,
      25–26, 105–07, 109
Benjamin, Walter 72–73
Bigelow, Kathryn
   Strange Days (1995) 78–79,
      127–28
biotechnology 6–7, 118–20,
   124–26, 129, 130, 134–35,
   139–40
   biopiracy 139–40, 146
blockbuster
   'high-concept' cinema 4, 5, 12,
      31–34, 36–37
   ideological relativism of 4, 37,
      40–41
   see also New Hollywood
Blomkamp, Neill 140
   Alive in Joburg (2006) 140,
      143–44
   District 9 (2009) 2, 6–7, 119–20,
      139–46, 160
Boyer, Herbert 119, 124
Brenner, Robert 20, 23–24

Bruce, Jim
   Money for Nothing (2013) 154
Cameron, James
   Terminator, The (1984) 4, 75, 77
capitalism 5, 7, 11–14, 19–27, 30,
   65, 72, 89–107, 109–10, 113–15,
   129, 130, 134–35, 137–38, 139,
   153, 159–60, 161–62
   formal freedom of 120, 127–29,
      130, 134–35, 142–43, 146
   and historical consciousness
      1–2, 12, 26–27
   imagining the end of 7, 169,
      171–80
   relationship to intellectual
      property 121–23
   'spatio-temporal fixes' 11–12,
      22–23, 25, 26–27, 72, 150
   'systemic cycles of accumulation'
      12, 24–27
   transition to 13–17
   see also commodification;
      economic crisis; enclosure;
      overaccumulation
'capitalist realism' 7, 169, 171–80
Chakrabarty, Ananda 124
Chandor, J. C.
   Margin Call (2011) 155
class 14, 21, 45, 53, 60–61, 65,
   77–78, 84, 112, 152, 176
   class struggle 19, 22–23, 37–39
Clinton, Hillary 167–68, 169

Cohen, Stanley 119, 124
Cole, Teju 144, 145
commodification 3, 4n6, 113, 121,
    125–26, 130n35, 146, 148
    see also capitalism; enclosure
commons 11, 14–18, 23, 63, 68,
    93, 102–03
    colonial commons 15–16,
        102
    common right 14–16, 100
    'information commons' 121,
        129–30
    see also property
Cruz, Ted 167
Cuarón, Alfonso
    Children of Men (2006) 7,
        173–76, 178–79

De Angelis, Massimo 18n25,
    20n32, 22, 23
Dean, Jodi 177
Debord, Guy 66, 67, 114–15
    Society of the Spectacle, The (1967)
        65–67, 138
DeMonaco, James
    Purge, The (2013) 2, 7, 146,
        148–49, 163–69
    Purge: Anarchy, The (2014) 167
    Purge: Election Year, The (2016)
        167–68
Detroit 51, 52, 55, 56, 57, 179
Dick, Philip K. 132n36
    *Do Androids Dream of Electric
        Sheep?* (1968) 74
    'We Can Remember It for You
        Wholesale' (1966) 61, 62n42
Directors Guild of America 35
dispossession 2, 5, 6, 12, 14,
    17–22, 86, 89, 103–04, 152,
    155–56, 178–79
    'accumulation by dispossession'
        19–20, 22, 96n15
    of Indigenous peoples 15–18,
        62–63
    see also enclosure; expropriation;
        primitive accumulation

dystopia 3, 91, 117, 119, 137, 148,
    172, 173, 175, 178–79
    anti-utopian dystopia 146–47,
        172, 178–80
    'critical dystopia' 111–15
    quantitative and particular
        character of 28–31, 33
    relationship to 'high-concept'
        cinema 12, 33–34, 36–41
    utopian dystopia 3, 6, 31, 41,
        57, 64, 67–68, 75, 85–86, 91,
        111–15, 138–39

economic crisis
    of 1970s 2, 4n6, 5, 11–12,
        23–25, 27, 45
    of 2007–08 2, 7, 27, 147–53,
        158, 163–66
    relationship to class struggle 23
    'signal' versus 'terminal' 24–25,
        27
    temporality of 147–48
    typical representations of in
        Hollywood 153–56
    see also overaccumulation
Eliot, T. S. 173
enclosure 1–7, 30, 45, 89–91,
    97–98, 104–06, 121, 129,
    145–46, 152, 180
    and discourse of 'improvement'
        6, 15–16n15, 64, 102–03, 10
    in England 14–15, 89, 93,
        95n14, 96–97, 98
    as foundation of impersonal
        domination 98–99, 105,
        112–13
    of Indigenous land 15–18
    'new' versus 'old' 5, 11–12,
        18–21, 120
    relationship to class struggle
        and economic crisis 22–25,
        148n3, 150
    temporality of 11
    and waning of historical
        consciousness 1–5, 12, 27–28,
        32, 113, 115

see also commodification; dispossession; expropriation; primitive accumulation
Ereky, Karl 129
expropriation 11–12, 15, 25, 93, 95, 102, 105, 120, 178–79
  'financial expropriation' 149, 164
  see also dispossession; enclosure; primitive accumulation
extrapolation 6–7, 59, 77–78, 146, 149, 161–62
  in 'high-concept' cinema 4, 12, 33–34, 36–37
  relationship to dystopia 12, 28–31, 175
  see also science fiction

Federal Reserve (United States) 25, 154
Ferguson, Charles
  Inside Job (2010) 153–54
finance 2, 7, 20n30, 23, 24–25, 118, 137–38, 147–64
Fisher, Mark 7, 171–77, 179
  Capitalist Realism (2009) 7, 171–79
  see also 'capitalist realism'
Fisher, William W. 121–22
Fitting, Peter 114–15
foreclosure 2, 7, 53n34, 147–65
  see also dispossession; expropriation
Friedman, Milton 55
  Capitalism and Freedom (1962) 47

gender 66–67n4, 140–41, 164–65
Gilliam, Terry
  Brazil (1985) 29
Gilman, Charlotte Perkins
  Herland (1915) 30
Goldman Sachs 155

Hanson, Curtis
  Too Big to Fail (2011) 154, 155

Harvey, David 11, 19–20, 22–23, 25, 72, 96n15, 149–50
Haussmann, Georges-Eugène 72–73
Hollywood 3–4, 5, 12, 31, 34–35, 43, 67, 79, 86, 119n8, 119–20n9, 132, 159–60n21, 176
  see also blockbuster; New Hollywood

imperialism 12, 15–17, 26, 64, 93, 123–24, 139
  'new imperialism' 25
intellectual property rights 122, 132
  Agreement on Trade-Related Aspects of Intellectual Property Rights (TRIPs) 118, 123–24
  Bayh–Dole Act 124–25
  Berne Convention 35, 123
  Clonus Associates v. *Dreamworks, LLC* 132–33
  Diamond v. *Chakrabarty* 124
  Digital Millennium Copyright Act (DMCA) 35, 123, 129–30
  expansion of 2, 6–7, 12, 25, 35, 118–26, 129–30
  as form of enclosure 12, 20, 121–23
  imperialist character of 118–19, 123–24
  patenting of life-forms 119–20, 124–26, 146
  and post-classical Hollywood 34–35
  'trademark placement' 132
  United States Patent and Trademark Office (USPTO) 125–26
  see also biotechnology

Jameson, Fredric 1, 4–5, 26, 27, 29n58, 37, 67, 74n32, 77n35, 101n29, 104n39, 104n40, 110n58, 113n62, 172–73, 175

Japan 6, 24, 36, 46, 58n38, 117–20, 123, 135–37, 149
Jensen, Kyle 125

Krugman, Paul 166
Kubrick, Stanley
   2001 (1968) 26, 31

Le Guin, Ursula
   Dispossessed, The (1974) 30
Lehman Brothers 147, 155
Levitas, Ruth 107–10, 139, 177
Locke, John 6
   Second Treatise of Government (1689) 102–03
Los Angeles
   privatisation of 2, 66, 68–74
   representations of 6, 73–79, 84, 85, 138, 149, 174
Lucas, George 34–35
   Star Wars (1977) 31, 34–35
Lukács, Georg 26, 91

Marx, Karl 90, 99, 100n28
   Capital (1867–94) 6, 13–15, 19, 20–21n33, 21, 70, 89–105, 111
   Grundrisse (1858) 98
   immanent critique 91–96
May, Christopher 122
McClanahan, Annie 151, 157–58
McKay, Adam
   Big Short, The (2015) 154, 155
Midnight Notes Collective 18–23
Moore, Michael
   Capitalism: A Love Story (2009) 153
More, Thomas 96, 101, 108, 113, 115
   Utopia (1516) 6, 30, 90–91, 97–105, 108, 109, 110, 112–13
Morley, David 117–18
Morris, William 106–07, 109
   News from Nowhere (1890) 26, 30, 106, 109

Motion Picture Association of America 35
Moylan, Tom 111–15
Murray, Fiona 125

neoliberalism 19, 20n30, 56, 111–13, 119–20n9, 127, 173
   ostensible utopianism of 109, 176–77
New Hollywood 4, 5, 12, 31–37
   see also blockbuster; Hollywood
New Urbanism 80–84
   'Charter of the New Urbanism' (1996) 81
Newman, Stuart 125–26
Nichols, Robert 17–18, 95n14, 178–79n18

Obama, Barack 153, 166, 168
Orwell, George
   1984 (1949) 26
overaccumulation 11, 20, 22–24, 72, 77, 113, 121–22, 150, 155n16
   see also capitalism; economic crisis
overpopulation 3, 102, 167, 179

Padilha, José
   RoboCop (2014) 3, 179–80
Park, Jane Chi Hyun 136
Parts: The Clonus Horror (1979) 132–33, 134, 137–38
Peterson, Marina 66–67, 71
political economy 6, 14, 89–96, 97, 101, 103–05, 107
postmodernism 4–5, 173
   postmodern urbanism 6, 66–76, 82, 117
Prawer, S. S. 97, 98
primitive accumulation 14, 17n24, 21, 22, 45
   Marx's critique of 6, 89–96, 101, 103
   as ongoing necessity for capital 18n26, 19–20, 96n15

see also capitalism; dispossession; enclosure; expropriation
privatisation 2, 5–6, 12, 20, 23, 51–56, 133, 179–80
  as concept 2, 5, 44–48
  in legislation 49
  of policing 3, 50–51, 71
  President's Commission on Privatization 44, 49–50
  of urban space 2, 5, 6, 25, 66, 68–75, 79, 81–82
product placement 132
property 20–21
  common 20, 27, 90, 98, 101, 103–05, 113
  private 16–17, 20, 27–28, 57, 62, 66, 80–82, 98, 101n31, 102–07, 113–14, 152, 169
  public 18, 20, 23, 27, 45–46
  see also commons; enclosure; privatisation

race 68–69, 81n45, 84, 125–26, 147, 151–52, 164
  representations of in Hollywood 2, 5, 75, 119–20, 131, 140, 143–46, 163–65, 178
  'techno-Orientalism' 6, 117–18, 120, 135–37
  white supremacy 7, 16–17, 62, 78–79, 128, 131, 134–35, 139, 161–62, 165, 168–69
Raimi, Sam
  Drag Me to Hell (2009) 155
Reagan, Ronald 5–6, 25, 44, 46, 47–48, 49, 50, 52–53, 54, 71, 111, 120, 172
Reeves, Keanu 136
Ricardo, David 91, 93
Robins, Kevin 117–18

Sapochnik, Miguel
  Repo Men (2010) 2, 5, 7, 146, 148–49, 156–62, 169
Schwarzenegger, Arnold 43, 45, 75, 159–60n21

science fiction
  as analogical genre 28–31
  and 'cognitive estrangement' 27–28
  history of 1–5, 26–27
  relationship to postmodernism 4–5
  and waning of historical consciousness 1–5, 26–27, 104n40
  see also extrapolation; science-fiction cinema
science-fiction cinema
  relationship to 'high-concept' cinema 4, 12, 32–34
  trajectory of in Hollywood 2–5, 12, 27–28, 31, 40–41, 115, 117–18, 138–39, 146, 149, 172, 180
  see also blockbuster; science fiction
Scott, Ridley 2, 117–18
  Alien (1979) 2, 3–4, 5, 26, 31, 34, 36–41, 117
  Blade Runner (1982) 5, 6, 26, 31, 41, 64, 67–68, 73–79, 84, 85, 111, 113, 117, 133, 139, 149, 161
Scott, Walter 1, 26
Seaside (Florida) 80–81, 84
  see also New Urbanism
Shakespeare, William 97, 98
Shelley, Mary
  Frankenstein (1888) 26
Shiva, Vandana 123
Smith, Adam 91, 93, 94, 96, 104
Sontag, Susan 31
Spielberg, Steven 33
  Close Encounters of the Third Kind (1977) 31, 34
  Jaws (1975) 32, 37
Steuart, James 93
Stone, Oliver
  Wall Street: Money Never Sleeps (2010) 154–55

Supreme Court (United States) 123, 124, 125
Suvin, Darko 25–26, 27n52, 28–29, 33, 34, 90n3

Thatcher, Margaret 46, 47, 111, 172
Todorov, Tzvetan 147
Trump, Donald 167–68

United States 133, 134, 137–38
  'American dream' 120, 138n44, 139, 162
  austerity economics in 148–49, 165–67
  economic crises in 147–53, 163
  enclosure as foundation of 15–17, 62–63
  expansion of intellectual property rights in 118–26, 129–30
  hegemony in the capitalist world-economy 5, 6, 22–25, 117–20
  privatisation in 44–51, 68–72, 80–82
  representations of American politics 52–53, 153–55, 167–69
utopia 3, 28, 41, 86, 138–39, 169, 176–77
  anti-utopia 3, 7, 91, 107, 109–11, 172, 176–80
  as critique of enclosure 6, 30, 89–91, 97–100, 103–10, 112–15, 172, 177–80
  neutral theorisations of 7, 107–10, 177

qualitative and universal character of 29–31, 33
relationship to 'high-concept' cinema 33
see also dystopia

Verhoeven, Paul 43–44, 64n43
  RoboCop (1987) 2, 3, 5–6, 33, 34, 41, 43–45, 46, 50, 51–58, 60, 64, 67, 77, 86, 139, 141, 179–80
  Total Recall (1990) 2, 3, 5–6, 26, 34, 41, 43–45, 46, 58–64, 67, 77, 86, 132n36, 139, 159–60n21, 179
Verne, Jules 1, 26
Villeneuve, Denis
  Blade Runner 2049 (2017) 2, 170

Wachowski, Lana and Lilly 136
  Matrix, The (1999) 6–7, 119–20, 123, 126–40, 146, 160
  Matrix Reloaded, The (2003) 127, 128n33, 130, 137
  Matrix Revolutions, The (2003) 127, 128n33, 130, 135, 137
Weir, Peter
  Truman Show, The (1998) 2, 3–4, 5, 6, 33, 41, 64, 67–68, 79–86, 111, 114–15, 137–39
Wells, H. G. 1, 26, 107
  A Modern Utopia (1905) 6, 107, 109
Wiseman, Len
  Total Recall (2012) 3, 179
Wyatt, Justin 33–34

Zer0 Books 171

www.ingramcontent.com/pod-product-compliance
Lightning Source LLC
Chambersburg PA
CBHW070740020526
44114CB00042B/2246